Archaeology
and Early History of
Angus

Archaeology
and Early History of
Angus

Andrew Dunwell and Ian Ralston

TEMPUS

First published 2008

Tempus Publishing
Cirencester Road, Chalford,
Stroud, Gloucestershire, GL6 8PE
www.tempus-publishing.com

Tempus Publishing is an imprint of The History Press

British Library Cataloguing in Publication Data.
A catalogue record for this book is available from the British Library.

ISBN 978 0 7524 4114 6

Typesetting and origination by The History Press
Printed in Great Britain by Ashford Colour Press Ltd., Gosport, Hants.

Contents

List of illustrations

COLOUR PLATES

Preface

Nowadays, visitors to Angus are welcomed by road-signs proclaiming it as 'Scotland's Birthplace'. The archaeological record of Angus, especially for the many centuries before and around the birth of Scotland as a nation, has long been recognised as rich and diverse. In recent years we have come to appreciate the severity of the threat to that record's survival, especially through rural economic activity but also through infrastructure development. In its desire to target efforts on the needs of the most important and most threatened sites and landscapes, Historic Scotland was hindered by the lack of a structured understanding of the temporal and functional relationships of the different elements revealed by field survey and aerial archaeology, and also of the processes by which destruction occurs.

Out of that need for knowledge, combined with the research interests and training needs of the Department of Archaeology of Edinburgh University and the extensive field experience of the Centre for Field Archaeology, the five-year campaign of investigations described in this volume was born. Focused largely on the gaps between the major upstanding monuments, the Angus and South Aberdeenshire Field School set out to investigate key site-types and to provide an expanded archaeological narrative for the region by linking these investigations to recent and older fieldwork undertaken by others. Readers will see for themselves that these objectives were met with a high degree of success, although many additional questions for future research were generated by the process of investigation. Such is the nature of archaeology.

The project reported here represents an excellent model of partnership working. All parties benefited in ways which met their expectations – perhaps most of all the many student archaeologists who trained on the project over the summers between 1996 and 2000. Hopefully some will return to Angus in future years to move forward the frontiers of knowledge. Until then, this report represents the most comprehensive account of the pre-medieval archaeology of any comparable-sized area of mainland Scotland, and I commend it to you.

Noel Fojut
Head of Archaeology
Historic Scotland

Acknowledgements

The idea for this book stemmed from the wish to present the research results of the Angus and South Aberdeenshire Field School, a collaborative project funded by Historic Scotland and the University of Edinburgh, with additional support provided by Aberdeenshire Council, to a wider readership. Other strands of the project – notably to do with the management of cropmark archaeology – will appear elsewhere. We are grateful for the advice and unstinting support received from Ian Armit, Sarah Govan, Mairi Davies and Noel Fojut of Historic Scotland, who at different times were responsible for overseeing the project on behalf of Historic Scotland. Thanks are also due to Peter Kemmis Betty and Tom Vivian at Tempus for managing the production of this volume, and for their patience.

We owe a particular debt to a considerable number of present and former colleagues at the Centre for Field Archaeology, located within the Department of Archaeology, University of Edinburgh until the autumn of 2000, and latterly at CFA Archaeology, Musselburgh. Many directed, or made major contributions to, the Field School investigations and other recent excavations discussed here. Numbers of the interpretations presented below are taken from, or are developed from those in, the individual site excavation reports, published in their own right by the excavation directors – Derek Alexander, Kirsty Cameron, Michael Cressey, Jamie Hamilton, Melanie Johnson, Catherine McGill, Tim Neighbour, Alastair Rees, Richard Strachan and Ian Suddaby. They are, of course, not to blame for the liberties that we have on occasion taken with the data they generated. Between 1996 and 2000 many undergraduate students of the Department of Archaeology gained their first experience of field archaeology at the Field School, and some obtained their first experience of excavation supervision, on the projects considered below. Other former members of the Edinburgh University Archaeology Department – both staff and postgraduates – contributed directly to the Field School or indirectly through their involvement in other research in the areas considered here. They include Geraint Coles, Mike Church, Graeme Warren and Shelly Werner.

Discussions with friends, associates and colleagues too numerous to mention have helped us to crystallise the views presented here. Lindsay Dunbar of AOC Archaeology/ Historic Scotland kindly provided a report on the excavations at Auchterforthar in advance of publication, and Murray Cook of AOC Archaeology shared as yet unpublished information on recent discoveries at Kintore.

Illustrators and sources of illustrations are credited in individual captions. Leeanne Whitelaw at CFA Archaeology produced most of the original illustrations, skilfully transforming our half-formed ideas into reality. Historic Scotland, the Royal Commission on the Ancient and Historical Monuments of Scotland, Aberdeenshire Archaeology Service (especially Moira Greig's aerial photographs), the National Museums of Scotland (per David Clarke, Trevor Cowie, Alan Saville and Alison Sheridan), the Society of Antiquaries of Scotland, D.C. Thomson Ltd and SUAT Ltd (per Derek Hall) supplied images for which we are very grateful. Ian Armit, Alan Braby, Colin Burgess and Ian Colquhoun, Euan MacKie and Graeme Warren kindly granted permission to reproduce certain images and illustrations. Certain other images are the authors'.

Noel Fojut, Jill Strobridge at CFA, and Ian Shepherd at Aberdeenshire Council commented upon earlier drafts of the text. Help from Gordon Barclay (HS) and Alison Sheridan (NMS) was invaluable in composing the chapter on the earlier prehistory. Thanks are also due to James Fraser at Edinburgh University for keeping us straight on some of the finer details of Pictish history. Sue Anderson at CFA Archaeology copy-edited the text. While we are very grateful to these and all others above-mentioned for their assistance, remaining errors and shortcomings are entirely our responsibility.

Finally, we hope that our long-suffering families – Alison, Louise and Jenny; Sandra, Tom and Natalie – can forgive us the long days and late nights of study.

Andrew Dunwell and Ian Ralston
Musselburgh, June 2007

1

Introduction

Forfarshire; Angus; Angus district; Angus again – over the last century the name and boundaries of the administrative county have changed on a number of occasions. The Angus of our title is not meant to correspond exactly to any of these, and indeed, especially where key sites are in close proximity whether in the City of Dundee, Perth and Kinross, north Fife, or the south of the Mearns (or Kincardineshire, Kincardine and Deeside district or now Aberdeenshire) we have allowed ourselves to stray. Our focus nonetheless lies to the west and south of Glen Esk and the course of the North Esk as it heads eastwards to debouch into the North Sea. Our study area extends as far as a line drawn approximately from the City of Dundee north-west through the Sidlaws around the conspicuous summit of Kinpurney Hill to join the middle reaches of the River Isla. The area considered extends into the southern Grampian Highlands as far as the ridge to the south of Loch Muick (*1*).

Included in this area of east-central Scotland are therefore a number of important tracts of prime agricultural lowlands, including part of the wide valley of Strathmore, the Howe of Angus, the lowlands around the Montrose basin, archaeologically important valleys such as that of the Lunan Water, and the coastal plain inland of Buddon Ness and Carnoustie. These comprise some of the richest farming country in Scotland, generally set in areas with a relatively kind – in Scottish terms – climate. It is therefore unsurprising that they have been settled and used almost as long as the country has been inhabited, even if, driving through these landscapes today, this is far from easy to appreciate. We hope that the following pages will help bring their archaeology to life.

Angus has long been a fertile hunting ground for antiquarians and archaeologists. In the middle of the eighteenth century, surveyors working for General William Roy produced plans of some of the county's premier ancient monuments. They include the White Caterthun hillfort, which still survives very much in the condition in which he saw it, and Kirkbuddo Roman camp, which has since been substantially eliminated as a surface monument and assuredly does not. Prominent among the Victorian investigators were Andrew Jervise of Brechin, who, amongst his other interests, examined several significant Iron Age sites (discussed below) and Alexander Hutcheson of Broughty Ferry. The most exhaustive early account of the history of the county was surely Alexander

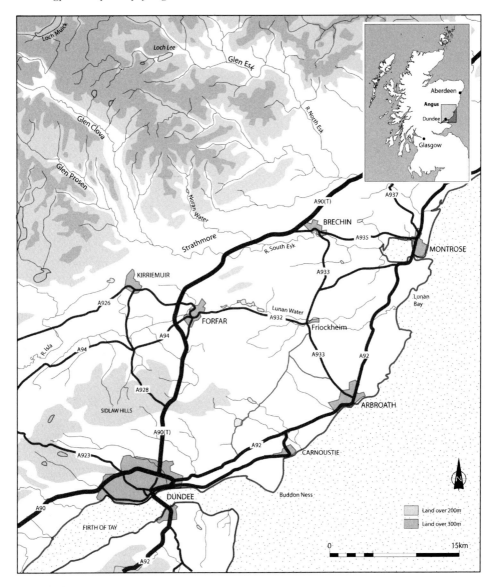

1 Angus: its topography and principal catchments, along with the main modern settlements and transport links. *Drawn by Leeanne Whitelaw, based on Ordnance Survey mapping: kind permission, 2003, Ordnance Survey*

Warden's five-volume *Angus or Forfarshire: the Land and People, Descriptive and Historical*, produced in instalments during the early 1880s.

Since the 1990s, a number of archaeological projects have been carried out in Angus, prompting this new overview. Most, though not all, were concentrated in the agricultural lowlands of the country, away from the famous, visible sites like the Caterthun hillforts near Brechin, or those on Turin Hill, to the east of Forfar. The arable fields of the county have long been known to reveal archaeological monuments, most famously the stone-lined passages called *souterrains*. These attracted the attention of, amongst others, Andrew Jervise, who has a strong claim to be considered the main pioneer of archaeological fieldwork in Angus. They were made more famous following investigations during the 1950s by Dr F.T. Wainwright, then of Queen's College, Dundee, and arguably the first lecturer in Dark Age archaeology in a British university. Towards the end of his sadly short life, Wainwright in 1963 published *The Souterrains of Southern Pictland*, an important account which, after some 40 years, is still the most recent general overview of a class of sites found in Angus and its environs.

A characteristic of research on souterrains is that it was spurred on by chance discoveries as farmers' ploughs, first pulled by Clydesdales and other heavy horses, and then after the Second World War by successive generations of increasingly powerful tractors, accidentally broke into their stonework. The archaeological response, necessarily mounted quickly, was part of what would now be called 'rescue archaeology'. Such field investigations, and the research that flows from them, have taken place because of the intrinsic interest of these remains as subjects for research and because the archaeological remains have been threatened by further damage. In many parts of Angus, as will become clear throughout this book, most of what we know about the prehistoric and early historic archaeology of the area has arisen in this way, as responses to chance discoveries, or damage to remains. The history of research on souterrains certainly illustrates this, but chance discoveries made during routine farming activities or in other ways also dominate what is known about, for example, Bronze Age burials (*2*).

THE IMPACT OF AERIAL PHOTOGRAPHY

Since the 1950s, but more particularly over the last 30 years, the application of a new technique has quietly revolutionised what we know about the archaeology of lowland Angus in particular, although it has also had a role to play – in a different variant – in the uplands of the county. This is archaeological aerial photography, undertaken from high-winged light aircraft, such as the *Cessna 150*. The underlying principles are fairly simple, although the results in favourable areas can be astonishing.

Anyone who has looked attentively at growing fields of cereal will be aware that, at certain times in most growing seasons, the crop looks very even in colour and as regular as a Brigade of Guards in height. In certain years, however, this is not the case. Some parts of the crop may be turning a range of yellows, whilst others remain stolidly green; in other areas bands of cereals within the fields may stand slightly proud of the neighbouring crop. There are a number of non-archaeological reasons why such differences develop: the uneven distribution of fertiliser, or the effects of localised crop diseases are two. Many such variations, however, are caused by the fact that plants growing in one part of a field may have access to water and nutrients to an extent that others growing nearby do not. Reasons for this state of affairs include the presence of greater depths of nutrient-rich soils, or deposits that retain moisture in times of near drought, at particular points under the growing crops. Factors which can account for

2 F.T. Wainwright (standing to left) supervises the excavation in October 1953 of a Bronze Age cist discovered by chance at Murton, Forfar. *Photograph copyright of D C Thomson & Co Ltd*

such differences in soil depths and fertility, and moisture-retaining qualities, can be natural or man-made. Natural features that can cause this kind of variation range from former stream channels, infilled with silts and no longer visible on the surface, to changes in the underlying bedrock; man-made ones include the 'tramline' effects of the old style of Scots cultivation, rig and furrow, often to be seen on prints of rural scenes in antique dealers' windows, and – importantly for us – indications of much more ancient human activities. In lowland Angus, these latter are caused by what archaeologists uninspiringly call 'negative features' – the gamut of pits, ditches, post-holes, graves, stone-holes, drains, slots, palisade trenches and other dug features that have disturbed the natural subsoil and have in due course been backfilled with other, richer, soil deposits (*colour plate 1*). Plants – especially cereals – growing above such features, and able to root in them, can thus develop differently from their neighbours.

An observer attuned to seeing such features whilst flying overhead at the right time – for visibility of such marks can often be very short-lived – can see patterns in differences of colour that may appear simply confusing and random at ground level. From the bird's eye view, these patterns – some simple and geometric, others much less so – in the growing crops can betray the presence of archaeological sites in landscapes where they have been very largely eliminated as upstanding features at ground level. The effect is somewhat like the difference between the impression a crawling baby has of a patterned carpet, and that gained by his mother towering above him – but with one crucial difference. In the landscape case, whether in lowland Angus or elsewhere, the whole pattern is never apparent at a single moment, since the colour differences are the result of the selection of crop, fertiliser and rainfall regimes, growing temperatures, underlying geomorpho-logical conditions – how free-draining the land is – and so on, all factors which vary very significantly across space and through time. The 'carpet pattern' therefore has to be assembled slowly, like a mosaic; and in some areas, because of soil or other conditions, it is very unlikely that coherent traces of the activities of the ancient populations of Angus will ever be seen from the elevated platform provided by light aircraft.

Where the technique works, however, it has utterly changed our impression of the previous human occupation of the areas concerned. The classic landscape within Angus in this regard is the valley of the Lunan Water, stretching east from Forfar to the North Sea at Lunan Bay, and more particularly the sectors of it south of the river course itself. In a good year for cropmark formation – when water is in short supply in the well-drained areas – extensive palimpsests of cropmarks occur just inland from the shore near Redcastle, and also over the free-draining sands and gravels of the middle valley, around Balneaves and Boysack. Other areas of Angus, too, produce cropmarks – from parts of the North Esk Valley almost to the coastal edge – but the valley of the Lunan Water provides many of the clearest and most extensive traces.

What differences do these cropmarks make to our appreciation of the long-term human past in Angus? Importantly, they allow the recognition of further examples of the kinds of sites that are already known about. In the case of souterrains, for example, we are no longer dependent, as Dr Wainwright was half a century ago, on the telephone call from farmer, policeman or minister to his university office to reveal the location of each new example. Of course, farmers do still occasionally find unrecorded souterrains, but the distribution of this class of site – one amongst several such in Angus – has been altered in a major way by aerial reconnaissance. Dark marks – often distinctively 'banana-shaped' – in the growing crops betray the presence of infilled souterrains, now lacking roofing slabs. In some cases, these marks have a pale margin to them – showing where the crop is growing more poorly over the stone walls edging these features – but others have no such traces and excavation sometimes shows them to have been timber-lined. In Angus and the neighbouring county of Perth and Kinross, there are now more souterrains known simply as cropmarks than those revealed by all other means. As the pair of Clydesdales were replaced by the grey Ferguson tractor pulling its plough as the main way of detecting souterrains in the 1950s, so tractors have now been displaced in turn by 'remote sensing' from light aircraft.

Three further general comments need to be made about aerial photography by way of introduction. The first is that cropmarks can often relate to the sites of former timber-built structures, including some souterrains. As will become clear, much of the architecture of lowland Angus in prehistoric times was of timber, probably used in association with turf and earth, and the former importance of this can only be assessed by the examination of the 'negative features' cut into subsoil that were listed above. The second is that – unlike souterrains, where surviving, visitable and cropmark examples are known – the cropmark record includes examples of types of sites of which there are no surviving upstanding examples where their layout can still be appreciated in three dimensions. This is especially the case when the cropmarks relate to former timber structures, for even sturdy wooden buildings have a limited lifespan in Scottish conditions. In their case, the assessment of the cropmarks as to their type and date has to be done by reference to parallels either nearby or distant, and this is always a procedure that is less than 100 per cent secure. Due to the fact that this kind of evidence is new, varied and widespread, there are some cropmark patterns that have never been sampled archaeologically. The last basic point to make about archaeological cropmarks is that they have something of the iceberg about them: in many cases, careful excavation demonstrates that far more features (especially small ones) survive in the ground than are apparent on the aerial imagery. That useful piece of computer jargon, 'WYSIWYG' – what you see is what you get – is rarely applicable to the excavation of aerial photographic sites. Once the ploughsoil is machined off, there are usually more features apparent than can easily be seen on the photographs that inspired the project in the first case. It therefore follows that interpreting an aerial photograph without resorting to digging, whilst often necessary, is also somewhat hazardous. The reader should bear this in mind: cropmark interpretation is not an exact science.

Aerial photography is also used on the uplands, but here not to reveal sites buried below the present-day surface. Rather, in both rough grassland and heather-covered moor, aerial photography in the right conditions – such as low sun and/or melting snow – can reveal patterns of relatively slight traces that correspond to the former stances of houses, old field boundaries and the like. However, in such tracts of landscape – what may be called from the archaeological perspective the 'zone of likely survival' – all the sites we know about are still visible on the surface, although some are much less distinct than others. The description of this zone refers to the fact that subsequent land-uses are much less likely to have entirely eliminated earlier sites than is the case in, for example, the ploughlands. These, contrastingly, form a 'zone of likely destruction' where – as we know from archaeological aerial photography in particular – sites have not been entirely eliminated, but rather they are no longer visible on the ground. In a few cases this is not entirely true, because scatters of stone or flint tools, even sherds of pottery, on the surface of the ploughed fields can betray the presence of underlying sites, but such scatters remain sufficiently rare within Angus that they are in effect the exceptions that prove the rule.

ANGUS AND SOUTH ABERDEENSHIRE FIELD SCHOOL

The principal project that lay behind the writing of this book was concerned with assessing the record of a range of cropmarked archaeological sites in the valleys of the Lunan Water, and South and North Esk rivers. Some of these sites had been selected for protection under the appropriate law – the Ancient Monuments and Archaeological Areas Act of 1979 – but others not, and Historic Scotland's Inspectorate of Ancient Monuments put forward an agenda of research and management issues relating to them. It was these questions that were examined as part of a Field School project for Edinburgh University's archaeology students.

The University of Edinburgh, Department of Archaeology and Centre for Field Archaeology ran the Field School for its intending Single and Joint Honours Archaeology and Environmental Archaeology undergraduate students between 1996 and 2000. A number of broad archaeological research themes were addressed by the Field School. The focus in this book is on settlement evidence and its patterning in the cropmark record. Others included environmental changes and their relationships to human activities, and management themes relating to the conservation of cropmark archaeology within the arable landscape. The results of these are considered elsewhere.

A review panel of archaeologists recently classed the later prehistoric record of Angus as being 'unsorted' and thus difficult to fit into wider views of that period in Scotland. Central to the aims of the Angus fieldwork was an effort to tackle that difficulty, by studying systematically, and with particular aims, a selection of the available evidence. A major aim was, therefore, to examine previously unexcavated or rarely excavated cropmark types in the area (e.g. enclosed settlements). Clarifying basic issues, such as the date range of particular sites, was essential to begin to allow the varying patterns of cropmarks to be understood as parts of archaeological landscapes (*colour plate 2*).

A period-by-period overview of the archaeological remains along the Lunan Valley was conducted to identify gaps in the dataset that could be targeted for future research. Most archaeological work on the prehistoric remains had focused inland, on the area west of Inverkeilor. By contrast, towards the coast only features at Ironshill had previously been examined in any detail. Work undertaken in the 1980s by the Lunan Valley Project, directed by Dave Pollock, had examined principally areas of medieval rural settlement along the river.

A comparison of the evidence recovered from the lowland cropmark record with that revealed by upland survey in nearby areas was considered essential. Investigation of the lowland zone was considered likely to increase the range of site types identifiable, perhaps particularly from later prehistory and the early historic period. Furthermore, the known sites included in the archaeological landscapes of the upland area are not all the same types as those in the lowlands, and the differences are clearly not just the result of differential preservation. This appears at its most obvious with the hilltop enclosures such as the Caterthuns, considered further below, where their summit positions were evidently significant to their builders, regardless of the functions of the enclosures themselves. However, even less certain was how these sites fitted into their wider landscape context, especially their relationship to the surrounding lowland areas, to which their topographic setting makes them necessarily peripheral. The chronological and/or social relationships of these upland hillforts to the smaller enclosed settlements identified on lower ground, largely through aerial survey, also required examination.

OTHER RECENT WORK

The nature of the archaeological record for Angus continues to evolve. Stray finds continue to be found, as do cropmark sites and other remains disturbed by ploughing. Field survey also leads to the identification of previously unrecorded sites. For nearly 20 years now, it has become increasingly the rule as a result of government guidance that major development projects, such as new roads, that may disrupt the archaeological record in their proposed path, need to be assessed to determine their likely impact on archaeological resources in advance (*colour plate 3*). Steps can then be taken to mitigate their impact, in the case of archaeological sites, either by avoiding them through the engineering of the project, or by excavating them in advance of the development and publishing the results. In effect, these procedures represent the extension of the 'polluter pays' approach favoured by government from purely environmental issues to cultural ones. As a result of archaeological involvement in development projects of this kind, new insights into the nature of the archaeological record of any given area can be obtained. Angus is no exception.

We have, therefore, widened our remit to include other projects, stemming from development proposals, undertaken recently in Angus by a range of individuals and organisations, amateur and professional. The significance of discoveries made during such development-led projects is duly acknowledged throughout this volume.

THE SCOPE OF THIS ACCOUNT

The main chronological focus of this book lies in later prehistory, not least because this long period is that most frequently revealed by rural archaeological fieldwork in the county. In essence, by this term we mean the 2000 years before about AD 1000, in conventional archaeological terms spanning the Late Bronze and Iron Ages, the Roman Iron Age and the Pictish and subsequent parts of the Early Historic period (*3*). We have made no effort to extend our cover to deal with the archaeologies of medieval and

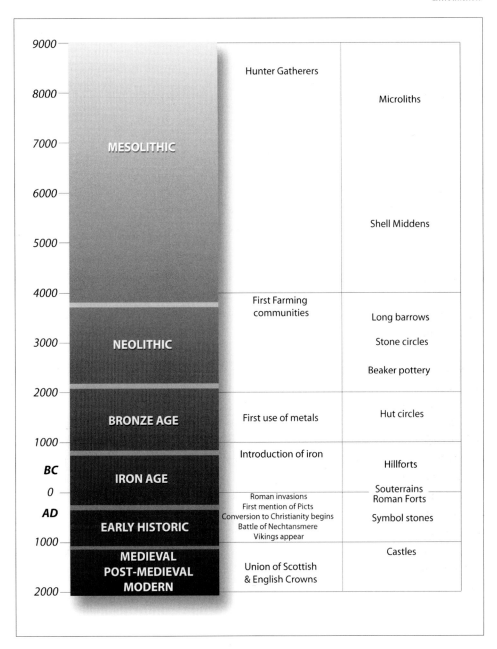

3 Outline chronology for the human occupation of eastern Scotland, showing the approximate dates of key events and the estimated appearance of well-known monument and artefact types

modern Angus here, but some of the evidence relating to the earlier prehistoric record, as yet fairly unknown, will be outlined. Where dates are given, even when these are derived from radiocarbon assay, the ranges we quote will generally be in true calendrical spans: the Appendix gives details as to how to obtain the original uncorrected determinations, should this be necessary.

It is also not possible to examine within a book of this kind all aspects of settlement and society in the first millennia BC and AD; there are, for example, many topics such as the Roman military presence for which little new information has come to light during recent projects. The result is not in any sense a definitive archaeology of Angus from its earliest occupation until *c.*AD 1000. Rather, the view presented here should be considered as a rather fuzzy snapshot in which some parts are in rather better focus than others. The clearer elements are as a result in some instances of good judgement in the selection of sites for examination, in others because of the serendipity of archaeological discoveries made in areas chosen for development of one kind of another. Despite the inevitable unevenness of treatment, we hope that what follows may stimulate others to work on the archaeology of this important area, which straddles lowland and highland, and also sits axially on the key routes between the central belt and the north-eastern lowlands of Scotland.

2

Hunter-gatherers in Angus

SETTLING SCOTLAND

Over recent years, many new sites relating to the initial colonisation of Scotland by hunter-gatherer-fisher groups have been found. The arrival of human communities perhaps some 10,000 years ago followed the appearance here of suitable species to hunt, themselves dependent on the establishment of vegetation to sustain them. As temperatures rose, forest-living animals, such as red deer, progressively replaced reindeer and other open tundra herd species. The underlying picture is of course one of improving climate associated with the downwasting of the final ice sheets of the last glacial period, coupled at times with rapidly rising sea-levels, as the melting waters of the remaining ice-sheets further north poured into the seas which in turn rose faster than the neighbouring land, flooding low-lying areas. The land too was rising after the removal of the immense weight represented by an ice-sheet which had been in excess of a kilometre thick over Scotland; the rate at which this occurred progressively slowed. The balance between 'isostatic rebound' (the process by which, freed from its heavy overburden of ice, the land rose) and changing sea-level was both dynamic and complex. Around 7000 years ago in the later Mesolithic period, for example, relative sea-level in the inner Tay Estuary may have been about about 7-8m higher than at present: radiocarbon dates for shells from a deposit stratified at this height near Inchture fit here (4). As an instance of the scale of the environmental changes that were then occurring, a deposit some 3m thick of carse clays, subsequently laid down as higher sea-levels again receded, lay on top of this shell horizon. The fertile soils of the Carse of Gowrie to the west of Dundee, an area probably not finally drained until medieval times, were also produced in this way.

Perhaps the most remarkable archaeological testimony to these dynamic changes was the late Victorian discovery of a dug-out canoe, probably worked from a single trunk of pine, further up the Tay at the former Friarton brickworks, near Perth. This craft was found lying on peat and sand that were in place before the final incursion of the sea that was responsible for the laying down of the clays that covered this canoe, helping to preserve it. Probably found at about 7-8m above present sea-level, this craft may be approximately contemporary with the Inchture shells. For our purposes, the key

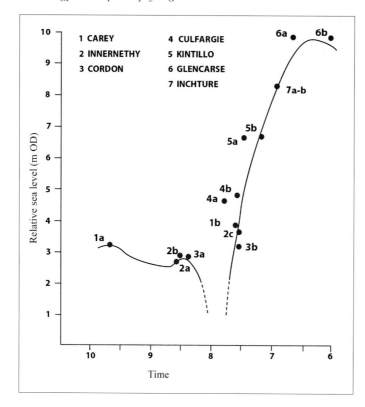

4 Diagram showing radiocarbon-dated evidence for relative sea-level changes in the Tay Estuary during early prehistoric times. The timescale is expressed in thousands of radiocarbon years before present. *Modified by Leeanne Whitelaw from Cressey et al. 2003*

outcome is that the coastline was not at its present position for much of this early period; consequently, some of the richest lowland environments that would have existed when relative sea-levels were lower have since been lost to ready archaeological inspection through coastal change and rising sea-levels. These areas may well have been preferred by the county's early Mesolithic inhabitants, so radically reducing the chances of discovering such evidence. The Mesolithic millennia were undoubtedly times of much greater environmental changes of this nature than subsequent periods.

This observation is important for several reasons. Whilst it is possible to overplay the importance of the subsistence economy – getting enough to eat – for these first settlers, the rich natural environments of coastal edge and estuary would have been very important sources of food. These first Mesolithic communities in the landscapes of Scotland generally lived at very low population densities. Comparisons with anthropological records of recent hunter-gatherers elsewhere indicate that group sizes were often small and kin-based, partly to keep population groups in line with the tasks to accomplish, but partly due to social considerations – not least the desire to keep order – although these are considerations at which we can now only guess. Estimates by Graeme Warren of Scotland's human population at this time hazard a figure of a few thousand. Of course, seasonal meetings and gatherings of larger groups would have occurred, but for much of the time populations would have been dispersed very thinly across the country. The best archaeological testament of this is the known distribution of sites (5).

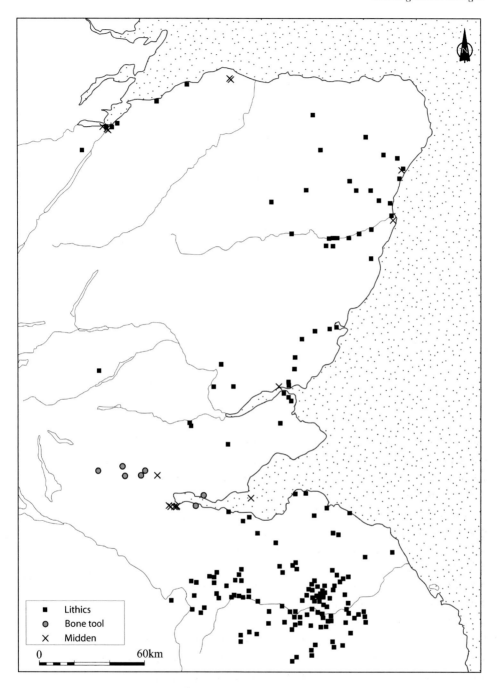

5 The distribution of hunter-gatherer sites in eastern Scotland as known from lithic scatters, finds of bone tools and Mesolithic shell middens. *Courtesy: Graeme Warren*

As environmental evidence accumulates, it has become clear that the forest cover over the country provided environments rich in animal and a wide range of plant resources. These were complemented by those of the sea, the shore and the major rivers. Whilst it is tempting to create a 'Garden of Eden' myth, with Angus's first settlers able, with little effort, to exploit the richest natural environment in Scotland during the last 10,000 years or so, such a view clearly over-eggs the pudding. The principal reason is the changing seasons, more particularly the severity of the winter months, during which edible plant resources – fruits, berries, fungi, tubers – would have been much less available. Some foodstuffs could have been stored, but seasonal changes would have encouraged people to move through the landscape to wherever the ecology was most productive, and in the Scotland of several millennia ago this tends to mean inland and upland towards summer, and down to the shore for the hardest months. The range of resources at the coast, particularly at estuaries, including accessible banks of shellfish, overwintering wildfowl and the odd stranded sea-mammal would have made bigger population aggregations feasible there. All kinds of social exchanges could have taken place in such settings.

FINDING HUNTER–GATHERERS IN ANGUS

From the perspective of the field-working archaeologist, what consequences of such mobile lifestyles in rapidly changing environments can we hope to detect in Angus? As regards the important coastal-edge environment, much evidence pre-dating the late Mesolithic is likely now to be dispersed offshore. Thereafter, middens, their contents dominated in visual terms by shellfish remains, may be anticipated. The alkaline environment resulting from the shells means that organic materials – such as animal bones – can survive here, whereas in other circumstances soil acidity will have destroyed them (7). Elsewhere, the easiest archaeological evidence to find consists of stone tools and the waste flakes and chips from making them. These are most likely to be spotted in disturbed ground – predominantly the ploughed fields – of the county. Flint – in Scotland available as a resource on some of the beaches, or from onshore deposits inland from Peterhead in Buchan – was certainly the favoured material, although other workable stones – including quartzes and agates – were certainly used. What we know of Mesolithic sites elsewhere in eastern Scotland suggests that structural evidence from them is likely to consist of slight traces of flimsy buildings – the holes for stakes that supported wind breaks and the like – such as were detected across the Tay Estuary in excavations at Morton in Fife. There were, however, more substantial buildings – one was found recently near Dunbar in East Lothian – but so far these are very rare. Surprisingly, despite certain evidence of their use elsewhere by Mesolithic communities – notably around Oban in Argyll – there is as yet no evidence for hunter-gatherers in Angus using natural caves. There are sea caves near Arbroath and St Vigeans, for example, one of which – Forbidden Cave – produced animal bones when it was examined just after the Second World War. However, further evidence may yet be there, waiting to be recognised!

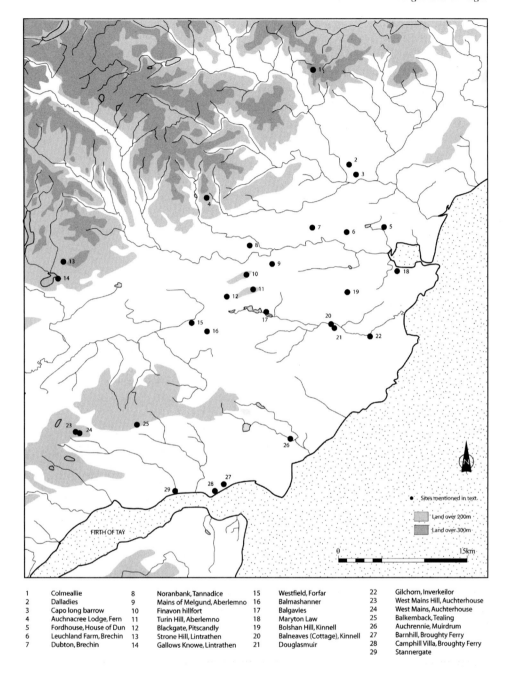

1	Colmeallie	8	Noranbank, Tannadice	15	Westfield, Forfar	22	Gilchorn, Inverkeilor
2	Dalladies	9	Mains of Melgund, Aberlemno	16	Balmashanner	23	West Mains Hill, Auchterhouse
3	Capo long barrow	10	Finavon hillfort	17	Balgavies	24	West Mains, Auchterhouse
4	Auchnacree Lodge, Fern	11	Turin Hill, Aberlemno	18	Maryton Law	25	Balkemback, Tealing
5	Fordhouse, House of Dun	12	Blackgate, Pitscandly	19	Bolshan Hill, Kinnell	26	Auchrennie, Muirdrum
6	Leuchland Farm, Brechin	13	Strone Hill, Lintrathen	20	Balneaves (Cottage), Kinnell	27	Barnhill, Broughty Ferry
7	Dubton, Brechin	14	Gallows Knowe, Lintrathen	21	Douglasmuir	28	Camphill Villa, Broughty Ferry
						29	Stannergate

6 Map showing key sites and finds mentioned in Chapters 2, 3 and 4. *Drawn by Leeanne Whitelaw, based on Ordnance Survey mapping: kind permission, 2003, Ordnance Survey*

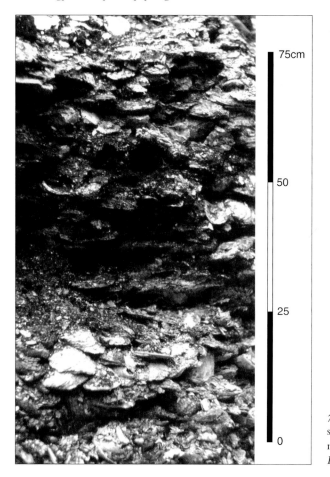

75cm

50

25

0

7 The alkaline environment of shell middens allows organic materials to survive. *Courtesy: Euan MacKie*

In eastern Scotland, several main developments have occurred in Mesolithic archaeology in recent years. One is that earlier and earlier radiocarbon dates have been produced for material from new open-air camp sites that have mainly been found by chance, including at Fife Ness and close to the Roman fort at Cramond on the outskirts of Edinburgh, both low-lying positions near the Forth Estuary. As the dates for the earliest known settlement of the country are pushed back – they now lie before 8000 BC – it is clear that for approximately half the span the country has been settled, its inhabitants depended on hunting, gathering wild plants, fishing and collecting shellfish. Their only domesticated animal would have been the dog, its developed sense of smell and excellent hearing key to the success of many hunting expeditions.

The second significant change has been the finding of traces of Mesolithic activity at high altitudes, for example around the Daer Reservoir in the Southern Uplands, or in the important landscape archaeology project – primarily targeted at evidence for much more recent times – at Ben Lawers above Loch Tay. Such high-altitude sites may also be found by examining peat erosion, or the upcast from forestry ploughing or ditching: in upland Angus, none has so far been detected.

Between the coastal edge and the uplands, in landscapes that were then heavily wooded, the lower terraces above main rivers provided the easiest-to-follow routes for both man and beast. Elsewhere in eastern Scotland, as around Crathes on Royal Deeside, or above the Tweed in Selkirkshire, particularly near confluences with tributary streams, substantial scatters of Mesolithic flints have been identified supporting this view.

For Angus itself, we can point to some evidence from the coastal edge, and to some use of the river systems. Shell middens attracted early archaeological attention. An example was recorded at the Stannergate, Dundee, in the 1870s, during the city's Victorian expansion. The former fishing port of Broughty Ferry also produced an extensive buried layer, some 2m down and 15m above sea-level, in digging the foundations for Camphill Villa in 1885: this black deposit contained quartzite pebbles and burnt wood as well as flints, none of which now survive. Both deposits were located on raised beaches and are therefore likely to relate to a period of higher sea-level within the Mesolithic era. The Broughty Ferry site may have been overwhelmed by a massive tsunami, generated by an offshore landslide close to Norway nearly 8000 years ago; this event, known as the Storegga Slide, is certainly credited with the destruction of a low-lying hunter-gatherer site in Inverness.

The Stannergate site, disturbed during harbour-works at Dundee, revealed complex archaeological stratification adjacent to the Tay Estuary (*colour plate 4*). This is still the most important Mesolithic site known in Angus. Overlying bedrock, a gravel horizon marked a raised beach, some 10m above present sea-level. The key horizon, labelled 'kitchen-midden' in the early account, overlay this. Much higher in the stratification, above 2m of accumulated soil, Bronze Age cist graves were encountered. These are both stratigraphically and chronologically separate from the early prehistoric material.

The Stannergate site appears to have been extensive; evidence for shell, charcoal and rotted wood, in a layer between 0.3 and 1m deep, was spread over a 30m by 17m area. To seaward, midden layers were mixed with beach sand and gravel, suggesting that then the site was much closer to the sea. A central hearth-stone was recovered within this deposit. The shells, mostly broken, included cockles, mussels, periwinkles, limpets and whelks, and other organic material included two red deer antler tines and some mammal bones, split to extract marrow. Flint items were few and hardly diagnostic as to period. Had the deposit been sieved, fish bones would assuredly have been recognised: notable finds from the Morton site near Tentsmuir across the estuary in Fife included the vertebra of a sturgeon that must have weighed around 250kg, as well as bones of large cod and medium-sized salmon.

These Stannergate finds remain our best evidence for a Mesolithic community established on the Angus coast. The site perhaps continued into the succeeding period, as a Neolithic stone axe was recovered, although its association with the animal bone and shell is not clear. However, it is far from necessary to require total breaks in the record of individual settlement sites, as we move from one archaeological period to another. Around Grangemouth on the Forth, Mesolithic shell midden sites – here predominantly of oysters – continued in use into the succeeding Neolithic period.

3

Farming communities of the Neolithic and Bronze Ages

INTRODUCTION: CONTRASTING ARCHAEOLOGICAL RECORDS

In this chapter, we briefly review the emerging evidence for early farming communities in Angus, without devoting the same degree of attention to these periods as to later prehistory, on which the work of the Field School was primarily focused. The Neolithic period in Angus remains comparatively poorly known; contrastingly its Bronze Age archaeology, dominated by visible, sometimes conspicuous, burial monuments and by finds of copper-alloy metalwork has, since the nineteenth century, attracted considerable attention. However, more recently work on this period has tended to be rescue-oriented, and there is no modern published overview. This contribution can only very partially address that lack.

This chapter thus covers the prehistory of the county over the period – in excess of 3000 years long – from the initial development of farming economies until the later Bronze Age. For the New Stone Age – the Neolithic, which starts a little after 4000 BC – the story is of the emergence of '… a rich archaeological landscape, which until recently has been physically hidden or has lain unrecognised', as Gordon Barclay has described it. The bulk of the available Bronze Age evidence, starting from about 2300 BC, is provided by graves and funerary monuments (many very degraded since they were first described in the nineteenth century) and by copper-alloy objects, usually deliberately deposited – although most likely for a variety of reasons – in hoards or as single items. Settlement evidence is still relatively rare and where it occurs – in the cropmark record and on the uplands – remains substantially for future investigation. Certain of the blocks needed to build a detailed consideration of Angus in this long period are already in place, including the studies of Gordon Barclay on the Neolithic of Tayside (more especially neighbouring Perthshire), the Royal Commission on the Ancient and Historical Monuments of Scotland (RCAHMS) surveys of major parts of the same county and the initial quantification of the available information contained in David Hunt's thesis. For the Bronze Age, a radiocarbon dating programme, principally on cremated bone, directed by Alison Sheridan of the Museum of Scotland, is doing much to clarify the chronological sequence.

In introducing a selection of the sites and finds that are or may be attributable to this extended period, we will not take a conventional approach, introducing the earlier Neolithic material first and running through successive stages to the Late Bronze Age. Rather, we hope to show using this material how our picture of the early prehistory of Angus has evolved as different kinds of evidence have come to light. We can demonstrate this approach, not by going back to the Victorian start of serious archaeological endeavour in Angus, but to relatively recent times.

A CHANGING RECORD: CASE STUDIES IN RECOGNISING SITES AND THEIR SIGNIFICANCE

From the mid 1960s, members of staff in Dundee and Angus Museums were frequently called out as ploughs pulled by the new generation of tractors on lowland Angus farms dislodged the sometimes massive capstones covering short cist graves. Their evocative name highlights their main feature: a rectilinear box, of four substantial, upright slabs of stone, set into a pre-dug pit and capped by a fifth. The contents normally consisted of a single, decayed skeleton, in a crouched or near-foetal position, sometimes accompanied by a pot, some flint tools or, occasionally, polished black jet jewellery. In the main, these belong to the end of the third millennium BC and the first part of the succeeding 1000 years. They have long been known as one of the most diagnostic characteristics of the earlier Bronze Age.

Their discovery signified that ploughing depths were increasing; buried remains, once out of reach, were now being disturbed. These were not the first cists to be brought to light by ploughing, and are unlikely to be the last, but the pages of *Discovery and Excavation in Scotland*, where such finds are recorded, show a quickening pace of discovery during this period (Table 1) akin to that in some decades of the previous century.

Table 1: Angus short cist burials identified through ploughing 1964-94 (from *Discovery and Excavation in Scotland*) by farm

East Drums, Brechin	(1964)
Ingliston, Eassie and Nevay	(1965)
Knockenny, Glamis	(1965)
Bractullo, Letham; Netherton, Aberlemno; and Reswallie Mains, Rescobie	(1967)
Melgund Bank, Aberlemno; and Backboath, Carmyllie	(1969)
Cookston, Airlie; Mains of Craichie; Dunnichen; and Hatton Mill, Kinnell	(1970)
White House, Tealing	(1970 and 1971)
Grange of Airlie	(1972)
East Hills, Carmyllie	(1973)
Drumachlie Farm, Brechin	(1975)

Mains of Melgund, Aberlemno	(1980)
Murton Farm, Forfar	(1984)
Mains of Melgund, Aberlemno	(1986)
East Campsie, Lintrathen	(1987)
Mains of Balgavies, Aberlemno	(1990)
West Scryne, Panbride	(1994)

Perhaps it is just chance – numbers are small and there is no reason to believe that all examples are reported – but it is interesting to note that eight were discovered in the five years from 1964, a further eight between 1970 and 1975, and only six since, with none detected in over a decade. These Bronze Age burials – far from the earliest material considered in this chapter – are, however, symptomatic of the character of the earlier prehistoric sites of Angus as many are now difficult to detect without assistance from the disturbances produced by modern activities. Into the 1960s, most new archaeological sites were thus found by chance through ploughing and similar activities.

UNDERSTANDING THE RECORD: THE AERIAL PHOTOGRAPHIC REVOLUTION

Aerial photography, notably by Dr St Joseph of Cambridge University, had been taken over Angus from the 1950s. It was not until the mid 1970s, however, that such photography specifically for archaeological purposes began to be routinely undertaken here. Although the new technique revealed extensive, sometimes spectacular, results from the Angus lowlands, this late start to systematic airborne reconnaissance means that only recently has it become possible to assimilate the results of the detection of cropmarks into accounts like this. It was, however, soon apparent that the ploughed-up short cists, and the odd standing stone or more-or-less dilapidated mound that by then stood proud of extensive croplands or improved pasture, were far from representative of the Neolithic and Bronze Age communities who had first farmed these areas.

EXPECTATIONS AND REALITIES

The Angus record considered here shows many aspects of the issues facing archaeologists – professional and amateur – as they set about finding new sites. One is to note their reluctance to recognise monuments different in their materials and size from those anticipated. Fieldworkers mostly find what they are looking for and, in Scottish landscapes, that has meant monuments built largely of stone. A century ago, almost all major prehistoric monument categories then known were stone-built. Crannogs, artificial timber-built islands, were the exception that proved the rule. Thereafter, Romanists, with Classical manuals as guides, found evidence for timber buildings inside Roman forts. By the Second World War, timber architecture of a variety of kinds and dates was identified in later prehistoric excavations. It is now a feature of all periods of prehistory and a great deal of the evidence only apparent from the air falls into this category.

There has also been an assumption that Scotland's prehistoric monuments are of relatively small size – smaller than the grander monuments found further south. The outcome of such deflated expectations has been that the biggest earlier prehistoric monuments have long escaped detection, or have been radically wrongly interpreted. Thus the longest Neolithic long mound in Scotland, at Auchenlaich near Callendar, was only recognised in the 1990s, having been previously explained as being a moraine from a downwasting ice-sheet and not a man-made feature. In Angus too, at least some earlier prehistoric monuments may have been 'missed' because they were bigger than expected.

THE EARLIER PREHISTORY OF ANGUS BEFORE AERIAL SURVEY

What was previously known of the earlier prehistory in Angus? The county's entries in general guides to Scottish archaeology concentrate on upland hillforts, stone-built souterrains, coastal promontory-forts and the magnificent Pictish sculpture – all distinctly later elements. These are the most visitable monuments here. With rare exceptions, except for Bronze Age burials, considered separately below, earlier prehistoric sites get short shrift.

Over much of Scotland, particularly the west and north, it was early established that Neolithic and Bronze Age communities built structures, some of monumental size, using stone and earth. Antiquarians and archaeologists could trace their former activities not simply by discovering discarded tools, as is largely the case for the Mesolithic, but also by identifying upstanding remains. In general, cycles of natural decay, agricultural and land improvement, neglect, quarrying, building and a host of other activities have depleted this earlier prehistoric record, whilst sometimes – as with cist burials – disturbing and thus drawing attention to it.

In 1970, Herbert Coutts' *Ancient Monuments of Tayside* outlined surviving categories of earlier prehistoric sites. Prominent amongst these are round mounds (dry-stone cairns) or earthen barrows. Examples survived in the inland glens and elsewhere as far as the coast, usually as isolated monuments. Numbers showed signs of earlier (either unrecorded or inadequately recorded) excavation. Such monuments, certainly in use in the earlier Bronze Age, about 4000 years ago, are now thought likely to include older examples. Coutts grouped other stone-built monuments as 'stone circles, stone settings and standing stones'; he readily conceded these to be 'modest affairs' compared with examples elsewhere. A boulder near Letham, later reused as a medieval boundary stone, but pecked with cup-and-ring markings millennia earlier, was one of few prehistoric carved stones then included. Further examples of all these classes of site have been discovered in the Angus countryside since 1970; the fieldworker John Sherriff had a particularly prolific time with cup-and-ring-marked rocks in the mid 1980s. None the less, compared to other areas of eastern Scotland north of the Forth subject to similar histories of land improvement, the tally of apparently ritual and funerary sites of these periods identified by fieldworkers seems a little disappointing and restricted in its range. This impression is, as we shall see, counteracted by new information for timber architecture in the lowland zone.

STONE CIRCLES AND STANDING STONES

Amongst the few long-known megalithic monuments of Angus are its series of stone circles. Several relate to classes distributed widely in eastern Scotland. Only in the case of one group, the 'four posters', are a significant proportion in Angus. Even for these, Angus has fewer than neighbouring Perthshire, and half the Angus cases are uncertain as a result of damage or stone removal. 'Four posters', as the name intimates, are arrangements of erect stones disposed in a rectangle, in classic cases aligned approximately east–west and north–south. One stone may be cup-marked; if so, this is most likely to be in the south-east. The tallest stone generally occurs in the south-west and there may be Bronze Age funerary deposits (three Angus examples dug into long ago, produced 'urns') in a pit or cist set within the circle. Such sites occur on upland terraces or the shoulders of hills, often at around 200m.

Four posters are late, usually small, examples of the stone circle building tradition of the British Isles. Angus includes 'a peculiar mixture of mini and maxi rings ranging from the tiny settings at Brankam to the enormous wreckage of Blackgate …' as Aubrey Burl described them. At Balkemback Cottages, near Tealing, on a south-facing terrace, all four stones survive, although two are lying prone. Here, the south-east stone carries elaborate cup and cup-and-ring marks on one face and simpler cups on the other. Possibly the grandest in size, if a distinctly uncertain example, is the very damaged site at Blackgate Smithy, Pitscandly, near Lunanhead. It has been much reduced since Victorian times, when the site consisted of a substantial cairn through which four stones protruded; that the stones were erected first is known because one of the original stone-holes has since been examined. The tallest surviving stone here is some 3.7m high. The collapse of another disturbed an urn containing cremated bone and digging in the 1850s produced a sandstone slab, now lost, which was elaborately carved. At Carse Gray, near Forfar, three stones, one tumbled, form the remains of a ruined four poster on a hill; during the re-erection of another stone, brought down by a tree throw, white quartz, perhaps of ritual significance, was recovered from its socket.

Most Angus stone circles were discovered long since. More recently, 'mini' examples of four posters were identified by John Sherriff in detailed fieldwork around Lintrathen in the 1980s. On Strone Hill in Lintrathen one upright stone 0.35m high, with three fallen stones nearby some 2.5m across, were set in a landscape with ring cairns, roundhouses, hut circles and more recent remains. This settlement evidence is considered further below. On Brankam Hill, two further diminutive four posters were found in a landscape with probable Bronze Age hut circles and kerb-cairns. The pairing of four posters is a trait recorded elsewhere.

A slightly more complicated plan occurs in a monument at Corogle Burn in Glen Prosen. Forming another 'ruined but recognisable' four poster in Burl's terminology, this is accompanied by an extra pair of stones, now fallen, lying some distance west of the four poster. Such outlying stones are known elsewhere and Professor Alexander Thom believed that the westerly stones at Corogle had been aligned on the most southerly setting of the moon.

One small circle, all its nine stones bar one fallen, at Balgarthno, now within the City of Dundee, was recognised as a 'Druidical Temple' in the nineteenth century, though limited excavations seem to have been entirely unproductive. It is worth a mention here, not least because it shows that small circles – in this case some 6m in diameter – could have more numerous stones. Some way up Glen Esk is the only surviving Angus candidate for membership of a class of circles, widely represented in Aberdeenshire and the Mearns, called Recumbent Stone Circles and belonging later in the third millennium BC. This is Colmeallie (*colour plate 5*), a heavily damaged site with, however, enough evidence to indicate the presence of the recumbent and one flanking stone, and the kerb of a probable ring-cairn. Further, the position of the recumbent slab and the alignment through it of a prominent hill and the setting position of the moon at midwinter strengthen this attribution. Gordon Barclay and Clive Ruggles linked Colmeallie to a small group of Recumbent Stone Circles represented south of the Mounth only in the Mearns. There is very little overlap between the distribution of these classic north-east sites and the henges (much more recently identified in Angus) discussed below (*9*).

Angus also includes examples of single standing stones (*colour plate 6*) as at Noranside, on a rise above the Noran Water, on the Hill of Kirriemuir, and at Lendrick Lodge, Airlie. Modern archaeological work at them has been rare and generally unproductive, although some certainly marked cremation burials. They remain amongst the most enigmatic of prehistoric monuments.

CUP–AND–RING–MARKED STONES

Over 50 cup and cup-and-ring-marked stones are now known from Angus, and have been particularly studied by John Sherriff (*10*); further examples continue to be identified by fieldwork and reported in *Discovery and Excavation*. They now appear to be particularly numerous on the upland around Turin Hill east of Forfar but others are known as far east as the coastal plain to the north-east of Dundee; some of these stones show signs that their decoration is of more than one phase. A simple cup-marked stone found during excavation at the Dalladies barrow (considered below) suggests that the oldest of these stones was pecked out during the earlier Neolithic era, but others (especially those with more elaborate designs) may belong later in that period. Some had likely been moved to their present locations in the Bronze Age. Their interpretation has been the subject of considerable speculation, often based on their prominent setting within the landscape, and sometimes connecting them to routeways.

A characteristic of the Angus series is that numbers were reused in still-later prehistoric monuments, of types discussed in later chapters. These notably include

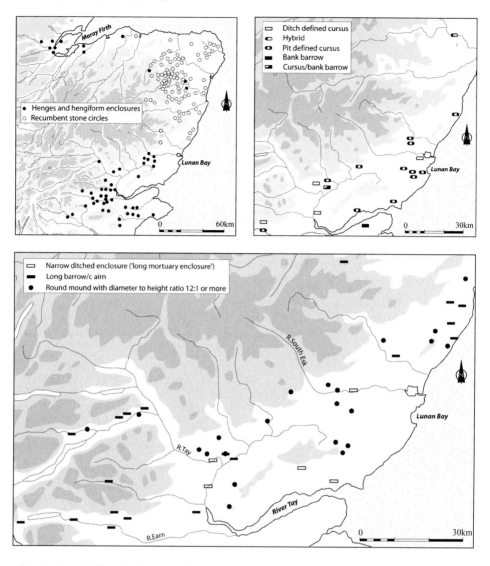

9 Regional variability in the Neolithic of eastern Scotland, as illustrated by different classes of Neolithic monuments. *Drawn by Leeanne Whitelaw after Barclay 1999 and Brophy 1998*

souterrains, as at Ardestie and Tealing (*colour plate 7*). However, the date at which a large cup-marked slab was hauled up the White Caterthun, eventually to lie between two of the outer enclosure lines (*22*), is uncertain. Other Angus cup-marked stones are also from forts – including both Finavon and the coastal promontory at Auchmithie. A cup-marked slab, the 'Girdle Stane of Dunnichen' at Letham, formed part of a medieval boundary, adding to the idea that some of these carvings had a marked cultural longevity.

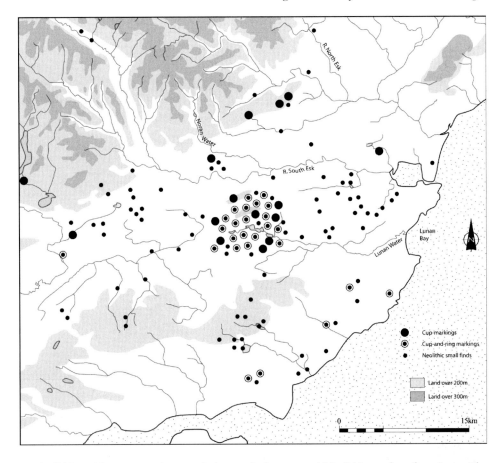

10 Neolithic and later cup- and cup-and-ring-marked stones, and Neolithic artefacts, from Angus. The distribution of the former is heavily focused on Turin Hill. *Drawn by Leeanne Whitelaw after Sherriff 1995, based on Ordnance Survey mapping: kind permission, 2003, Ordnance Survey*

ARTEFACTS AND THE DISTRIBUTION OF NEOLITHIC AND BRONZE AGE SITES

Another good indicator of early occupation is provided by the recovery of stone and flint debris. Again, some of this material has been known since the nineteenth century. Stone axes, for example, of which 'stray finds' have long been recorded throughout the county, were mapped by David Hunt. These include prosaic items used to ring-bark or fell trees, as well as other, much finer, examples. The latter, sometimes of exotic geological types, were undoubtedly prestige possessions.

A small axe from Stannergate, Dundee, hints that this locale, already used by hunter-gatherers, was still frequented by early farmers. Recurrent use of parts of the landscape is also suggested by Graeme Warren's analysis of mixed flint debris found in the ploughed fields at various points in the Lunan Valley. These include Neolithic scatters with possible Mesolithic elements. Other flint collections are more surely of Neolithic or

Neolithic-and-later character, for example the unusual flint flakes and blades recovered near Myreside, Lunanhead. For these, an Early Neolithic date was proposed by Caroline Wickham-Jones. Contrastingly, a leaf-shaped and a barbed-and-tanged arrowhead recovered from gravels at Keithock Mill, Newtonmill, Brechin suggest losses later in the Neolithic; the latter projectile is of a type found in short cist burials.

This material can be instructive in a number of ways. If flint debris includes waste that was simply discarded, the finest stone axes are unlikely to be casual losses. They may have been offerings or items hoarded for some reason. The ethnographic record indicates that making and finishing a finely polished stone tool represents an important investment of labour. Whatever view – ritual deposition or not – is taken of why serviceable equipment was placed in the ground in the Angus countryside, their findspots are direct indications of a Neolithic presence. Finds of axes continue to be made; near-complete examples are more likely to be found by chance than in conventional archaeological excavations. Stray finds have recently come to light in a Montrose garden and on Monifieth Golf Course, as well as on Easter Ingliston Farm, Forfar. The outstanding find, however, was made near the top of Bolshan Hill, Kinnell, in the upland tract between the Lunan Valley and the South Esk (*colour plate 8*). Alan Saville studied this highly polished flint axe-head – too fine ever to have been used, unlikely even to have been hafted. He compared it to other exceptional finds from eastern Scotland, notably a hoard from Smerrick, the Enzie, Banffshire. Another, more usual axehead was found on Bolshan in 1985, but the flint example stands out as a status symbol, perhaps even an import across the North Sea from Denmark, where there was a tradition of manufacturing similar items.

ROUND MOUNDS – AND LONG ONES?

Round mounds, often tree-covered, have long been appreciated as a component of the earlier prehistoric landscapes of Angus. In the nineteenth century, they attracted the attention of the first serious excavators in the county. Classic, Bronze Age examples will be considered later in this chapter.

In the 1960s, however, the examination of a site up Strathtay at Pitnacree provided a first indication that some large round mounds in Tayside might be Neolithic, rather than Bronze Age as was conventionally assumed. Pitnacree was a complex construction initially dating from the mid fourth millennium BC. A noteworthy feature is that early activity here included the building of a 'mortuary structure' of earth and timber, of a type discussed further below. For a long time, however, the Pitnacree mound seemed an isolated Neolithic funerary site between the Tay Valley and the skirts of the upland Mounth, an area where excavated round mounds of a variety of sizes seemed to date later, usually producing burials attributable to the Bronze Age. For RCAHMS, for instance, Angus was mapped in the 1990s as very largely a 'black hole', essentially devoid of Neolithic funerary monuments and with henges considered very rare.

Could more round mounds be Neolithic in date? As with other under-studied monument classes, different perspectives are possible, since there is little evidence from excavation. New discoveries of mounds, such as those at Culhawk Hill, Kirriemuir (16m in diameter and 1.5m high, although disturbed), Wester Coul Farm, Lintrathen and Balgavies House, Aberlemno (both 15m in diameter) emphasise that sizeable features still lie unrecorded in as well-peopled a landscape as Angus. Using a comparison of the sizes and profiles of known Neolithic barrows in Perth and Kinross and in the north-east, Gordon Barclay proposes that Angus round barrows can be subdivided into two broad classes. He suggests that earlier mounds have diameters above 20m and a flattish profile – a diameter:height ratio of 12:1 or greater. At least six candidates exist in Angus; some support for a Neolithic date for these comes from his recognition that the primary monument at the remarkable Neolithic bank barrow at the Cleaven Dyke (near Meikleour in Perth and Kinross) was an oval barrow akin to these examples.

A COMPLEX SITE AT THE HOUSE OF DUN – THE IMPACT OF EXCAVATION

In the 1990s, one of the first projects set up by the National Trust for Scotland archaeologists was at House of Dun, north of the Montrose Basin. This account of the complex barrow there draws on interim reports by its excavators; these demonstrate how new fieldwork can challenge and perhaps overturn assumptions in under-prospected areas such as Angus. The Fordhouse mound was considerably damaged before archaeological intervention, inevitably making its interpretation difficult. Traces of activity, with a north-west–south-east axis, preceded its construction; these comprised posts, apparently burnt in situ, slots that could have held further timbers, and pits containing Arran pitchstone, widely traded over Neolithic Scotland. The initial wooden structures seem to have been built in the Early Neolithic period – just after 4000 BC, to judge from radiocarbon dates. They too may have formed the kind of precinct described as a 'mortuary structure', a component of an initial long, rather than round, barrow. Radiocarbon dates suggest that burnt hazelnuts in other pits were collected during a first, hunter-gatherer, use of the location.

The successive accumulations covering these structures ultimately formed a mound of conventional Bronze Age appearance that incorporated flint items and sherds of beaker, food vessel and urn types. Whilst some of the pottery related to Bronze Age cremation burials, other sherds were not in situ. Sherds from Early Neolithic vessels were also found redeposited in later disturbance. One small stone-lined cist, containing two cremations and burnt objects including a flint and a bone pin, was identified. This late addition to the mound suggests sequential activity within the Bronze Age. After a capping of glacial boulders was installed, further burial deposits, some accompanied by Collared Urns, were inserted into the mound.

In the last excavation season, an astonishing discovery was made. This consisted of a pit, lined with dry-stone walling placed centrally beneath the mound (close to the burnt timberwork already identified) comprising a short passage, accessing a chamber 2m in diameter. Seemingly unfinished, it is proposed as a passage grave – a chamber tomb marked by use of massive stones. Such monuments are generally found in western Britain and Ireland. The chamber floor produced redeposited flints and cremated bone, dated to later in the Neolithic period, while the passage blocking contained earlier pottery. The excavators noted that stones in the chamber walls oversailed each other, as expected beneath the stone-built roof in a chambered tomb, but no such roofing was present.

A full report will be required to understand this composite monument. The complex history of the mound's accumulation, the recognition of earlier activity on the old ground surface and the sequential burials are elements attested elsewhere. What is altogether unexpected, however, is the internal chamber with its 'blind' access passage. Chambered cairns containing passage graves date from the Neolithic period and, as evidenced from new work at the Clava Cairns near Inverness, from the earlier Bronze Age. Within Scotland, however, such features are characteristic of the Atlantic west, the northern mainland and the islands. East of Drumalban, the chambered cairns nearest Fordhouse are known from western Perth and Kinross. If confirmed as a passage grave this example will therefore radically alter archaeologists' views on the nature of the Tayside Neolithic.

Aerial photography and the timber architecture it reveals have revolutionised our understanding of Neolithic archaeology in the Angus lowlands. Although they have often been known for much longer, we must allow the possibility that the examination of upstanding stone monuments might equally necessitate radical rethinking about the characteristics of such sites. The semi-subterranean chamber at Fordhouse is highly unusual. What is not in doubt, however, is that there was Mesolithic, Neolithic and Bronze Age activity here, testifying to recurrent use of this place near the Montrose Basin.

LONG BARROWS ACROSS THE NORTH ESK: DALLADIES AND CAPO

As major monuments of Neolithic date may be constructed of earth, turf or timber, their traces in Angus may be very sparse. Thus unchambered long barrows, widely distributed in southern and eastern Britain, have now been found in some numbers in Aberdeenshire, extending south to the North Esk Valley near Edzell. Here, two examples have been known since the late 1960s. One, Dalladies, was excavated 30 years ago before the extension of a gravel quarry. Stuart Piggott's excavations showed it to be a long mound, built of cut turfs, higher and wider at its eastern end; this covered a 'mortuary structure'. The mound was edged by a ditch running parallel to each of its long sides. Gordon Noble proposes a rather different nature and function for the initial construction, stressing its relationship with the original forest cover, but the mortuary structure was undoubtedly of two phases, secondarily consisting of a small, low stone-built enclosure. This surrounded three massive, and two smaller, posts which may originally have supported a raised platform on which, based on anthropological parallels and limited excavation evidence, the dead may have been exposed. Alternatively the posts may simply have been free-standing. Eventually the surviving timber elements were destroyed by fire and the feature was sealed by the mound, which had side revetting walls and a façade of upright stones, superficially like that of a chambered cairn but not giving entry to the mound's interior. Much later, Early Bronze Age cists were inserted into the ridge of this mound, as elsewhere they were dug into the summits of rises within formerly glaciated terrain. An even more massive long barrow survives nearby, at Capo, within a coniferous forest. A resistivity imaging survey at Capo undertaken in association with the Field School demonstrated that this mound likely contains architectural elements not dissimilar to Dalladies (*colour plate 9*). It was not for another generation, with the Fordhouse excavation in the 1990s, that a similar long barrow was identified in Angus.

Further long mounds, in the form of stone-built cairns that apparently lack internal chambers, are known in Perthshire (*9*). An important and as yet unanswered question is whether the distribution gap between these two areas is real (i.e. that similar sites never existed elsewhere in Angus) or not. It is certainly possible that upstanding sites may survive, unrecognised, in the county; Dalladies and Capo (just into Aberdeenshire) were only recognised a generation ago by an amateur archaeologist with an excellent eye for his local terrain. These sites had previously been considered geomorphological features. Alternatively, any such monument in the Angus lowlands may have been ploughed to the extent that its only means of identification will be by cropmarks indicating the paired, slightly converging, ditches that once edged the trapezoidal mound. If Ladbrokes ran an archaeological betting service, they would find individuals prepared to back both options! There is, however, no compelling reason for there ever having been earthen long mounds in any number in the county. Other evidence strongly points to substantial regional diversity during this period and it is perfectly possible that the inhabitants of Angus devised ways of disposing of their dead, and venerating them, that did not involve constructions of this type.

EXPLOITING THE LOWLAND RECORD FOR NEOLITHIC SITES: CURSUS MONUMENTS, TIMBER HALLS AND PIT ALIGNMENTS

Having considered some of the upstanding stone monuments and the possibility of others built primarily of earth or turf, it is time to turn to the lowland zone of destruction, where few early archaeological sites survive as visible features in the landscape. Shortly after the first discoveries of potentially early prehistoric cropmarks in the lowland zone, one of the clearest sites then identified had to be wholly excavated before the building of a 1980s gas compressor station. This lay in the middle valley of the Lunan Water, at Douglasmuir (*11*). Here, Jill Kendrick revealed a substantial enclosure defined by pits (more tightly bunched on one side than the other and deeper at the narrower ends) that had held upright oak timbers. The enclosure measured some 65m by 20m, far too substantial ever to have been roofed. It had a central division, also post-defined; the enclosure's two halves differ in plan, suggesting it was built sequentially. Charcoal from three post-holes suggests the structure was deliberately burnt down – a fate shared with other earlier Neolithic wooden structures in eastern Scotland – in the earlier fourth millennium BC.

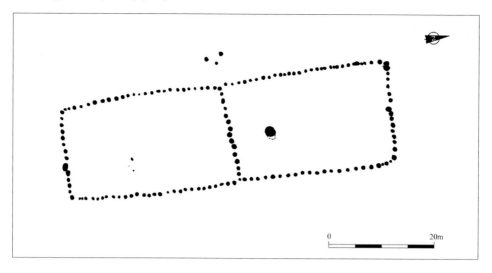

0   20m

11 The Neolithic pit-defined enclosure and associated features excavated at Douglasmuir. Irregularities in its plan suggest it may be of two phases. *Drawn by Leeanne Whitelaw after Kendrick 1995*

Douglasmuir is amongst the smallest of the cursus monuments of Scotland. These monuments are generally in river valleys like their better-known southern parallels. Remarkable for their diversity, they are long enclosures, all known only as cropmarks, with each side defined by a single ditch or (more often in Scotland) a row of pits. These may or may not have held posts. Cursus monuments can also be the focus for much later activity and provide a good indication of the opening up of the landscape and the removal of woodland. Kenny Brophy envisages them as part of '... increasing attempts, through monumentality ... to connect aspects of social life from burial to domestic life and ritual, and to merge the natural with the cultural'. Numbers of examples are now known in Angus, particularly in the Lunan Valley. Some are much more extensive than Douglasmuir.

Pit alignments – single rows, more or less regular, of pits running straight or crookedly across the landscape and not closed forms like the cursus type – are also known in Angus exclusively as cropmarks. They are harder to classify and well-nigh impossible to date in some instances. In some parts of Scotland, notably the south-east, regular alignments form parts of Iron Age systems of land division (Chapter 6) whereas north of the Mounth a set in the grounds of Crathes Castle on Deeside seem initially to have been dug by hunter-gatherers. A North Fife example examined by Stephen Carter was radiocarbon dated by elements in its fill to the later Neolithic period. Whilst this last might have been an anthropogenic feature, it could also have been the by-product of tree-throw. In other cases, recovering evidence to date the features and identify their use can be problematic; this was the case with examples investigated at Hatton Mill Farm, Kinnell, by CFA in the early 1990s. It would be unreasonable to assume that the initial excavations of all categories of cropmark features will unambiguously clarify their date and function, and pit alignments certainly demonstrate that.

NORANBANK, TIMBER HALLS AND OTHER EVIDENCE OF NEOLITHIC SETTLEMENT

If major architectural statements such as cursus monuments were unroofed structures, assumed to have fulfilled ceremonial functions, aerial photography has also revealed a scatter of 'timber halls', apparently originally roofed, over eastern Scotland as far north as Aberdeenshire. Assumed initially to be Early Historic buildings – providing settings similar to those in which Dark Age epics such as Beowulf unfolded – it is now clear that some such buildings, generally isolated, belong to the earlier Neolithic period. The closest excavated examples geographically lie in Royal Deeside at Balbridie and Crathes, and others have since been examined by Gordon Barclay in Perthshire and particularly at Claish in Stirlingshire. All these sites have been discovered from the air since 1976. They are now known to represent Neolithic buildings and have spearheaded the recognition of Neolithic settlement evidence from the lowlands. None of this evidence was apparent when Herbert Coutts was writing in 1970. At least one of the Angus cropmarks (at Noranbank) so closely resembles the form studied by Barclay at Claish that an earlier Neolithic date for it is very probable. The internal post-hole arrangements at the Aberdeenshire and Stirlingshire examples indicate buildings that could have been covered by steeply pitched roofs – with ridges perhaps 8m above the ground in the grandest examples.

It is clear that Scottish timber halls were unusual buildings for their time. As imposing structures, they indicate more substantial investments of labour and resources than the fragile remains now characteristic of most Neolithic settlements in Angus. Where evidence of these has come to light, it has usually been as a by-product of other work or as a component of 'catch-all' exercises in areas scheduled for major development. This has encouraged the view that most of the other settlement evidence betokens relatively short-lived communities, perhaps retaining some of the mobility of the hunter-gatherers who had preceded them. Such a perspective is not necessary, however, as the apparent slightness of the remains has much to do with subsequent damage rather than necessarily demonstrating the original character of these sites.

Indicative of the lesser Neolithic sites are Dubton near Brechin and Carlogie on the outskirts of Carnoustie. Arguably the most extensive of these sites is Dubton, where extensive stripping of topsoil revealed a scatter of pits, mixed with later Iron Age evidence. The earlier Neolithic pits were in a range of sizes and contained both Early Neolithic pottery and, in some smaller examples, later Neolithic material. Plant remains suggest a sophisticated cropping regime for cereals here and the ingathering of a variety of wild products. The nature of the pit-fills suggests a pattern of deliberate deposition of materials; this is not simply haphazardly discarded waste. Pits at Carlogie were encountered on the upgrade of the A92; two contained a few sherds of coarse Late Neolithic pottery, but there were no associated traces of buildings such as post-holes. Such ephemeral remains prove difficult to interpret. Other examples were discovered on the road line, for example at Mains of Kelly, where another pit contained diagnostically later Neolithic Grooved Ware. Further examples of pits with Neolithic pottery have since been revealed during other projects, as at Newton Farm, Carnoustie, suggesting that the the type of occupation they represent may have been widespread on the Angus lowlands in Neolithic times. It would be premature to infer from the nature of these sites and the apparent lack of distinct houses that they were necessarily ephemeral places incorporated by early farmers into cycles of movement through the landscape.

HENGES AND HENGIFORM ENCLOSURES

Other categories of Neolithic site are now recognised in the cropmark record from the county. These include henges, although none has been excavated in Angus (*9*). Their characteristic feature is a delimiting, near-circular or ovate ditch accompanied by an outer bank, punctuated by one or two entrances. None survives as an upstanding monument and RCAHMS, in its consideration of such sites as cropmarks in Tayside was very circumspect in its assessment. Gordon Barclay has recently taken a more optimistic reading of the evidence, seeing in particular one site within a cluster of cropmarks at Westfield (with the well-known site of Brogar on Orkney) as one of the biggest of Scotland's henges. Westfield (south of the Loch of Forfar) has an extensive grouping of such sites, which have now principally been recorded within Scotland in the eastern lowlands between the Forth Estuary and the southern skirts of the Mounth. Most activity on excavated henges in Scotland dates to the later Neolithic or earlier part of the Bronze Age. It is often very varied in character but can include stone circles, their timber equivalents, burials or other more enigmatic features. It is demonstrable that the ditch and its external bank were in some instances a later addition, to contain the other elements, rather than being the original features. That might go some way to explaining the variability that these sites show.

ROUND CAIRNS AND OTHER EVIDENCE FOR BURIAL FROM THE LATE NEOLITHIC AND BRONZE AGE

In the preceding sections of this chapter, we have demonstrated how the archaeological record has evolved through time. In this section, the most extensive evidence for Bronze Age burial will be outlined. Although Bronze Age burials also appear in various guises in the cropmark record, what we currently know about them mostly comes from older, often nineteenth-century, excavations.

The round cairns of Angus have a strong claim to be the category of sites both most examined since the early nineteenth century and most significantly degraded since that period. Many are now distinctly damaged, but it is still possible to see how imposing some examples must originally have been. Whilst archaeological classification often separates earthen barrows from stone cairns and both from 'flat' short cist burials and cremation cemeteries, in reality these differences reflect not only access to different materials and different funerary practices, but also the outcomes of subsequent damage. It is likely that burials were inserted secondarily into mounds and that in other cases mounds were erected over earlier burials. Cropmark 'ring-ditches' some of which represent the remains of annular depressions around ploughed-out mounds, further complicate the picture. Their detection emphasises the fact that some upstanding barrows, now surviving as singletons, were originally part of more extensive cemeteries. These sites indicate, from the efforts made by Bronze Age communities to celebrate or commemorate their dead, the prosperity of their elite members much more readily than does the more ephemeral or marginal evidence for settlement. However, although it may appear that Bronze Age burials are an ubiquitous component of the Angus archaeological record, it remains possible to undertake substantial projects without adding significantly to the tally – the A92 corridor is a case in point.

In a number of cases burial mounds seem deliberately to have been sited so as to be conspicuous. A recently examined example at Maryton Law demonstrated degradation resulting from rabbit burrowing, livestock poaching and quarrying. This imposing mound (34m in diameter and 6m high) was set on the northern edge of the hills immediately south of the Montrose Basin. To judge from the pottery recovered (sherds of beaker and of food vessel) it had been in use primarily in the Early Bronze Age. Gallows Knowe at Lintrathen, dug into since the earlier nineteenth century when two cists were found, and disturbed anew during the Second World War by the construction of an Air Ministry brick shelter, when another cist containing cremated remains and white quartz were found, nonetheless retains something of the imposing profile of these monuments. Set on a rounded summit above the Loch of Lintrathen, it is 30m in diameter and 3m high (*colour plate 10*).

The cairn set on the summit of West Mains Hill, at Auchterhouse in the Sidlaw Hills, is still a potent symbol of the significance of such structures. Some 20m in diameter by 2.5m high (but now crowned by a pillar celebrating Queen Victoria's Jubilee of 1887 and an OS trig point) it is hard to avoid the term 'landmark' in describing this site. At the end of the nineteenth century the landowner had it opened. A local archaeologist, Alexander Hutcheson, provided a good account of the work, which consisted of cutting a trench in from the north side. The mound contained a central, double cist, the joints between its slabs well-sealed with clay. Two cremations and a bronze dagger lay in one half and a further cremation in the other. Such remains suggest a relationship amongst those included, but the details now elude us. The dagger had a horn hilt and fragments of its sheath, probably of skin, also survived. The mound was of composite construction; the cist was covered by boulders, then a turf pile edged by a kerb of large stones, then finally a stone capping, itself with a kerb – a rather more elaborate construction than its final appearance perhaps suggests.

Recently obtained radiocarbon dates suggest the cremation accompanying the dagger dates to around the twentieth century BC, probably broadly contemporary with another rich find – the knife-dagger from a cist at Barnhill, near Broughty Ferry (found during Victorian road construction). Both these finds indicate stylistic links with the south of Britain, in the case of Barnhill this is marked by the presence of two gold discs paralleled from a burial on the south coast of England, at Hengistbury Head beside Poole in Dorset (*colour plate 11*).

12 The surviving elements of the jet necklace and bracelet, both with spacer-plates, from Bell Hillock, East Kinwhirrie, Kirriemuir. The maximum diameter of the necklace was approximately 230mm. *Drawn by Helen Jackson. Courtesy: Alison Sheridan*

Other high-status jewellery from Bronze Age graves was made of a fine black material: jet from Whitby on the Yorkshire coast. In the second of three known excavations in 1919 at the Bell Hillock (an earth and stone mound on East Kinwhirrie, Kirriemuir) a cist containing a Food Vessel and numbers of jet beads, representing about two-thirds of a necklace, were unearthed. The accompanying burial may have been a cremation. The jet necklace, not much worn when put in the grave, had been made by a highly skilled worker and was – unusually – accompanied by a bracelet, also of jet (*12*). Stylistically it resembles another example, one of two accompanying an inhumation in a short cist (also with a food vessel and a bracelet) from Pitreuchie, Forfar, which was reported in the previous decade.

If much of the remaining settlement evidence and indeed some of the burial sites, provide few indications of hierarchy or long-distance links, such artefacts show that the Bronze Age inhabitants of Angus had access – perhaps indirectly and at second or third hand, but nonetheless access – to exotic materials. Burial in round mounds continued well into the second millennium BC. A mound at Gilchorn Farm, Inverkeilor, in the lower Lunan Valley, produced a cremation deposit in a Collared Urn, a pottery type now known to be in use in Scotland from about 1900 to 1550 BC, as well as a flint and a smaller ceramic vessel. A bronze blade was found nearby in a mound that had been disturbed earlier and which contained other urns as well as a central cist. The date for this urn is the latest at present for a pot of this type in Scotland. Its association with a

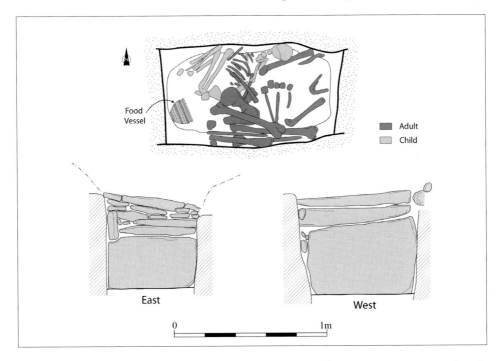

13 Mains of Melgund, Aberlemno: short cist excavated in 1986. This grave included an adult male of about 30 years of age, accompanied by a 7/9 year-old child, buried with a food vessel. The end slabs (illustrated) required levelling up to seat the cap-stone. Radiocarbon dating confirms that the interments belong to the first half of the second millennium BC. *Drawn by Leeanne Whitelaw after Rideout and Russell-White in Taylor et al. 1998*

glass bead (once thought the earliest glass from Scotland) can no longer be maintained, but another exotic material – the blue vitreous paste called faience – has now been discovered at the Fordhouse barrow.

To adequately consider the extensive evidence for Bronze Age burial in Angus would require far more space than can be devoted to the topic here, and should await the fuller outcome of Alison Sheridan's painstaking development of the radiocarbon dating of finds old and new. Although recent accounts have summarised many of the new discoveries, the most recent published attempts to map all this data were undertaken by the distinguished local archaeologist, David Taylor, in 1968, and by David Hunt 20 years later. The latter's data aggregate Angus with Perthshire, but make plain the wealth of information that remains to be analysed.

What is clear from the tighter chronological control that is now possible as more radiocarbon dates are obtained, is that the classic sequence suggested for pottery at this time (with beakers spanning the end of the Neolithic and the earlier part of the Bronze Age, giving way to varieties of food vessel and thereafter to various types of cinerary urn) actually conceals considerable overlaps amongst the use of these types. It is also the case that the main ritual represented – inhumation and thereafter cremation – is also not a straightforward substitution. Sometimes cremation was practised early in the

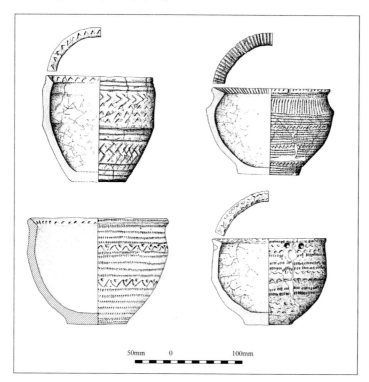

50mm   0   100mm

14 Amongst decorated pottery from Angus cists, the numbers of food vessels are particularly remarkable. These examples are from short cists at Murton, Forfar, Hare Cairn, Pitkennedy, Mains of Melgund, Aberlemno (*13*) and Barnyards, Tannadice. *Drawings modified by Leeanne Whitelaw from Taylor et al. 1998; Courtesy: Trevor Cowie*

sequence, but it seems never wholly to have ousted inhumation. Where it is possible – in an elaborate barrow for example – to identify the relationships between the main pottery types, beakers are invariably associated with the primary deposit; urns belong at the end of the sequence. The likely factors behind such sequencing are to do with the social and ideological meanings of the burials, rather than straightforward changing ceramic fashions. A major difference that needs an explanation, looking at a wider geographical compass, is that beakers (which flourished between *c*.2300 and 2000 BC) are proportionately more common than food vessels (which began about two centuries later) in Aberdeenshire, whereas the reverse is true for Angus (*13* and *14*). Not all single graves were accompanied by grave goods, however, there being numerous unaccompanied inhumations or cremations in short cists in Angus. It may be that this indicates that the tradition of this style of burial was a long-lived one in Angus – extending beyond its earlier Bronze Age floruit – but more radiocarbon determinations would be required to demonstrate this.

Cropmarks of Bronze Age funerary monuments have, to date, rarely been examined in Angus. At Balneaves Cottage in the Lunan Valley, however, a small (7m across) enclosed cremation cemetery consisted of a series of cremation burials delimited by a penannular ditch. Of the cremations, four were in large urns, placed upside-down in the pits. It is possible that there had originally been a stone setting inside this monument, but the displacement of a large stone to prepare the ground for agriculture means that the indications are ambiguous. This is the only excavated example of this type of site in Angus, but others surely lurk in the cropmark record.

BRONZE AGE SETTLEMENT

Work on the A92 corridor provided important evidence for Bronze Age settlement in the Angus lowlands which, though long suspected, had proved to be elusive. While many timber-built settlements have now been identified from the air, this site, above the Monikie Burn at Auchrennie near Muirdrum, was only located by machine-topsoiling. Two structures, which had successively occupied the site, and associated features indicating a small farmstead, were examined. The larger was a house a little over 8m in diameter, with its entrance, apparently lacking a porch, on the south-east. It had an internal ring-ditch initially providing extra storage capacity within the building, which showed considerable evidence for repair. It had replaced an earlier, rather smaller, timber roundhouse. Small finds are few, and the best way of dating Structure A here is by radiocarbon dating. Although the ring-ditch type of house has become predominantly associated with the earlier first millennium BC, the radiocarbon determinations showed that this structure had been in use during the period 1600-1100 BC. Chapter 6 considers the evidence from Angus for this type of house in the following millennium.

HUT CIRCLES; THE STONE FOOTINGS OF ROUNDHOUSES

The better-known evidence for Bronze Age settlement in Angus comes from the upland areas, notably from several of the Angus Glens – generally speaking zones of archaeological survival where subsequent land-use has been less damaging to slight, but upstanding, remains. Stone-walled roundhouses have been found at approaching 100 locations in Angus, their landscape settings have been analysed by Shelly Werner. They concentrate along the flanks of the main glens flowing southwards out of the Mounth – Glen Prosen, Glen Clova, Noran Water, West Water and Glen Esk. Their recorded numbers have increased substantially in recent years as a result of field surveys, particularly in Glen Clova, and there is a suspicion that many more remain to be discovered in out-of-the-way corners.

These sites principally consist of penannular stony banks delimiting houses, sometimes strung along the contours and potentially representing a prolonged phase of use of the hillier terrain in the county. Although not securely established in the case of the Angus examples, which are unexcavated, parallels elsewhere in Scotland north of the Forth-Clyde isthmus indicate that this move upslope was well under way in the Bronze Age. In some instances the houses are accompanied by traces, often fairly vestigial, of field boundaries. Elsewhere, the footings are interspersed with other more fragile remains, notably of the leveled aprons of small platforms which suggest that in these areas too there were sometimes 'all-wood' houses as well. Whether the Angus examples are indicative of relatively short-lived settlement on the uplands, consisting of small-scale populations frequently rebuilding their houses, or larger and more permanent communities settled in such locales, will require more substantial field interventions to ascertain.

A good example of such a landscape with roundhouses is provided by detailed fieldwork carried out by John Sheriff on Strone Hill, Lintrathen, less than a kilometre

from the Gallows Knowe mound discussed previously. Strone Hill offers a tract of archaeological survival in an area where geomorphology and subsequent land-uses dictate that such survival is discontinuous and patchy. The pre-medieval visible archaeology in this landscape includes diminutive examples of monument categories – ring-cairns and the possible 'four poster' discussed previously – as well as other larger burial monuments, which may tentatively be attributed to the centuries after *c.*2000 BC. Also occupying this landscape are single- and double-walled stone-footed roundhouses, the latter of so-called 'Dalrulzion' type, as well as others containing internal ring-ditches (as encountered in the lowlands at Auchrennie). There are clear indications that not all were contemporary and whilst numbers date to the last millennium BC, some may well be earlier. Set through this landscape too are low rickles of stone defining small plots of land, and stone clearance heaps produced by de-stoning areas for cultivation; dating these too is difficult, although some displaced stonework suggests that at least parts of the system are more recent than at least some of the houses. From surface fieldwork it is also possible to infer that certain houses display more than one phase of construction. In such cases, the usual trend is for them to decrease in size over time, an observation of potential social or economic significance.

METALWORK: COPPER AND ITS ALLOYS

Metalwork in copper and its alloys is represented throughout the Bronze Age of Angus. It is introduced here not in order to consider the records from Angus in detail, but to outline how this material has come to archaeological attention. Leaving to one side the relatively few items recovered from burials, most of the key finds have been made during farming operations and that is certainly true of the earliest of the hoards, the Early Bronze Age Auchnacree Lodge hoard found just after the First World War. This contained nine items, including axes, fragments of axes, two knife-daggers – one a very worn example – and two bracelets. Such hoards, and other, slightly later ones that have come to light since, such as two flanged axe-heads of Early Bronze Age type from Balluderon Hill, Tealing, were clearly deliberately deposited. This find was reported by responsible metal-detectorists – users of another of the techniques which can reveal significant components of the earlier prehistoric record.

Whether as gifts to the gods or not, the spread of such practices of deliberate deposition indicates the existence of, literally, disposable wealth at this time in Angus. Given that copper-alloy objects always required rare resources (though copper could be obtained locally, tin could not) many archaeologists now believe that many of the metal finds once dismissed as casual losses and recovered as 'stray finds' are unlikely to have been so. Their deposition, like the placing of significant, wealthy, sometimes exotic, items in graves, had most likely much to do with the celebration of those who had gone before, and the marking – by hoards, or by graves within large, prominent mounds – of the landscape in very human ways. Hoards, however, are almost universally added to the archaeological record as a result of chance finds, not made in routine archaeological fieldwork or excavation.

CONCLUSION

This rapid review of some of the archaeological evidence from Neolithic and earlier Bronze Age Angus highlights both how extensive and varied these records now are, as well as something of the scope for future work on a wide range of topics. Whilst the small stone circles and the upstanding traces of abandoned upland field systems and hut circles hint that some societies at this time may have been relatively small-scale, or indeed forced to survive in relatively marginal habitats, the accumulating evidence perhaps suggests that these were the exceptions rather than the rule. Much more of the evidence, including that now available for the Neolithic period, points in the direction that the major funerary monuments of the earlier Bronze Age in particular have long indicated. Their scale, their often prominent settings across the landscapes of Angus, and the wealth and quality of some of the grave goods they contain, suggest that some of the population by that time were notably prosperous. That prosperity is most likely to have been founded on the rich agricultural resources on the county. The Neolithic sites considered here, only a small fraction of the record that is apparent now solely as cropmarks, suggest that agriculture was already to the fore in earlier millennia.

route north through Strathmore and into the Mearns. Within Scotland, Angus is thus approximately in mid league in these terms, less affected it may be argued than areas to the south of the Forth-Clyde isthmus and the Antonine Wall, more so than the Highland heartland.

The start of the early, pre-Roman Iron Age is marked by the demise of the copper-alloy industries at the end of the conventional Bronze Age (after which bronze was not significantly employed for edge-tools such as axes or swords). At this stage the downgrading of copper alloys, through the consignment of quantities of material into the ground in hoards, may be read as an indirect indicator of its widespread replacement, at least after some time, by the new metal.

Much later, the local appearance of the legions of Imperial Rome in the late 70s AD is significant in that during these centuries we increasingly move from a purely prehistoric archaeology (one where only the sites and artefacts survive) to one which is protohistoric. That is to say there are also the first near-contemporary documents, although these are very sparse and are written about 'the Other' (the barbarian inhabitants of Scotland) by people from the very different cultural background furnished by the Classical civilisations of the Mediterranean basin. However, the scale and nature of these changes are probably hugely less significant than those that happened further south, within the Roman province of Britannia. In the first millennium AD, archaeology continues to be 'text-aided', although the nature of the historical sources changed to those ultimately written down primarily in monasteries and mostly locally within the northern half of Britain. It can be argued that it is only rather later that a step-change in the volume of historical records occurs. This is the Early Historic period, including famous named 'peoples' such as the Picts and Scots. Technologically this was still an 'Iron Age', with some earlier categories of site still used.

If, in the longer term, the move to the use of iron as the dominant material from which tools, weapons and the like were fashioned was to be very significant, it is certainly possible to overplay the initial impact of this technology. Given iron's propensity to rust away, its presence, and more especially the initial scale of its use, are hard to quantify in Scotland. Numbers of settlement sites provide a little evidence of iron-working − slags, hammerscale perhaps, elements of simple furnaces − but in general the extent of this is very limited. The prevailing impression is, therefore, of small-scale black-smithing, and trying to fix the start date of this technological innovation from settlement contexts − as with metalworking debris recovered by Gordon Childe from Finavon fort, a key Angus site discussed further in subsequent chapters − is difficult. In this regard, iron finds directly associated with other metal items are highly important; here we are primarily concerned with instances of Bronze Age hoarding − the deliberate deposition in the ground or in watery contexts of collections of material culture. Some, although not all, hoards seem to have been inserted into the ground (or thrown into rivers or other wetland settings) as single acts, from which it is reasonable to surmise that the objects included in them were broadly contemporary, although some may clearly have been older than others at the stage they were deliberately removed from circulation.

THE BALMASHANNER HOARD

Within Angus, a key find for recognising the local appearance of iron was made over a century ago during late Victorian ploughing on the farm of Balmashanner, set around a hill immediately to the south of Forfar. Apparently contained in a pottery urn, possibly placed in the ground upside-down and in any case shattered on impact, this included an unusual, miscast bronze bowl, a broken socketed axe and, in keeping with several other hoards of the final phases of the Late Bronze Age in north-east Scotland, a collection of personal jewellery items. These included five jet and over 20 amber beads, 11 armlets, and rings of a variety of types (*colour plate 12*). Whilst the majority of this material is of copper alloy, some of the smaller rings (perhaps hair ornaments as well as 'ring-money' – the latter a type with a preponderantly Irish distribution) are gold or gilded over copper cores. One ring, some 4cm in diameter is, however, of iron (not shown on *colour plate 12*). This last, clearly too small to have been an armlet, was most likely a component of a composite piece; it has been suggested by Alison Sheridan to have been an import ultimately from the east Alpine area. Typological considerations would attribute the Balmashanner hoard to the penultimate phase of the British Late Bronze Age, called Ewart Park/Covesea, and now attributable to the tenth to eighth centuries BC. Items in the Balmashanner hoard display not only evidence of contacts with continental Europe, but also with Ireland, and offer a corrective to archaeological views drawn largely from the settlement record which tend to emphasise the purely local dimensions of later Bronze Age societies. Some of these links are also shared more widely across north-east Scotland, as is shown by the distribution of penannular bronze bracelets of Covesea type – named after a key cave site on the Moray coast from which they have been found. The iron ring is a precocious find in this material, but it may be significant, as Colin Burgess noted, that there was also an iron ring recovered in rampart debris at the vitrified fort at Finavon. A smaller and rather later iron ring was found on the floor of a hut at the Early Iron Age palisaded site of Staple Howe, Yorkshire, which also produced Hallstatt C period metalwork. Iron rings are thus one of the few items in this still-scarce material which seem also to occur on British settlement sites at the outset of the Iron Age.

THE SWORDS FROM LEUCHLAND FARM, BRECHIN

Another find of particular interest from Angus, in terms of indicating participation in a wider world, is that from Leuchland Farm, near the South Esk River to the east of Brechin (*15*). Comprising two swords of 'Group VII', these are variants on the dominant model of weapon found in Hallstatt C, the first period of the temperate European Iron Age and contemporary in Britain with the final, Llyn Fawr, phase of the British Late Bronze Age (of approximately the eighth century BC) during which evidence for iron-working in these islands starts to accumulate. The Leuchland Farm swords comprise the northernmost exemplars of a distribution that in Britain is resolutely eastern and related to major river valleys, as Burgess noted long ago. In views expressed by

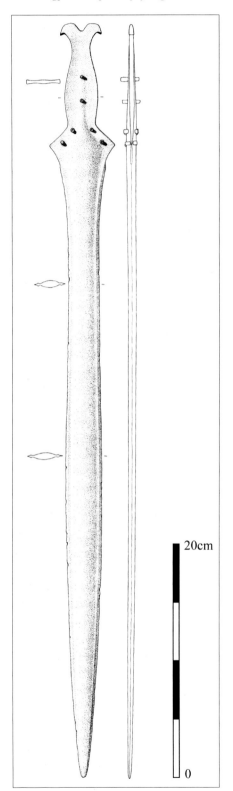

20cm

0

15 One of the Gundlingen variant copper-alloy swords of the beginning of the Iron Age found on Leuchland Farm, Brechin. *Courtesy: Colin Burgess and Ian Colquhoun*

previous generations of archaeologists, such material may be intimately linked with patterns of trading and raiding from adjacent portions of continental Europe. The circumstances of the Leuchland discovery are rather uncertain, but suggestions that this was a burial seem very unlikely, given that in those areas of the continent where weapons in burials occur, they are inevitably singletons. Only a portion of the Hallstatt C material from Britain is definitely imported, with rather more (this is especially the case with swords) representing local derivatives of the imported types. However, Burgess has noted that the widespread nature of Hallstatt C material over Britain and Ireland indicates 'more than normal cultural contact' and has been associated with the diffusion of working methods related to the processing of the new metal, iron.

Such material as the Balmashanner and Leuchland finds brings into question the nature of the Scottish Iron Age and the extent to which it was part of a wider temperate European sphere, embracing not only the remainder of the British Isles, but also the nearer continent. Archaeological perspectives since the Second World War have oscillated between envisaging the Scottish pre-Roman Iron Age as profoundly influenced from outside but only two or three centuries long, to much more indigenously focused, with a substantial inheritance from the preceding Bronze Age and three-quarters of a millennium in duration. The position advocated here is one where there were recurrent contacts with areas outside the country, but where the scale and impact of these are relatively muted. What gets adopted and what gets adapted are thus, it would seem, largely a matter of cultural selection, rather than imposition at the hands of substantial troops of invaders.

IDEAS OF CELTICITY

It follows that there is no straightforward answer to the question of whether the pre-Roman Iron Age of Angus was Celtic, given the Classical uses of that term to describe peoples of some portions of continental Europe. Little skeletal material from the ancient inhabitants survives and of that which does, none has yet been subject to the emerging technologies of genetic testing that may in due course make one kind of response to this question possible. At another level, the cases rehearsed above suggest that at least some of the inhabitants of later prehistoric Angus were aware of wider technological developments, some of which were taken over in modified form for local use. Of course, studies of DNA will never isolate that kind of cultural adoption. A further component of the debate that has been going on amongst archaeologists at least since the 1960s is the issue of language and at what stage a language or languages in the family subsequently labelled 'Celtic' may have begun to be spoken, in our case within Angus. Whilst all agree that languages cannot spread in prehistoric, non-literate societies without face-to-face contact, the prevailing view as recently expressed by Dennis Harding has been that it is 'unlikely that there was any significant element of colonisation from the south or directly from Continental Europe earlier in the Iron Age', so that the Celtic languages either have to be established here earlier (as Colin Renfrew suggested) or developed by other means.

The demonstration of the inadequacy of the archaeological basis for inferring invasion or migration as a means of explaining cultural change or the adoption of a particular language in Britain has for long been a major archaeological activity. Such widescale population movements did indeed occur in the European Iron Age, however, and it is salient to bear in mind that the technologies and resources to make them possible probably existed by the Iron Age, particularly its developed phases, in quantities not present in earlier times. Lighter wheeled carts and wagons, sea-going vessels and harbour facilities, more and bigger ponies, all these are demonstrably present by the last centuries BC and some were in use considerably earlier. The reason to rehearse this material is emphatically not to revive ideas of mass population displacements, peaceful or military in intent, into or within Britain. Rather it is to suggest that the possibility of such major, even catastrophic, interactions has deflected thought from the sorts of movement that were undoubtedly happening and which could have contributed over time to substantial changes. Examples of this include the fosterage of children, the movement away of younger sons or nephews whose rise to influence was checked by their in-laws, and perhaps most of all what anthropologists class as exogamous marriage – the marrying off of daughters and sisters to allies, real or hoped-for, in support of a range of political, social or economic interests. Such social movements, coupled with some trade and the search for raw products (for example, suitable iron ores), the transhumance of livestock to profit from upland summer pastures, and similar practices may have played a bigger role in bringing different people into contact with each other and thus influencing what we can now see archaeologically of the characteristics of Iron Age Angus.

5

Up hill and down dale – the forts of Angus

We begin our later prehistoric survey with an examination of the forts of Angus, since these include the largest and most conspicuous surviving features of the landscape of the region (*16*). Our starting point is the approximately 25 surviving archaeological sites and monuments in Angus that have been classified previously as forts of one kind or another and that have been interpreted as belonging to the first millennia BC and/or AD. The fortified sites are remarkable for their variability in terms of topographic setting, their size, the scale and nature of their enclosing works and potentially also their date and functions (*17*). The Caterthun forts represent individually the largest visible monuments of later prehistoric occupation in Angus although, as we shall see in later chapters, the forts as a group occupy a far smaller landscape footprint than the extensive spreads of settlements now for the most part ploughed flat and visible only as cropmarks.

Hillforts are, of course, major monuments that loom large in much of the archaeological literature on the Iron Age in Britain and indeed beyond. They include the first sites in temperate Europe for which we have other than archaeological evidence, in that some at least were visited, even attacked, by people or armies from the Mediterranean south. Classical authors thus give us descriptions of some examples that can be combined with their physical remains to enlighten us. In some countries – as at Numantia in Spain, or Alesia in France – sieges at such sites mean that they have become key places in what might be termed national origin myths. In Britain, examples have also become celebrated through their association with famous archaeologists – the great site of Maiden Castle outside Dorchester in Dorset, sheltering behind its series of massive ramparts and ditches in the heart of Wessex and famously dug by Sir Mortimer Wheeler in the years before the Second World War, is emblematic of a perspective on these sites which sees them in military terms, as the architectural consequences of episodes of venture and resistance. As the evidence accumulates, it remains to some extent true that the varying (sometimes elaborate but sometimes basic, hurried or even ill-maintained) architecture of their enclosures suggests that they were indeed fortifications. However this is far from universally the case. In other instances, the indications are that enclosure served other purposes, in much the same way as did medieval town walls. There is every likelihood that the hill- and promontory forts of Angus similarly served different purposes at different times, and this is a concept we shall try to expand upon here.

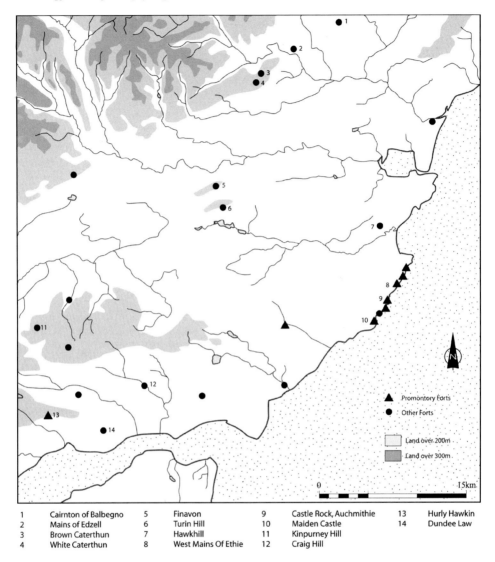

1	Cairnton of Balbegno	5	Finavon	9	Castle Rock, Auchmithie	13	Hurly Hawkin
2	Mains of Edzell	6	Turin Hill	10	Maiden Castle	14	Dundee Law
3	Brown Caterthun	7	Hawkhill	11	Kinpurney Hill		
4	White Caterthun	8	West Mains Of Ethie	12	Craig Hill		

16 Distribution map of forts, identifying key sites mentioned in text. *Drawn by Leeanne Whitelaw, based on Ordnance Survey mapping: kind permission, 2003, Ordnance Survey*

The siting of these forts, often on hilltops or at inland or coastal cliff edges beyond or at the margins of now continuously cultivated land, has tended to protect them from the deleterious effects of ploughing and other destructive modern land-uses. Unlike in areas farther south, almost all are also free of woodland cover, and are thus readily appreciable in heathland or rough grassland. The majority survive as visible earthworks, though varying substantially in their scale from the relatively low relief multiple ramparts and ditches witnessed at Auchterhouse to the very substantial walls and ramparts that define some of the most impressive prehistoric monuments in northern Britain, in particular the spectacular walled fort crowning the summit of the White Caterthun (*18*). Some

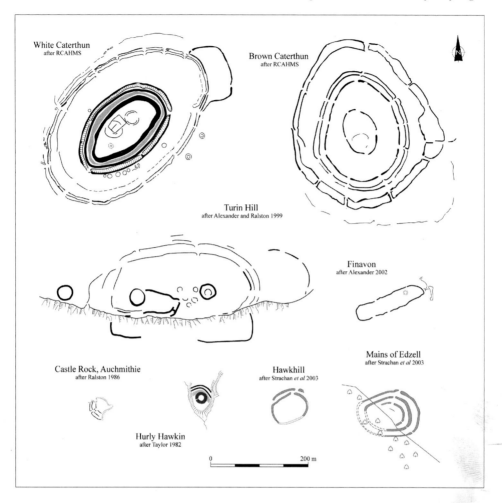

17 Comparative plans of Angus hill- and promontory forts to the same scale. Drawn by Leeanne Whitelaw, based on sources cited

forts that are located within the arable zone, however, have been entirely levelled by the plough and are now only detectable from the air – examples include the double-ditched D-shaped fort at Craigmill near Panbride and the two multiple-ditched enclosures examined during the course of the Field School at Mains of Edzell and Hawkhill.

The number and frequency of detected forts in Angus is low compared to certain other parts of northern and western Britain, and in particular areas such as the Scottish Border counties or the Welsh Marches, and there are reasons to suspect that the surviving population underestimates the original numbers. Documentary references point to other fortified sites apparently once present in Angus but since destroyed without record and others still may have evaded detection, such as plough-truncated buried sites located on soils that are not susceptible to revealing cropmarks. Compass Hill, overlooking the Lunan Valley near Boysack, is a good example. John Carrie reported in 1881 that earthworks of a fort were visible on the hill until the early nineteenth century.

18 Aerial view of White Caterthun fort from the south-east. The multiple lines of enclosing works are visible, with the major wall with its pitted upper surface particularly clear. This envelops two annular, and a later rectangular, enclosures and a depression marking a cistern or well. *Courtesy: Aberdeen Archaeological Surveys*

These appear to have been levelled by ploughing by early Victorian times, since the fort was no longer visible by the 1850s, is absent from any Ordnance Survey map coverage and has not been detected by aerial photography. The hill has now been heavily nibbled into by stone quarries.

In what follows the Angus forts are considered in three broad groupings – hillforts located on or around the summits of hills, a series of small multiple-ditched enclosures occupying or encircling low rises or knolls, which are particularly prevalent in the area, and comparatively tiny promontory forts, both coastal and inland. These groupings are defined on the basis of morphological and locational characteristics, rather than on what we envisage may have been the functions intended by those who built, used and modified such sites. Omitted from consideration here are the many cropmark single-ditched and palisaded enclosures, which evidence from Angus and elsewhere suggests were simply enclosed settlements where the enclosure was certainly less defensive in intent. These are addressed in Chapter 6. The rather artificial and potentially misleading nature of distinguishing between forts and enclosed settlements is recognised here, not for the first time, as a thorny issue. This will become evident when the functions of these sites are considered, but the reader should bear in mind that the decision to allocate a particular site to the 'fort' or 'enclosed settlement' category is a value judgement that often has to be made without excavation evidence that could, for example, clarify the real scale of the original enclosing works.

PREVIOUS INVESTIGATIONS

The Angus forts have long attracted the attentions of antiquarians and archaeologists. Many of the earthwork monuments, although surprisingly as yet not all (e.g. Kinpurney Hill), have benefited from detailed topographic surveys. The first systematic planning of hillforts was undertaken by David Christison in the 1890s. Some interesting details were provided by a remarkable pioneering female archaeologist, Christian Maclagan, although some of her views – for example that White Caterthun was an oversize broch – are distinctly idiosyncratic. The most recent and by far the most reliable monument plans are those produced from the 1950s onwards by the RCAHMS. Perhaps the earliest detailed survey was the somewhat schematic plan and profile of the White Caterthun produced under the direction of General William Roy in the middle of the eighteenth century and published posthumously in 1793 in his *Military Antiquities of the Romans in North Britain*.

The detail obtained from surface observation has proved crucial to our understanding of the character, sequence, functions and dating of these structures, since prior to the Field School researches there had been relatively little systematic or extensive archaeological investigation of these sites. Certain forts, notably Laws of Monifieth, were subject to antiquarian investigations in the nineteenth century, but the accounts of these works are generally brief and confusing. Only two Angus hillforts were excavated and reported to modern standards in the twentieth century. Finavon has been explored on two separate occasions, in the 1930s and 1960s (see further below), and in 1993 excavations by Stephen Driscoll on Dundee Law associated with environmental improvements there, located the disturbed remains of a vitrified timber-laced rampart belonging to an Iron Age hillfort of unknown form. The earthwork remains on the hilltop are of much more recent origins, possibly belonging to the sixteenth or seventeenth century. Coastal promontory forts were investigated at West Mains of Ethie by the Abertay Historical Society (1962-71) and at Castle Rock, Auchmithie, by the Arbroath Antiquary Club (1967-74). A remarkable inland promontory fort (with secondary broch and souterrain) at Hurly Hawkin, west of Dundee, was extensively examined by David Taylor (1958-68).

HILLFORTS

As the descriptor suggests, Angus hillforts tend to dominate their surroundings from elevated positions (*colour plate 13*). The majority are defined by one or more lines of enclosure generally following the contours around the slopes and thus encircling the summit, as is exemplified on the Brown Caterthun (*17*). However, in the case of the oblong forts, considered further below, the alignment of the enclosure wall does not conform to the natural topography of the hill. The wall on the summit of the White Caterthun is so substantial a feature that it has recast the profile of the summit, giving it a distinctive flat-topped appearance when viewed from a distance, effectively remaking the hill in a visibly cultural form. This contrasts markedly with the natural gently rounded top of the neighbouring Brown Caterthun, a profile which the White Caterthun assuredly once possessed before the truly massive wall was built. Not all forts enclosed the very top of the hill, thus dominating their local landscapes in the way suggested above. For example, the multivallate construction on Auchterhouse Hill is sited on a plateau below the summit.

Their positioning on prominent hilltop locations provided extensive views that were evidently fundamental to the siting of many of these monuments. Those who reach the summit of either of the Caterthun forts, for example, are rewarded on a clear day with panoramic views to the east and south across the fertile lowlands of the Mearns and Strathmore, across Fife as far south as East Lothian, whereas to the north the Highland edge – in the form of the Grampian Mountains – looms much closer. There are extensive views along Strathmore and over the Lunan Valley to be gained from the summit of Turin Hill, where Kemp's Castle is set on a distinctive hill ridge in mid Angus. However, what are absent from Angus are the spectacularly high eminence hillforts – notably the Mither Tap o'Bennachie and Tap o'Noth – characteristic of the area north of the Mounth.

As has already been suggested, the layout of many hillforts in plan is directly related to the topographic detail of the landscape into which they are set (*colour plate 13*). Rounded summits, falling away evenly in all directions, tend to be crowned by sites whose enveloping banks closely approach the circular in plan. At the other extreme, craggy outcrops may be defended economically by only fortifying those sectors not adequately safeguarded naturally. Effectively, between these two extremes, a wide variety of forms is found – some conditioned by the detail of their architecture, such as the inclusion of straight lengths of structural timber in their walls. What is very rare amongst hillforts at the European scale are sites which are regularly geometrical in form regardless of the local topography, to the extent that where these occur it is reasonable to see in them the outcome of cultural choices.

The scale of enclosing works is a vexed question and it has straight away to be admitted that many examples in Angus (and indeed elsewhere in Scotland) are puny compared to the most substantial of the White Caterthun walls. Confronted with this variation, many archaeologists are increasingly uncomfortable with the hallowed term 'hillfort' since many of the alleged 'defences', particularly as they now appear, seem inadequate for defensive requirements. In considering what follows, however, the reader needs to bear in mind that these are sites which at most may have been designed against relatively small war-bands using hand-to-hand fighting techniques and whose missiles – javelins, slingstones, very rarely perhaps arrows – were limited to those launched by strong right arms. They were not designed to repel a Roman mechanised army equipped with ballista and stone-throwing catapult.

Cistern

Vitrification

0   50m

19 Finavon fort, as planned by Derek Alexander. *Modified by Leeanne Whitelaw from an original by George Mudie*

OBLONG FORTS

The most distinctive structural form of hillfort architecture recorded in Angus and indeed in north-east Scotland more generally (where its occurrence is concentrated) is the oblong fort, typically defined by a single, massive wall within which – highly unusually – no trace of an entrance break can be seen. Entry must have been gained either through passages set into the wall that are obscured by tumble, or over the wallhead using steps or ladders. If the former suggestion is preferred, it is extraordinary that no such passage is now detectable in field inspection. The handful of structures of this type occur either in isolation as the sole enclosing feature, as at Finavon, or as elements of more complex and thus apparently longer-lived hillforts such as Kemp's Castle on Turin Hill. The spectacular wall crowning the White Caterthun appears to form a larger variant of this series (*c.*1ha). The walls of oblong forts, including those at Finavon (very visibly) and White Caterthun (much more locally) commonly display evidence of vitrification, suggesting that destruction occurred through the burning of the internal timber frameworks, whether by accident or by design, that held the dry-stone walls together.

Finavon is the best known of the Angus examples. Professor Gordon Childe dug here in 1933-4 and Dr Euan MacKie initiated a brief campaign in 1966, expressly to apply the then-new technique of radiocarbon dating to carbonised wood from the site. A new topographic survey of the fort (mapped by Childe before the War) was conducted by Derek Alexander as part of the Field School (*19*).

The fort is located on the summit of Finavon Hill and is *c*.150m long by *c*.50m wide (0.7ha). It is defined by a massive (and in places heavily vitrified) wall demonstrated by previous excavation to be *c*.6m wide and surviving up to 5m high (*20*) with a distinctive T-shaped outwork projecting at its eastern end. The wall alignment, disregarding the natural topography of the hill, is set back some metres from a pronounced free-face which it might reasonably have crowned, and includes at its west end a large and apparently natural depression. Its tumbled remains display no trace of an original entrance. The wall sections at Finavon may intimate a later refortification, given the existence of dumped stones higher than the vitrified portions of the wall, but this may simply indicate the contemporary slumping of the upper part of the wall. In any case, the material culture strongly indicates a pre-Roman date for the occupation deposits. Childe reported a folk memory that a partition wall, of which nothing now remains, once separated the western hollow from the rest of the interior.

Much that is now visible within the fort consists of the spoilheaps of previous excavators as well as despoliation from nineteenth-century quarrying activities that have heavily disfigured sections of the wall. A well or cistern, once visible in the western hollow, is no longer apparent. Towards the eastern end can be seen the infilled remains of a 6.5m deep rock-cut pit, excavated by Childe, which can be interpreted as a water cistern or, since fragments of human skull were found in it, a ritual shaft in which the inhabitants deposited significant material to propitiate their gods or for an equivalent purpose. Excavations within the fort and adjacent to the wall revealed occupation debris, in places rich in utilitarian artefacts associated with cooking and eating, and the remains of hearths and other possible structural features sealed beneath masses of tumbled wall debris.

If the oblong forts are characterised by their lack of evident gates, the circuits surrounding other Angus hillforts are punctuated by more entrances than would appear either practically necessary for access or defensibly advisable (since by their nature entrances represent weak points in defensive enceintes). Most of the Brown Caterthun

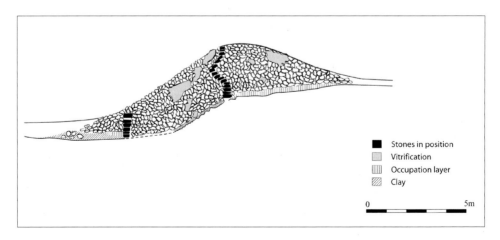

Stones in position
Vitrification
Occupation layer
Clay

0   5m

20 A cross-section of the fort wall at Finavon, showing the quantity of surviving construction material and the varied positions of vitrified masses. *Drawn by Leanne Whitelaw after Childe 1935*

enclosure lines are pierced by nine entrances spread around the slopes (*17*). An even greater number of breaks are visible in the outermost works of the White Caterthun, in stark contrast to the unbroken circuit of the walled enclosure on its summit. The apparently segmented nature of these earthworks on the Caterthuns had led to suggestions prior to the Field School excavations that what were conventionally viewed as Iron Age hillforts might even have Neolithic origins on the basis of the morphological similarities to 'causewayed enclosures', a form of Early Neolithic site widely distributed across southern Britain but otherwise without definite examples in Scotland – although a handful of possible such sites has come to light through aerial photography.

'UNFINISHED' FORTS

We have a tendency to envisage the surviving plans of hillforts as completed schemes, but the outer works of both Caterthuns are strong intimations that what now confronts us are the degraded remains of 'works in progress', structures effectively frozen in time during building and very probably marked by uncompleted repairs and additions underway when construction was abandoned. It is of course very hard to be categorical that such 'unfinished' schemes were not complemented by other features, such as thorn hedges, now difficult to detect archaeologically. Other sites do, however, seem to have been abandoned in a much more preliminary state. Kinpurney Hill, on the Sidlaws close to the Angus–Perthshire border, fits into this category. Only parts of its enclosure, including an impressive entranceway, moulded into the landscape and pointing towards Schiehallion, look as if they had been taken far before this building project was seemingly abandoned. The recognition that these schemes may often have come down to us in an unfinished state of course does not bring with it the suggestion that there is a simple event-based cause for that incompleteness – and perhaps especially no need to invoke the Romans as the reason why numbers of sites particularly in parts of eastern Scotland seem never to have been completed.

SEQUENCE AND DATING OF THE ANGUS HILLFORTS

Finavon

The problems of determining the date of Finavon fort are well documented, most recently in Derek Alexander's review of the contradictory results obtained from different dating techniques. The artefacts recovered during the excavations are not closely datable; MacKie attributed them to his 'Abernethy culture' for which a broad pre-Roman date would be not unreasonable. Radiocarbon dates from wood charcoal sampled by MacKie from planked structures of uncertain character immediately inside the fort wall initially suggested Early Iron Age occupation in the middle of the first millennium cal. BC. In the early 1980s thermoluminescence (TL) dating of samples of vitrified material by David Sanderson and others returned a date in the middle of the first millennium AD for the destruction of the wall. Other vitrified forts sampled and dated by TL methods at the same time were of different ages – the oblong fort on Tap o'Noth in Aberdeenshire, for example, returned dates late in the Neolithic period. In the early 1990s archaeomagnetic dating of vitrified material sampled by Doug Gentles provided a much more chrono-logically consistent series of determinations for Scottish vitrified forts and suggested the destruction of the Finavon wall at some point in the last two centuries BC.

These varying results had the effect that different commentators tended to choose the dates which best suited their theories. Recently, however, the precision of the error ranges of the radiocarbon dates (some of the earliest Scottish Iron Age samples to be dated) has been challenged, such that we can only be confident that the recalibrated dates now span almost all of the first millennium BC. Recent researches by Kresten and others in Sweden have suggested that TL dating results are very much affected by the degree of heating undergone by particular samples, and are thus in part a by-product of their positions within the vitrified wall. These findings cast considerable doubt upon the reliability of the TL dates obtained from the oblong forts. These recent developments have almost brought us full circle; we have returned to a position where a first millennium BC date for the construction and destruction of the vitrified fort best fits the available evidence. Furthermore, although there are some grounds to suggest the existence of a dump of additional stone over the top of the vitrified wall (although this may simply represent the collapse of the upper, unvitrified part of the same structure) there is no need whatsoever to push any such refurbishment into Pictish times.

Kemp's Castle, Turin Hill

More common are hillforts where an enclosure sequence is demonstrable readily from surface inspection of the earthwork evidence alone. The fort on the summit of Turin Hill, only 2km south-east of Finavon, provides a case in point. Derek Alexander again carried out a topographic survey of this site, also known as Kemp's Castle, as part of the Field School (*21*). This built on previous surveys by Christison in the 1890s and RCAHMS in the 1950s. The new survey confirmed previous interpretations: three main structural phases are detectable in the enclosing works from surface inspection.

The earliest detectable construction is a 2.7ha work, enclosed by a pair of walls and thus 'bivallate', apparently deliberately constructed so that a cliff edge defined its south side where no ramparts were required. An associated outwork rampart is visible downslope to the east; this appears to define an external 'annex' at least superficially comparable to that visible on the east slope of the White Caterthun (*17*). Some time later, a smaller stone-walled oblong fort of the kind previously considered was built beside the cliff-edge on the very summit of the hill, its western side apparently reshaping part of the equivalent side of the earlier bivallate fort. Although poorly preserved and heavily robbed of stone, its area and shape are comparable to those of the Finavon fort, although the surviving works are far from suggestive of a wall of equivalent scale. Later still, three circular structures of similar dimensions, which might be described either as circular homesteads or duns, were built in a line at *c*.120m intervals across the summit, although there is presently no convincing means of establishing whether they were contemporary

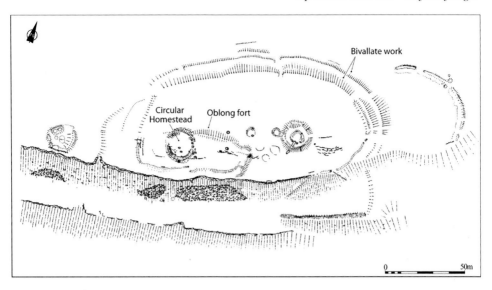

21 Simplified plan of Kemp's Castle fort, Turin Hill. Modified by Leeanne Whitelaw from an original published by Alexander and Ralston 1999

with each other. The central and best-preserved example is clearly built over the remains of the oblong fort, helping to sequence these remains. Its massive wall, up to 4m thick, may have consumed some of the stone formerly in the wall of the oblong fort, although the modern stone dyke crossing the summit no doubt also reused stone from both the oblong fort and its successors. Further consideration of these later structures is reserved for the following chapter.

The foregoing description incorporates only those remains capable of being sequenced with some confidence and omits many other features, major and minor, where interpretation of their phasing descends below the horizons of certainty and probability and into the realms of possibility and intuitive guesswork. Principal amongst these features which cannot readily be attributed to the structural phases identified are two hut-circles and the probable stances of several timber roundhouses, located between the oblong fort and the easternmost circular homestead. The surveyors posited that they were most likely associated with the bivallate work, although of course they could entirely pre-date the hillfort.

The fort on Turin Hill is unexcavated. There is no independent dating of any of its structural phases, and we are restricted to the inexact and unsatisfactory approach of dating by morphological parallels. The bivallate work may date to the middle of the first millennium BC; the basis for this is its similarity in terms of earthwork detail and enclosure size to what was demonstrated by excavation to be the earliest enclosing work examined on the Brown Caterthun (see below). When we turn to the later phases, equivalent uncertainties prevail. The dating of oblong forts, as Finavon demonstrated, is problematic, although a later pre-Roman Iron Age origin can now be reasserted with something approaching confidence. The dating of circular homesteads, formerly called ring-forts, has also proved contentious although, as set out in the following chapter, a date not before the early first millennium AD seems likely.

Thus it is possible to hazard a chronological sequence for the principal recognisable constructions beginning perhaps around 500 BC and ending with the circular structures being built not before the early centuries AD. Such a scheme needs to be treated with caution: there is no substitute for solidly based dating such as can be provided by securely recovered materials from archaeological excavation. Irrespective of the absolute dates for the structural phases of Kemp's Castle, however, the distinctive variations amongst them indicate that the patterns of use of the hilltop changed over time. The classification of Kemp's Castle simply as a hillfort at the very least underplays, if not caricatures, what was undoubtedly a more complex history of enclosure and use of this hilltop.

Brown and White Caterthuns

The real limitations in interpreting the character, sequence, complexity and dating of hillforts such as Kemp's Castle solely from surface examination of their earthwork remains become apparent when excavations take place. The Field School investigations of the Caterthun forts provide examples par excellence.

The White and Brown Caterthun hillforts stand less than 1km apart on twin summits of an undulating ridge, here separated from the Grampian Mountains by the valley of the West Water (*colour plate 14*). The opportunity to excavate at the sites arose from an unlikely source – ongoing, seriously deleterious damage to the ramparts around both summits caused by rabbit burrowing. The excavations, directed by Andrew Dunwell and Richard Strachan, concentrated on the Brown Caterthun, with only exploratory trenches opened on its neighbour. The investigations by necessity focused upon the enclosing works in damaged areas, although some examination of undamaged sectors of earthworks and the zones between them was possible. These are scheduled sites, protected under the first Ancient Monuments Act of 1882 and never excavated since. Historic Scotland were understandably keen to restrict the scale of these interventions, which nonetheless represent the most extensive hillfort excavations in Scotland north of the Forth-Clyde isthmus.

It had long been recognised that the six enclosure lines encircling the summit of the Brown Caterthun were the result of different phases of construction (*22*) since the earthworks can be resolved into three non-concentric systems. The innermost is a 0.4ha enclosure bounded by a low bank containing potentially five entrance breaks (A). It was suggested in the 1960s by Richard Feachem as the remains of a late citadel, but more recently had been interpreted by RCAHMS staff, who resurveyed the hillfort in 1989, as a comparatively early wall robbed to build its successor downslope (B). The medial system is a 2.3ha enclosure bounded by an overgrown wall and fronted by two terraces (B-D) each punctuated by nine axially aligned entrance corridors. This second system had been variously interpreted as a single concept or as a sequence of constructions, with the terraces pre-dating the wall (owing to the presence of an additional entrance gap in the terraces which is blocked in the wall

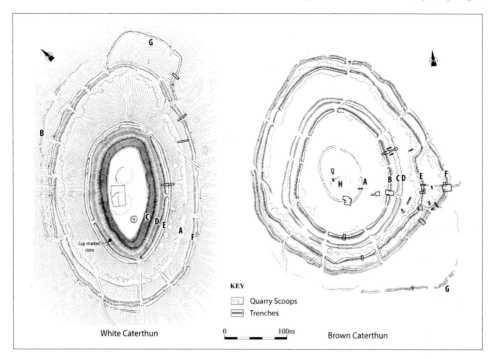

22 Plans of White Caterthun and Brown Caterthun forts, with CFA trenches added. *Basal plans Courtesy RCAHMS: Crown Copyright*

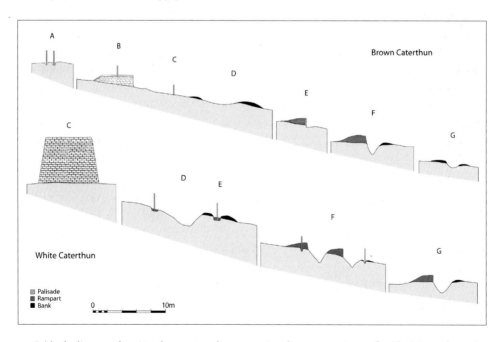

23 A block diagram showing the suggested cross-sectional reconstructions of enclosing works at the Caterthuns. The heights of palisades and the original scale of the innermost wall on White Caterthun are conjectural. Other dimensions are taken, or extrapolated, from excavation data. The vertical and horizontal distances between each individual block of defences are not to scale. *Drawn by Leeanne Whitelaw*

73

24 The best-preserved wall (B) on Brown Caterthun, showing its inner face. *Crown Copyright: Historic Scotland*

on the south-west flank of the hill). The outermost two ramparts (E-F) also broken by nine entrance corridors (of which six align with those through Wall B) form the third system, enclosing 6ha. They were generally considered to be contemporary with each other, owing to their roughly parallel alignments, their connection by avenues running upslope from entrance break to entrance break, and the co-ordinated appearance on plan of their 'dog-legs' on the eastern flank. Lines E-F were also posited as later than circuits B-D upslope. Traces of an outermost low discontinuous earthwork (G) have been interpreted either as an unfinished attempt to extend the enclosed zone or a marker trench for an abortive alignment of F that was never completed before that circuit was realigned. In addition, part of an unsequenced ditched enclosure, now feebly marked on the ground, has been identified on the very summit of the hill (H).

Aided by radiocarbon dates and the evidence of structural detail and phasing within enclosing works that could not be determined from surface traces alone, the excavation results revealed a complex history of construction and maintenance. Enclosing works of different character (*23*) spanning several centuries throughout the Early (pre-Roman) Iron Age, were identifiable. When this architectural evidence is considered in tandem with the nuances of the earthwork evidence, appreciated in plan, our understanding of the development of enclosure on the hill over time is much enhanced.

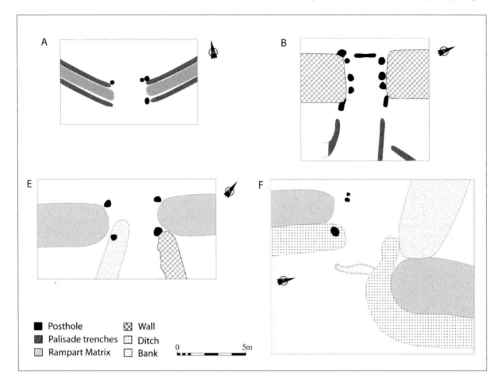

25 Comparative plans of the excavated entrances in enclosure lines A, B, E and F at the Brown Caterthun. *Drawn by Leeanne Whitelaw*

Phase 1: Wall and terraces

The earliest detectable enclosure of the hilltop occurred prior to 400 BC with the construction of the wall (B) and associated terraces (C–D) around the upper slopes of the hill. Where excavated, the wall was excellently preserved, *c.*4.5m wide and surviving up to 1.3m high, with a roughly faced boulder and cobble base overlain by a turf capping (probably utilising turf stripped from the wall line before construction began). The stone base was still intact at one location examined, which is testament to both the skill and care taken in its construction (*24*). At some point after its construction the wall was modified: a timber hurdle fence or breastwork was set into the turf capping, but only after a quantity of the original capping material had eroded off the wall. We know of the existence of this breastwork because it burnt down and its charred remains were found buried beneath yet another capping of turf. The external terraces were defined on excavation as low banks with little evident structural purpose. A foundation trench that once supported a fence or palisade ran immediately along the inside of the upper terrace, one of several such features on the Caterthuns not at all visible from surface inspection.

One entrance through these works was examined, revealing careful control of access both through and along the earthwork lines. The 2.5m wide passage through Wall B had been provided with a timber-framed gateway structure (*25*) which had been rebuilt on at least one occasion. The small size and disposition of the post sockets, however, combined with the low relief of the wall as it survived here, do not suggest the presence of a substantial or elaborate gate-tower oversailing the entrance passage. The approach to the gateway from downhill, passing between the terraces, was also carefully controlled, with visitors having to walk within a passage fenced on both sides. Further gates, set opposite each other in the avenue fences outside Wall B, indicate an additional concern for controlling access along the contours of the hill between the enclosing works, a trait not otherwise recorded to our knowledge in hillfort gateway arrangements.

Phase 2: Rampart E

The enclosed area was expanded with the construction of Rampart E at some stage also before 400 BC. This rampart was a substantial and complex timber-laced earthen construction with an outer stone kerb or revetment and was enlarged on at least one occasion. Where excavated, the rampart was 3.5-4m wide and survived up to 0.8m high, although once it must have been considerably taller since much eroded material was present. At one point adjacent to an entrance, a rock-cut terrace not visible prior to excavation, was identified immediately outside the rampart and probably acted both as a quarry for the rampart core material and to increase the height of the outer rampart face. One entrance passage through Rampart E was examined, revealing what were most likely two sequential gate positions. The putatively original gate position was at the outer margin of the rampart; thereafter the gate may have been moved upslope to the inner edge of the rampart, contemporary with the construction of a secondary avenue leading downhill from the entrance.

Phase 3: Rampart F

The maximal extent of the hillfort was reached with the construction at some point between *c.*400 and 200 BC of a glacis-style dump rampart, up to 3.5m wide at the base but only surviving up to 0.6m high. This was constructed with material principally derived from an external V-profiled, rock-cut quarry ditch up to 2.4m wide and 1.7m deep. The original height of the rampart is a matter for speculation; assuming that it was composed entirely of material sourced from the ditch, a height no more than 1.5m would seem appropriate. An entrance examined on the east flank revealed no certain evidence for a gate, although the passage did appear to have been narrowed by the modification of the ditch terminals. A secondary bank represents an attempt to extend the entrance passage upslope towards Rampart E.

The excavation results provided support for the interpretation of Rampart G as an unfinished rampart and ditch, and probably the marker for a planned alignment of Rampart F that was never built. The digging of the ditch here involved the excavation of subsoil to create a low bank, probably never more than 0.5m high, adjacent to it.

Phase 4: Palisaded enclosure A

The process of expansion of the enclosed area was reversed with the emplacement of a smaller enclosure on the summit. The excavation revealed that Bank A was not the remains of a wall, but part of a palisaded enclosure with an associated bank that had been defined by two separate fence slots standing around 1m apart. Its date of construction is not known exactly, but it cannot have been before 350 BC based on a radiocarbon date obtained from charcoal sealed beneath the accompanying bank. Confident reconstruction of the form of this feature is not possible, given the insufficiency of the archaeological evidence. Previous researchers have interpreted similar excavated structures elsewhere in northern Britain variously as the remains of two separate freestanding fences, two fences infilled with core material, and as narrow timber-framed box ramparts, as known more particularly in southern Britain. The examined southern entrance through the palisades was about 3m wide and appears to have been gated, possibly with separate gates present between both palisade lines.

These excavations therefore made several important contributions to appreciating the complex development of the enclosing works of this hillfort. Firstly, they clarified the character of the principal works encircling the summit, revealing each to be of different construction, together encapsulating the range of structural forms – fence, wall, dump rampart – characteristic of the hillforts of Britain and beyond. The construction sequence was not as had been anticipated prior to excavation, with the chronological separation of the outermost two ramparts and a late palisaded structure coming as something of a surprise. With hindsight, it is apparent that the sequence proposed from surface fieldwork is entirely logical, albeit not the only possibility. It simply happens not to match the excavation results, an outcome that must be borne in mind when reading some of our other more-or-less confident assertions based on surface appearances about enclosure sequences.

Another important finding was that the enclosing works and entrances through them routinely showed evidence of modification. Although different walls and banks in different styles were built over time, it appears that the existing ones were not forgotten but were remodelled. Regrettably the imprecisions of radiocarbon dating coupled with the restricted number of suitable samples for dating recovered are such that we cannot link chronologically the modification of any one enclosing work to either the creation or modification of another. As a result it is unknown whether the hillfort in its final form is the result of a few well-separated construction 'events' as opposed to a more gradual, perhaps even continuous, development and modification of its enclosing works. In a similar vein we should avoid assuming that the finalised form of the hillfort cumulatively incorporated all such features identified archaeologically, since some features of the earlier enclosing works, particularly the timber palisades and entrance structures, could well have decayed and disappeared before the later use of the site occurred. Some of the timber features (such as the Wall B breastwork) had demonstrably been replaced early within the enclosure sequence.

The construction of these enclosing works required the consumption of considerable quantities of natural resources. Whilst the outer ramparts had been constructed primarily of earth and turf won from the hill itself, other enclosing works needed raw materials to be brought up from the surrounding landscape. Wall B is estimated to contain 2500 cubic metres of stone, much of which is water-rounded and was thus not quarried from the hillside, nor gathered from its surface. Large amounts of timber, some of it admittedly relatively slight roundwood, would have been required to erect the various palisades, rampart lacings and breastworks that were identified (and since none of these timber features were visible prior to excavation there is the potential for the buried remains of other, still undetected, structures to be present). If the palisade line identified running between circuits B and C extends around the whole hill, with a circumference of around 1.25km this would represent one of the largest later prehistoric palisaded works recorded in Scotland, albeit not quite on the scale postulated from Burnswark in Annandale. Pollen evidence from the excavations suggests that during the use of the hillfort the hill supported, as today, a cover of grass and heather, and thus that the timber came from coppiced woodland elsewhere. Alder, willow and cherry would have been exploited from the margins of waterlogged areas within the lower ground in the vicinity of the Caterthuns. Birch, oak and hazel would have been major components of woodland in the surrounding upland areas. The volumes of raw materials won, transported to the hill and used to create the enclosing works emphasise that considerable time and labour would have been expended on these works, a factor surely relevant to appreciating the social context within which these impressive structures were created, adapted and used. The implications too, are that resources and labour could be called on repeatedly.

WHITE CATERTHUN

Similar themes arise when the neighbouring fort on the White Caterthun is considered. At first sight the two Caterthun forts appear vastly different as a result of what appear to be very different structures present on their summits. However, dig deeper, as the Field School did on a more limited scale than on its neighbour, and you find that there are many more similarities than differences, indicating that the two sites were closely related elements in the landscape. Even though there are no absolute dates for White Caterthun, based on the character of the features examined there seems little doubt that the uses of both Caterthuns overlapped significantly. The two hillforts should be considered together, perhaps even – more controversially – as components of a single entity. In each case it is only the summit of the neighbouring hill which blocks an all-round view, a factor that may have been relevant in determining the construction of these neighbouring sites. There is no de facto reason to assume that two millennia ago the Caterthuns were conceived as two distinct locales, as opposed to two elements of one significant place.

The summit of White Caterthun is wholly or partly encircled by six earthworks of varying size, forming two distinct groups (*22*). The outer is defined by a series of low ramparts (A-B, F) incorporating multiple entrance breaks, which are reminiscent of the Brown Caterthun hillfort. The inner is dominated by the massive wall of the oblong fort (C), a truly immense bank of densely packed rubble about 20m wide and up to 4m high. Discoveries of vitrified stones indicate that this was once a timber-framed wall, although all are individual finds and there are no signs of the more extensive solidified blocks seen, for example, at Finavon. The remains of a potential second wall and a substantial ditch with pronounced counterscarp bank running concentrically outside it (D-E) have been regarded as outworks of the summit fort. Apart from what may be an original gap in the ditch on the east slope, these inner features are noteworthy for the absence of entrances.

Where excavated, the earthworks again revealed structural detail and complexity not evident from superficial inspection. This is demonstrated most clearly with regard to enclosing work F, visible on the ground as two closely spaced low ramparts with a ditch between them, enclosing an area of 6.8ha and punctuated by 13 gaps, of which at least 10 look original. Excavation revealed a double rampart and ditch that appear to have formed a single unit 12m wide and with an estimated total relief from ditch bottom to rampart crest of up to 2.5m (*23*). However, two palisade trenches were also identified. These may well relate to an earlier enclosing work following on the same alignment. Similarly, further palisade trenches were identified running along the inner lip of the rock-cut ditch (D) and also cut through the counterscarp bank (E).

The construction of these earthworks again indicates considerable consumption of both human labour and natural resources, the latter either local to the hill or brought in from the surrounding area. The summit wall includes both sandstone blocks that could have been won from the hill (and possibly through the excavation of ditch E) and waterworn cobbles from the vicinity of one of the nearby watercourses.

Given the great variety and number of features recovered by excavation, and in the absence of datable artefacts or radiocarbon determinations, it would be unwise to propose a detailed sequencing and chronology for the enclosing works at White Caterthun. However, the dichotomy between the highly segmented outer earthworks, each with several axially aligned entrances, and the inner works, which display a contrasting lack of entrances, is very marked. This distinction surely reflects different organising principles and radically different perceptions of the functions of the enclosed space. The outer works were designed to facilitate access and, even allowing for the earthworks originally to have been more substantial than they currently are, the enclosed area could very largely be seen from outside. The inner works were concerned with exclusion; the architecture indicates much tighter control of access and the massive wall entirely blocked the innermost area from the view of those outside. This distinction could simply reflect zonation within features that were all essentially contemporary, with easy entry to the lower slopes and highly restricted access to the summit, but it is more likely to relate to fundamental changes over time in the function of the site.

Intuitively, it could be argued that the lower, segmented earthworks, similar in many ways to several of the Brown Caterthun enclosures, are probably the earlier, belonging to the second half (perhaps the earlier part of the second half) of the first millennium BC. However, the physical relationships detectable in these earthworks and the additional elements recognised in unit F as revealed by excavation, demonstrate that the outer works are the product of a developing sequence of enclosure, rather than constituting a single phase. The oblong fort is argued as a more recent addition, since other oblong forts in north-east Scotland, such as that on the summit of Tap o'Noth in Aberdeenshire, often appear to be a secondary element of enclosure. We should also not be blind to the possibility that the ditch and associated features downslope from the massive bank in fact represent a separate and potentially intermediate phase of enclosure, more recent than the outer works but preceding the oblong fort, rather than simply outworks of the latter.

FUNCTIONS OF HILLFORTS

What were Angus hillforts used for? Their heterogeneity certainly allows for functional variability across time and space to be proposed, although definite evidence of the specific function or functions of any of the partially excavated examples is hard to come by. Across the wide area of Europe where variants of these sites occur, they are no longer all accepted uncritically as defensive structures, as the descriptor 'fort' might imply. An interpretation of at least some hillforts as non-defensive locations for communal and ritual activities has gained widespread acceptance in recent years, although their use in warfare, either real or ritualised and at least intermittently, has been maintained by others. Symbolic aspects of the boundaries that define them – the earthworks we have considered above – are now widely regarded as of importance in understanding the functions of enclosures. However, proposing a single function for most of these sites – into which so much effort and resources were poured in the Iron Age centuries – is probably entirely illusory.

A range of potential functions for the enclosing works and by extension the internal spaces they enveloped (not necessarily mutually exclusive) can be envisaged. They may indeed have functioned as defensive features, but equally to delimit areas for particular ritual or mundane activities, to define boundaries between communities, directly for display or as elevated platforms that could literally heighten such performances, to bolster the status of their inhabitants (i.e. as elite settlements) and as legal, juridical or similar boundaries. The social context of the erection of the enclosing works at such sites may have been as influential on their forms as the availability of resources of timber, stone and earth. The various types of enclosing work possibly reflect individual preferences and changing fashions as much as developments in the techniques of warfare requiring concomitant changes in earthwork style, although it is perhaps unlikely that no thought at all was given to defensibility when these significant engineering undertakings were commissioned. Moreover, the enclosing works need not have been imposing structures when first built in order to convey social meaning or significance, nor need the meaning of the boundaries have been readily interpretable by all contemporary observers.

The possibility that hillforts were hilltop towns or settlements merits attention and in this regard the critical archaeological evidence lies inside or between the lines of enclosure. Again, taking a wider view, it is plain that at least some of the larger hillfort sites of continental Europe had become complex and sizeable settlements by the last two centuries BC, with concentrated evidence for crafts and long-distance trade amongst other activities represented within them. The places subjugated by Julius Caesar in the 50s BC – called oppida because that is the Latin tag he gave them – include some that we might accept as 'towns', with commercial, administrative and cognate roles. Had any Scottish hillfort sites attained this level? It has certainly been proposed. For example, Gordon Childe in the only substantial twentieth-century synthesis of Scottish archaeology, talks of 'hilltop towns' in

1935, while a generation later Richard Feachem speaks of some of the more extensive eastern Scottish sites as 'minor oppida'. Does what we know now sustain such a view?

Certain hillforts contain visible remains of structures reasonably interpreted as houses. Previously mentioned are the hut-circles and circular homesteads on Turin Hill (although at least one of the circular homesteads arguably was built after the disuse of the enclosures) and hut-circles are also visible within Craig Hill fort. At White Caterthun eight shallow circular scoops are strung out along a contour on the eastern slopes. One of these appears to be a house of ring-ditch type (see Chapter 6). Its rear scarp was apparently overlain by the counterscarp bank of circuit E, suggesting it lies early in the visible occupation sequence on the hill. A well or cistern and two circular, possibly palisaded, enclosures (and a probably even more recent rectilinear turf-and-stone banked enclosure) are visible within the oblong fort, although these need not relate to domestic occupation. It is not known confidently how any of these structures fit within the development of enclosure at the site, but some may well indicate occupation at one or more stages. In light of the fragility of the traces which define them, those on the summit are much more likely to date to late rather than early in the sequence of the hill's use.

Childe's exploratory excavations at Finavon found layers of debris that indicated occupation within the oblong fort, but no coherent structural remains that can be confirmed as internal buildings comparable to the vernacular roundhouses evident in the lowland archaeological record (Chapter 6) were identified during his campaigns. So whilst we understand that people were active within the enclosed area at Finavon, it is presently unclear from this evidence why they were there and in what nature of abode they were living; some form of lean-to structures, perhaps keyed into the inner face of the timber-laced and subsequently vitrified wall, may hesitantly be put forward.

Similar issues – that settlement evidence if not fugitive is at least quantitatively not overwhelming – arise when we consider the results of the Brown Caterthun excavations. Where areas between enclosing works were examined, scatters of features were encountered and are testament to activities of uncertain longevity, date and character (and quite possibly a palimpsest of activity extending over centuries of use). On the east flank what may be the remains of one or more timber roundhouse around 7m in diameter, as yet undated, were partly exposed. A spread of pits and post-holes was present immediately inside the southern entrance of enclosure A, but formed no recognisable pattern. A rock-cut pit, 2.3m wide and up to 0.8m deep, on the very summit of the hill had been used – at least latterly – as a hearth or kiln (although perhaps only once) since its edges were burnt and its upper fills were rich in charred cereal processing debris. This exposed location is such an unlikely locus for drying grain that perhaps the activities were ritual, rather than domestic. These cereal remains provided radiocarbon dates spanning the eighth to sixth centuries BC. Therefore, this was a very early feature of the hilltop and could have even pre-dated all the known enclosures. The paucity of artefacts recovered that might relate to use of the hillfort – a few scraps of pottery, a handful of stone tools and an iron knife blade – hardly suggests permanent or prolonged occupation, when compared to the amount of material recovered during the Field School excavations at Hawkhill settlement or Redcastle souterrain (Chapter 6) or by others at promontory forts. There was very little evidence of surviving occupation layers or of settlement debris having been washed downslope to collect behind the rampart lines, where sediment traps might be anticipated. The entrance passages through the ramparts, through which access was channelled, showed little evidence of hollowing or rutting indicative of heavy usage by animals, wheeled vehicles or even human traffic.

The evidence as presently available for advocating Angus hillforts as permanent settlements is unconvincing, and as hilltop towns non-existent. Perhaps then the case for viewing them as defensive structures is not strong? Here we must return to consideration of the scale and architecture of the enclosing works. The scale of the enclosing banks and related works on the Caterthuns is generally small, a characteristic shared by many Scottish hillforts. Most of the enclosing works need not have substantially exceeded 2m in height, although arguably this would have been sufficient for warfare conducted on foot and without mechanised artillery. Whilst these would have provided solid barriers, they cannot be envisaged as insurmountable under concerted assault by determined assailants. However, the provision of multiple routes of access, at least through enclosing works B-F on Brown Caterthun and the outer ramparts of White Caterthun tellingly opposes a primarily military function. The provision of multiple entrances runs contrary to principles of defence, since entrances are unavoidably potential weak spots, requiring additional protection in terms of structures or manpower and thus never duplicated where this can be avoided.

The over-provision of entrances at the Caterthuns can be understood in terms of promoting access to a communal meeting place for the inhabitants of the surrounding landscape, with the entrances perhaps symbolically radiating out towards the places where these communities lived. It seems reasonable to suggest that it was people living 'off-site' who both used this communal facility (and thus justified its scale in the absence of evidence for much permanent occupation within it) and no doubt also supplied the labour that built, extended and maintained it. The reasons why some of the original entrances through Wall B were later blocked contemporary with the construction of ramparts further downhill, which in turn incorporated other entrances not matched directly upslope, are inevitably lost in the mists of time. However, the fact that the majority of the entrance alignments were retained when subsequent enclosure circuits were built indicates that the concerns that affected the form of the original enclosure continued to be relevant as the hillfort expanded. Access to the hilltop was however never unrestricted, either physically or socially, but controlled laterally by gates in certain enclosing works and longitudinally by the creation of corridors delimited by fences or similar features running across the contours between enclosing works. The use of free-standing timber-defined corridors on the external approach to Wall B suggests from the likely quantities of exposed wood that there was little concern for the possibility of arson. Whilst it could not be demonstrated archaeologically that all the excavated gates were contemporary, the evidence of increasing complexity in gateway and entrance arrangements towards the summit might reflect a hierarchical zoning of access.

Contrastingly, the massive wall of the White Caterthun oblong fort was surely intended to convey a different meaning from the segmented outer enclosures downslope.

Without firm evidence of chronology and sequence it would be unwise to push this distinction too far, although its appearance may have marked a transformation in the use of, or at least access to, the activities that took place on that hill. The massive-walled, apparently gateless oblong forts provide the impression of impregnable strongholds. Yet, Harding has recently argued, in the case of Finavon, the fact that the wall runs across the contours, combined with the absence of an external ditch, does not fit with one conventional view of how hillfort defences may have been intended to function. Supported by the recovery of a few human bone fragments from the rock-cut pit and rather disparate continental parallels for similarly shaped enclosures, he has suggested that the oblong forts functioned as ceremonial enclosures. However, this seems an excessive retreat; not all hillfort enclosures are accompanied by ditches and indeed in the case of White Caterthun there is a ditch outside the lower stone wall that parallels the major one. Furthermore, at least some of the oblong forts contain evidence of occupation. Indeed, in the case of Dunagoil on Bute which Harding himself republished, there is an argument that, given the restricted scale of the 1920s excavation, this is, on any 'square metres dug to finds made' ratio, the richest hillfort settlement in Scotland.

We should be wary of generalising as to the functions of all Angus hillforts from the Caterthuns, since they are among the largest examples and no other known hillfort in northern Britain takes the multiplication of entrances to this extreme.

SMALL FORTS

Apparently distinct from the bigger hillforts in Angus is a series of enclosures defined by one or more ditch, that occupy locally prominent knolls rather than hilltops. Lying largely within the arable lands, these are now recorded mainly as cropmarks on aerial photographs. Certainly those enclosures defined by multiple ditches have at face value the appearance in plan view of miniature hillforts, with their enclosures encircling a smaller internal area generally considerably less than a hectare in extent. However, the same questions relating to function raised in relation to the hillforts discussed above can also be levelled at these smaller sites – were they defended refuges, elite settlements, communal meeting places, a combination of these or something else altogether? Without the benefit of archaeological excavation there was no way of telling what these Angus ditched enclosures contained, and why and when they might have been built. The Field School examined two examples, with the aim of modelling their character, chronology and functions. Although restricted in scale, these were the first excavations ever on this set of sites in the county.

The triple-ditched cropmark enclosure at Mains of Edzell occupies a low knoll and extends into a mature beech plantation where the lack of either cropmark or earthwork evidence did not permit the full extent and form of the site to be established (*26*). Two axially aligned breaks in the ditches are located on the north and south-east of the circuits respectively. Excavation in 1998 revealed the enclosure to measure *c*.40m across within the inner ditch and 80-100m across externally (*27*). The ditches were substantial,

26 Aerial photograph of Mains of Edzell, showing the cropmarks of the three ditches of the fort; the remaining defences are concealed in woodland. *Courtesy RCAHMS: Crown Copyright*

2-3m wide and a little over 1m deep. Almost all traces of the dump ramparts, presumably formed from the ditch upcast, and which ran inside and between the ditches, had been ploughed away (and mostly back into the ditches). The entrance through the inner ditch on the south-east side of the hill was exposed, but without revealing any certain evidence for a gate or other constructional features.

Attempts to understand the patterns of use of the interior of the enclosure were confounded by the effects of plough-truncation, even within the beech plantation, thus suggesting that damage here happened some considerable time ago. A scatter of shallow pits and discontinuous lengths of palisade was concentrated in the northern sector of the interior, but there was nothing that could be confirmed as the ground-plan of a building

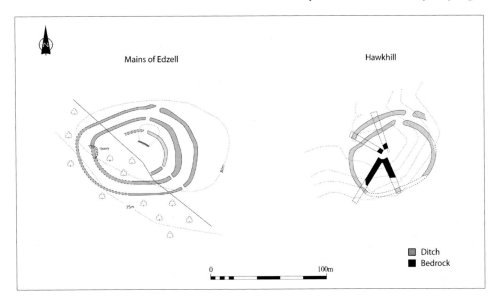

27 Plans of the Mains of Edzell and Hawkhill forts, as revealed by the Field School investigations. *Drawn by Leeanne Whitelaw*

or other interpretable structure. The distribution of archaeological features is likely to reflect chance patterns of archaeological survival as much as the real patterning of past activities within the enclosure. Notwithstanding this, there was some further evidence to suggest occupation of the site. A few scraps of pottery were recovered, although mostly from residual contexts; their chronological relationship to the use of the enclosure is uncertain. Occasional deposits of burnt material identified within the ditches were probably the residues of activities that took place within the enclosure and suggest the former presence of hearths that have not survived within the examined parts of the site.

Radiocarbon dates obtained from two burnt deposits in the ditches suggest that the site belongs to the earlier Iron Age and dates most probably to around the middle of the first millennium BC. However, the absence of any coherent structural information and datable artefactual materials precludes an assessment of the permanence, longevity or character of its occupation. Given that only 25 per cent of the total surface area of the site is contained within the enclosing works, we cannot lightly dismiss its defensive properties.

If the quality of preservation of the Mains of Edzell enclosure site was poor, that of the Hawkhill enclosure was even worse. This sub-circular enclosure (27) double-ditched around at least part of its circuit, encircles a prominent knoll offering extensive views across the Lunan Valley not far from Lunan Bay itself. Exploratory trenching and geophysical survey were carried out in 1999, with what can only be described as disappointing results. The enclosure was confirmed as measuring around 65m by 45m within the inner ditch, with at least one entrance passage, on its north side. No trace remained of any rampart.

The complete lack of archaeological remains from the interior of the enclosure was purely an artefact of wholesale plough-truncation of all buried deposits, a salutary case study in the complete, if unconscious, obliteration of an archaeological record. The summit of the knoll was so heavily plough-scored that fractured bedrock was encountered directly beneath topsoil no more than 0.1m deep. A fragment of later prehistoric pottery was all that was found; no material suitable for radiocarbon dating survived. The basic form and size, the character of its enclosing works and the topographic setting of the Hawkhill enclosure, are all closely comparable to Mains of Edzell. While this suggests that a first millennium BC date can be proposed for the Hawkhill enclosure, no actual evidence for the nature or date of activities that took place here was recovered. Cropmarks are intrinsically indicative of damaged sites, perhaps never more so than here.

With the input of aerial photography, the small fort at Cairnton of Balbegno, a little south-west of Fettercairn, only around 5km from Mains of Edzell but just beyond the county line in Kincardineshire, has been demonstrated to share certain characteristics with those examined at Mains of Edzell and Hawkhill. At Balbegno a small fort, around 50m by 18m in extent within a denuded vitrified wall up to 9m thick, is visible on the summit of a pronounced low knoll (*colour plate 1*). Partial excavations were conducted by Laurie Wedderburn in 1973-4 and published radiocarbon dates indicate occupation of the fort in the second half of the first millennium BC. More recently, however, aerial photography has confirmed that three ditches extend around at least part of the knoll, with those enclosing works being of similar scale and defining a similar area to the broadly contemporary and similarly topographically located small fort at Main of Edzell. The investigations at Mains of Edzell and Hawkhill, however, located no evidence for the former presence of vitrified walls, either surviving in situ or as debris collected in the enclosing ditches. This suggests that, just as no two of the Angus hillforts are identical in form or development, there may have been considerable variation between the particular forms and histories of these small forts.

PROMONTORY FORTS

At the opposite end of the spectrum to the Caterthun forts are the promontory forts. All the Angus examples are very small, enclosing only a fraction of a hectare. Most are on stretches of rocky coastline. They are all therefore subject to active erosion, but even allowing for this must always have been small sites. It could be argued that the only real similarity between these small, usually sea-girt, sites and the upland enclosures which extend to several hectares is the common use of ramparts to define their boundaries.

The most distinctive promontory forts are the six perched on the tops of precipitous coastal cliffs between Arbroath and Lunan Bay. They are edged by vertical drops on three sides, their often-narrow landward ends being defined by enclosing banks and ditching. In three cases these take the form of a single rampart (Maiden Castle, Lud Castle and Red Head (*colour plate 15*) whereas the other three display multiple ramparts (Castle Rock, Auchmithie; West Mains of Ethie and Prail Castle). The ramparts are accompanied by external ditches or natural gullies. At Maiden Castle the spectacular rampart stands over 4m high internally and 11m high externally (*colour plate 16*).

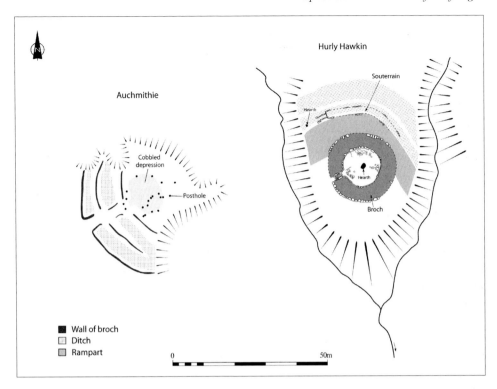

28 Plans of the coastal promontory fort at Castle Rock, Auchmithie and plan of Hurly Hawkin inland promontory fort, partly extrapolated from excavation results and with its rampart partially overlain by the broch. *Drawn by Leeanne Whitelaw after Ralston 1986 and Taylor 1982*

The two promontories that have been investigated by excavation – West Mains of Ethie and Auchmithie – provided complementary results. The tiny enclosed space at Auchmithie, only *c.*30m across, was accessed by a causeway through the bivallate enclosing work (*28*). The enclosed space contained a large cobbled depression and a series of post-holes and hearths that may be interpreted minimally as a series of windbreaks, but not improbably – despite the varying size of the post-holes – as the remains of a single timber-built roundhouse. Evidence of modifications took the form of secondary pathways. Whatever the exact structural connotations of these remains, the stratified finds assemblage points to Iron Age domestic activity. At West Mains of Ethie a complex suite of features was found in the landward end of the enclosed zone, which might relate to lean-to structures and other buildings associated with hearths constructed in the lee of the inner rampart. The artefact assemblage from this site again indicates domestic activity, including querns and stone lamps. It also notably includes a sherd of Roman samian pottery, two bronze brooches and a segment of a glass bangle that date to the first two centuries AD. These items indicate contacts, however indirectly, between the inhabitants of this promontory and the Roman world.

Quite why such extreme environments were selected for occupation is not readily answerable. Previous suggestions that they were constructed by refugees fleeing the

Roman occupation further south now meet with little support, not least since the origins of these sites seem to be 'Iron Age' in the traditional, pre-Roman sense, with their occupation straying at latest into the centuries contemporary with Rome's northward advances. Despite their locations, these promontories do not appear sensible as defensive refuges, since there is no escape from them in the face of land-based assailants. Perhaps we should be looking to other explanations for the settlement and enclosure of these windswept and hazardous locations, for example as the settlements of 'special' members of societies. Here a parallel with the isolated and marginal locations in the west chosen by Early Christian monks may be advanced, although there is nothing to suggest the survival of any of these sites into that period. The presence of workshops for particular activities such as metalworking is attested archaeologically at Auchmithie and this is a characteristic shared with long-lived promontory forts on the south coast of the Moray Firth, notably at Cullykhan. Nor should we forget that these locations offer wide prospects over the sea; two (Red Head and Prail Castle) were again occupied as military observation posts in the very different circumstances of the twentieth century.

The only excavated example of the very few inland promontory forts in our area is that at Hurly Hawkin, just outside Dundee. This site, located at the confluence of two streams, was enclosed with the addition of a rampart and two ditches across the promontory. The original use of this small promontory fort is uncertain, since its interior was heavily disturbed when a broch and souterrain were constructed, in the process also slighting the original enclosing works (discussed in Chapter 6). A circular, apparently palisaded structure around 15m in diameter, was traced beneath the broch wall, but its relationship to the enclosing works is uncertain. The excavator, David Taylor, interpreted this structure, which he considered could not have been roofed, as pre-dating the promontory fort. The date of the promontory fort is not confirmed, but is very likely to be pre-Roman Iron Age, since the secondary broch and souterrain were occupied in the early centuries AD. These secondary structures at Hurly Hawkin are notably different in character from the broadly contemporary structures identified at West Mains of Ethie.

PICTISH FORTS?

In a classic paper written a generation ago, Alan Small and Barry Cottam considered the hillforts of Angus as components of the area's Pictish occupation. Perhaps surprisingly, this hypothesis has not been borne out by subsequent work. With the exception of the contentious thermoluminescence dates for Finavon, there is as yet no incontrovertible evidence that any of the Angus forts was either created or reoccupied and refortified in Pictish times. There are a number of Pictish fortifications in surrounding counties – including the 'royal' nuclear fort at Dundurn in the upper Earn Valley, and the hillfort, much more conventional in plan but now completely removed, on Clatchard Craig in Fife. The putative power centre at Dunnottar near Stonehaven is referred to in documentary sources but has yet to be confirmed on the ground. The evidence of comparable (or even less grand) Early Historic fortifications in Angus is presently missing. Perhaps it is purely chance, the outcome of research bias and the fact that we still have no dating evidence whatsoever for a clear majority of Angus forts. This is, however, in marked contrast with the pattern north of the Mounth, where later Iron Age, Early Historic occupation or reoccupation of forts has been demonstrated in the more substantial excavations undertaken to date at Cullykhan, Green Castle Portknockie, Burghead and Craig Phadrig. However, perhaps the absence is real and reflects a lack of Pictish power centres of this type within the county and that what archaeologists should be seeking – maybe near one of the square barrow cemeteries (Chapter 8) – is a lowland site akin to that at Forteviot in the Earn Valley, or Scone, both in neighbouring Perthshire.

The forts of Angus, be they on hills or coastal promontories, thus appear to have their origins within the Early Iron Age, around the middle of the first millennium BC. Some, such as Brown Caterthun, appear to have fallen out of use, or at least new enclosing works ceased to be built there, sufficiently prior to the Roman incursions into the area that any effort to correlate hillfort abandonment with Roman activity is unsustainable. Others, such as the coastal promontories, seem to continue in occupation into the early centuries AD. Some of the latest structures detectable at these sites appear to be substantial stone roundhouses dating to, at the earliest, the early centuries AD and that in some cases are built over the earlier enclosing works, perhaps deliberately, and appear testament to a change in the way hilltops were used. It is to these roundhouses, not just in stone but also in timber, and associated settlement remains, that we turn next.

6

Round the houses –
Iron Age settlement and farming

We now turn to the archaeological evidence for Iron Age settlement and farming in Angus (*29*) from the eighth century BC until Pictish times. Here our focus moves away from the hilltops, knolls and coastal promontories that attracted the enclosed settlements considered in Chapter 5 to consider the fertile valleys and plains, where there are now virtually no visible remains from this period apart from the occasional defended site previously discussed and a handful of excavated souterrains that have been consolidated and are open to the public.

Aerial reconnaissance and archaeological investigations have identified plentiful evidence for timber-built roundhouses and souterrains characteristic of Iron Age settlements in the area, indicating that the lowland landscape was extensively and densely settled and farmed in later prehistory. To these can be added a handful of substantial stone roundhouses, some of which have been mentioned in the previous chapter. The accent on the lowlands does not imply that the inland glens in the north of the county were necessarily deserted. The remains of stone-walled roundhouses, conventionally termed hut-circles, are to be found in such areas. These buildings have traditionally been regarded as Bronze Age constructions, but there is growing evidence to suggest that their currency extended well into the Iron Age. There are also upstanding examples on the higher ground of the types of buildings that are also recognisable in the low-lying areas from cropmarks and archaeological rescue excavations.

The recurrence of particular structural types in different topographic settings across the county warns us against drawing an artificial distinction between the buildings of the low-lying and hilly areas, when to a good degree many elements that make up the apparent distinctions are the result of preservation biases. Excavations have demonstrated that timber roundhouses incorporated stone, turf and earth in their constructions, and stone-walled roundhouses likewise incorporated timber, turf and earth. The distinction is therefore one of degree, rather than absolute difference.

In this chapter we consider firstly the variability of the Iron Age housing stock in Angus, before examining the evidence for agricultural production. On a wider canvas, it is clear that many of the types encountered in eastern Scotland are the direct descendants from, and typologically close to, Bronze Age houses (Chapter 3). However, Bronze Age houses much older than the later span of that period remain elusive within the confines of Angus. Finally, we address the issues of settlement form and settlement development over time. The interpretive leap from identifying and excavating the cropmarks of roundhouses and souterrains to defining settlements is far from straightforward.

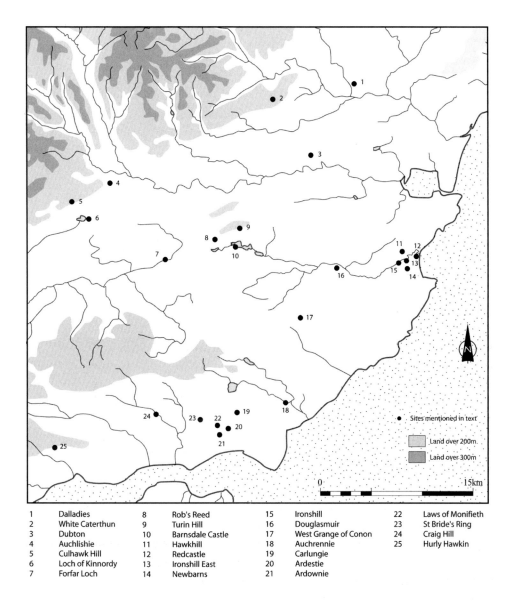

1	Dalladies	8	Rob's Reed	15	Ironshill	22	Laws of Monifieth
2	White Caterthun	9	Turin Hill	16	Douglasmuir	23	St Bride's Ring
3	Dubton	10	Barnsdale Castle	17	West Grange of Conon	24	Craig Hill
4	Auchlishie	11	Hawkhill	18	Auchrennie	25	Hurly Hawkin
5	Culhawk Hill	12	Redcastle	19	Carlungie		
6	Loch of Kinnordy	13	Ironshill East	20	Ardestie		
7	Forfar Loch	14	Newbarns	21	Ardownie		

29 Locations of key sites mentioned in Chapter 6. Drawn by Leeanne Whitelaw, based on Ordnance Survey mapping: kind permission, 2003, Ordnance Survey

TIMBER ROUNDHOUSES

Within the low-lying areas of Angus, it is very likely that the majority of the Iron Age population lived in timber-built roundhouses. The timber superstructures of such buildings are of course long gone – whether removed and reused, burnt down or allowed to rot away – and archaeologists must reconstruct what these roundhouses looked like primarily from their foundations, and in some cases floor levels, that survive buried beneath the cultivated soils. Only in exceptional circumstances, for example where structures have been terraced into sloping ground and/or have been concealed beneath deep accumulations of soil that have protected them from the bite of the plough, does anything above floor-level survive in the present-day arable land.

It was not until the 1970s that systematic examination and radiometric dating of timber roundhouses began to take place in Angus and neighbouring counties. At that time, important rescue excavations of Iron Age settlements were undertaken in advance of development – road development, gravel quarrying, gas installations – by Trevor Watkins at Newmill, Bankfoot, Perthshire and at Dalladies, beside the North Esk near Edzell; and by Jill Kendrick at Douglasmuir in the Lunan Valley. During the same decade, aerial photography by the first Scottish-based practitioners began rapidly to accrue a considerable body of cropmark information to supplement the few sites already identified by this means. The 'bird's eye view' had a massive impact upon what is known of the quantity, variety, associations and contexts of timber roundhouses in these areas.

In the early 1980s Lesley Macinnes attempted to model the potential chronological, functional and social inter-relationships between certain recurring structural and settlement forms in eastern Angus that were already evident in the newly emerging cropmark record. She recognised the limitations of the analysis that was feasible at that time; a lack of excavated data meant that her hypotheses could not be controlled by evidence obtained in this way. Over the last decade, the advent of 'developer-funded' archaeology has allowed the excavation of more extensive areas than was possible with state-funded individual rescue projects as at Newmill. The results of such projects, coupled with the researches of the Angus Field School, allow fresh insights.

In our area, timber roundhouses with three distinctive ground-plans are recurrently identified, although each type occurs more widely across Scotland and in some cases beyond. Based on the distinctive characteristics of their ground-plans (as these can be seen cut into the subsoil) they are commonly referred to as post-ring houses, ring-groove houses and ring-ditch houses. These structural features are not mutually exclusive and represent variations on a theme. Timber-built structures located on artificial or natural islands within lochs, known as crannogs, were also occupied in later prehistory over considerable parts of Scotland. However, the evidence for crannogs in Angus is scant, not least because of the relatively scarcity of lochs.

POST–RING HOUSES

In terms of their ground plan, post-ring houses are the least complex, their cropmarks generally consisting of a single ring of pits (*30*). There have been concerns expressed in the past that such morphologically simple cropmarks might not all relate to structures of the same period or function, and indeed in other parts of Scotland the origins of simple post-ring houses have been traced back into earlier prehistory. However, where examples have been excavated in Angus they have been demonstrated to be timber roundhouses dating to between the latter half of the first millennium BC and the early centuries AD.

Several poorly preserved structures of this type were identified at Dalladies, the variously circular and oval post-rings there varying between 5m and 11m across, and the largest example potentially incorporating two roughly concentric post-rings. At one location Trevor Watkins interpreted a complex arrangement of post-holes as the remains of several houses that had been built successively on the same spot. The post-ring houses were closely associated with a series of ditches, including some inter-cutting and thus successive constructions, that can now be recognised as small, timber-lined souterrains. A small number of radiocarbon dates from material in the backfill of some of these souterrains have ranges (recalibrated by the authors using a more recent calibration package than that employed in the original report) that span the fourth century BC to the third century AD, which by association provides a likely chronology for the otherwise undatable post-ring houses.

A similar structure was investigated at Ironshill, Inverkeilor by Dave Pollock in 1982-3 as part of a study of settlement patterns in the Lunan Valley. Excavation demonstrated that a large building with a diameter of around 18m had been built on a terrace cut

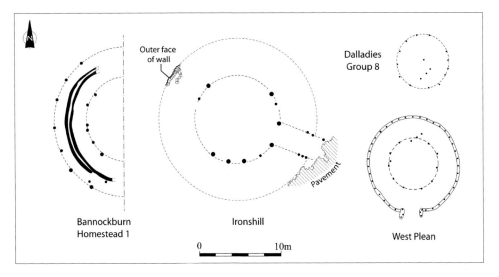

30 Comparative plans of a selection of excavated post-ring and ring-groove timber roundhouses in eastern Scotland. *Drawn by Leeanne Whitelaw after Rideout 1996 (Bannockburn), Pollock 1997 (Ironshill), Watkins 1980 (Dalladies) and Steer 1957 (West Plean)*

the wall-head, projected slightly as eaves, or indeed extended beyond the proposed outer wall to meet the ground-surface outside the roundhouse. In no case in Angus has any archaeological evidence survived to support the last of these possibilities. At least some of these buildings appear to have been provided with timber-framed entrance porches that projected out beyond the wall-line, making access easier and providing a covered, but reasonably lit, area where more delicate tasks could be undertaken in decent light. It is generally assumed that these buildings lacked windows.

Archaeologists have attempted to estimate the diameters of the many post-ring houses where no archaeological trace of the external wall survives. Over 20 years ago Peter Hill suggested on the basis of empirical data that the wall-to-wall diameter of such houses was in the order of 40 per cent greater than the post-ring diameter. On this basis the houses at Dalladies would have varied between 7m and 14m in diameter, although this range should be treated as an estimate since there is scope for variation, not least if the roofs were pitched slightly differently. There are excavated examples of roundhouses that have a different ratio between post-ring and overall diameters (for example, the diameter of the Ironshill house is 80 per cent greater than that of the post-ring).

Reconstruction of the form and scale of double-ring buildings is not straight-forward. If it is assumed that the outer post-ring defined the external wall-line (rather than that this lay yet further out) the Ironshill East building excavated by McGill would have been similar in size to the single post-ring building examined by Pollock nearby but utilising a different external wall construction. On the other hand, we could hypothesise the presence of a truly substantial roundhouse well over 20m in diameter, requiring two internal post-rings to support the roof and again assuming the outer wall had left no archaeologically recognisable trace. This would make it one of the most substantial of Scottish timber roundhouses, akin in scale to the example dug by Gerhard Bersu in pioneering work on such buildings at Scotstarvit in Fife. Whatever its size, the location of this building within its own enclosure set it apart from others in the surrounding landscape, both physically and conceptually.

Estimation of the height of these buildings involves the calculation of the estimated floor diameter of the building, secondly the post-ring diameter, and most importantly the assumed pitch of the roof (often estimated to be 45 degrees). Taking these considerations into account, it is apparent that the apex of the roof would have been several metres off the ground and thus all but the smallest post-ring buildings would have been capable of incorporating an upper storey, which potentially could have been used as a storage loft, or additional sleeping and living quarters, perhaps disposed in a circular gallery around the edge of the building. Of course, whether any buildings actually had upper storeys is pure conjecture, and there are reasons to suggest that such a feature would have been less than wholly practical. These buildings, of course, lacked chimneys and the main way for smoke from the central hearth to have escaped is through the thatch. In reconstructions it has been noted that smoke tends to 'hang' in the apex of the roof – unproblematic for people at ground level, but potentially troublesome in terms of smoke inhalation and the like for anyone in the roofspace of

1 An example of the impact of aerial photography is exemplified by the small vitrified fort at Cairnton of Balbegno, near Fettercairn just over the county line into Aberdeenshire. The fort was first dug by Sir Walter Scott in his only excavation and more recently (the trenches are still visible) in the 1970s by Laurie Wedderburn. The external ditches (disrupted on the left by an abandoned gravel quarry) were later discovered as cropmarks through aerial photography. *Courtesy: Moira Greig: Aberdeenshire Archaeology Service*

2 Features showing very clearly during Field School excavations at Redcastle, with the North Sea beyond

3 One man and his machine: many new archaeological sites are now initially identified by attentive surveillance during sampling programmes as here on the line of a road upgrade near Dundee

4 The estuary of the Tay, one of the great rivers of eastern Scotland, looking north to Dundee. The summit of Dundee Law and the industrial area (centre right), which occupies the Stannergate where early occupation was identified in the nineteenth century, are apparent

Above: 5 A southern outlier of the
Recumbent Stone Circles of north–east
Scotland occurs up the narrow valley of the
River North Esk at Colmeallie, albeit in a
rather mauled condition

Right: 6 A single standing stone survives
near Caddam on the northern outskirts of
Kirriemuir

9 This great long barrow, higher and wider at its eastern end, is a pair for the now-destroyed Dalladies. Now cleared of trees, the Capo barrow survives as a rare lowland monument within a Forestry Commission plantation north of the North Esk and thus within Aberdeenshire

10 Gallows Knowe, Lintrathen. Although damaged by excavation and by an Air Ministry installation – itself now archaeological as the Defence of Britain project has shown – this round barrow set on a summit is still a conspicuous landscape feature overlooking the Loch of Lintrathen

Opposite above: 7 This substantial cup- and cup-and-ring-marked stone has been incorporated into the basal course of the masonry of the souterrain at Tealing. *Crown Copyright, 2007, Historic Scotland Images*

Opposite below: 8 The finely polished flint axe discovered on the Hill of Bolshan, now in Montrose Museum. *Courtesy: Treasure Trove Unit. Crown Copyright*

11 Barnhill, Broughty Ferry: artefacts from a short cist discovered in 1876. The gold discs, perhaps button covers (diameter 33mm), are similar to Southern English finds, suggesting long distance links. *Courtesy: Trustees of the National Museums of Scotland*

Opposite above: 12 Balmashanner hoard, Angus: a substantial part of the Late Bronze Age hoard discovered in 1892 and comprising a variety of copper-alloy and gold pennannular rings, amber beads etc. found with a fragmentary socketed axe. The inclusion of a precocious find of an iron ring is important. *Courtesy: Trustees of the National Museums of Scotland*

Opposite below: 13 The well-preserved hillfort on Denoon Law. The internal rectilinear foundations are of more recent date. *Courtesy: Moira Greig, Aberdeenshire Archaeology Service*

14 Aerial photograph of the Caterthun hillforts. Brown Caterthun is in the foreground, with the inner wall of the White Caterthun showing in the middle distance. *Crown Copyright, 2007, Historic Scotland Images*

Ditch

15 The ditch of the small cliff-edged coastal promontory fort at Red Head south of Lunan Bay. *Courtesy: Moira Greig, Aberdeenshire Archaeology Service*

16 The impressive rampart and ditch of Maiden Castle promontory fort, near Arbroath

19 The Ardownie souterrain under excavation. *Courtesy RCAHMS: Crown Copyright*

Opposite above: 17 The Hawkhill (Angus) scooped building under excavation. This view gives an impression of how well – on occasion and in particular circumstances – archaeological sites can survive in the arable zone

Opposite below: 18 At Lochty, some 5km west-north-west of Brechin, the rather unevenly distributed pits of a single irregular pit alignment are visible against the paler cereals. Dating of such features is problematic. *Courtesy: Moira Greig, Aberdeenshire Archaeology Service*

20 The Aberlemno symbol stone, an unshaped boulder with three incised symbols – serpent, double disc and Z-rod, mirror and comb – on one face is perhaps the quintessential Class I sculpture in Angus. *Crown Copyright, 2007, Historic Scotland Images*

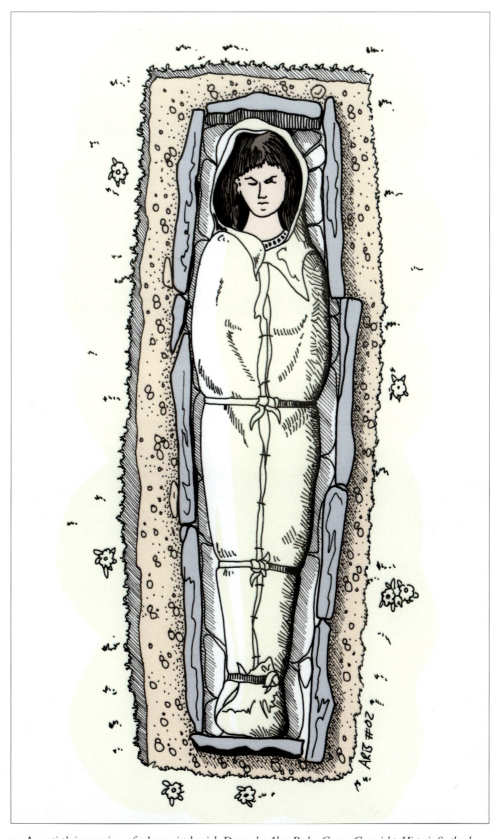

21 An artist's impression of a long cist burial. *Drawn by Alan Braby. Crown Copyright: Historic Scotland*

22 The largest square barrow at Redcastle is shown clearly after surface cleaning and before excavation. *Crown Copyright: Historic Scotland*

23 Cropmarks of the west part of the perimeter ditch of a Roman temporary camp of late first-century (Flavian) date at Stracathro. Midway along the complete side is a distinctive *clavicula* entrance, a defensive feature designed to restrict access to the camp. *Courtesy: Moira Greig: Aberdeenshire Archaeology Service*

24 Aberlemno churchyard cross-slab. On the reverse face from the deeply carved cross, below two Pictish symbols, is the depiction of a battle in three registers. This is often suggested to represent the events of 20 May 685, with helmeted Angles defeated by long-haired Picts. *Crown Copyright, 2007, Historic Scotland Images*

Left: 25 Restenneth Priory: the narrow round-headed door and its surrounding masonry at the base of this tower have been claimed as the remains of the church built by Northumbrian masons 'in the Roman manner' early in the eighth century. Recent analysts think the work is likely to be of more recent date

Below: 26 The modern church at St Vigeans crowns this highly unusual mound, from which much Early Historic sculpture was recovered, beside the Brothock Water just inland of Arbroath

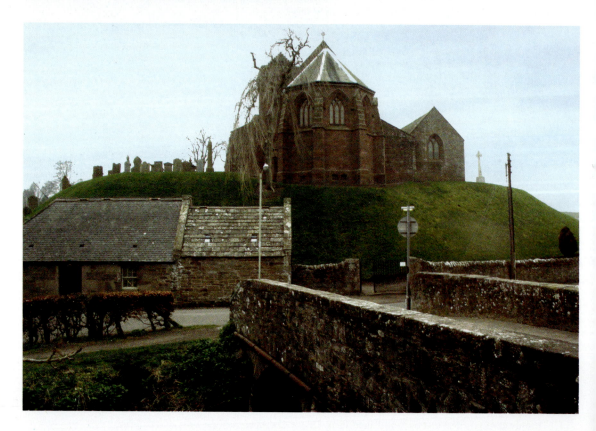

such a building. Some notes on visitable reconstructions not too far from Angus are included in the final section of this book.

RING–GROOVE HOUSES

Houses incorporating ring-groove foundations occur commonly across Scotland, but to date have been recorded relatively infrequently in Angus. The key archaeologically detectable characteristic of the ring-groove house is a narrow penannular trench, broken at the location of the entrance to the building, that provided the earth-fast foundation for the external wall, constructed either of timberwork (planking for instance) or timber-framed wattle and daub. As for post-ring houses, the floor diameters of such buildings vary from around 5m to approaching 20m, indicating the construction of roundhouses of very different scales in this style.

In smaller structures the ring-groove is often the only archaeologically evident means of supporting the roof, although in larger examples of these it is possible that additional internal roof supports were founded on stone post-pads at ground level that have not survived. For smaller examples such a possibility may be discounted as superfluous. However, also common are structures where the ring-groove surrounds a single post-ring – the Scottish type-site for such ring-groove houses, excavated at West Plean (*30*) in the Upper Forth Valley by Kenneth Steer in the 1950s, is of this form. These ground-plans in fact probably represent the remains of buildings that were originally little different in external appearance and internal arrangements from post-ring houses – the ring-groove, whilst giving the impression of a different building, is actually no more than a structural device related to a particular method of construction of the roundhouse wall (*32* B). The external appearance would only have been different where this held a continuous plank-built wall, rather than a wattle and daub wall, such as might also have been constructed over a framework of individual posts in double-post-ring constructions.

The largest structures might require more complex foundations, as was demonstrated by James Rideout's excavations at Bannockburn, also in Stirlingshire. At that site two Early Iron Age roundhouses, one rebuilt on the same spot and located centrally within a palisaded enclosure, had diameters of at least 18m and incorporated two concentric post-rings located on either side of a ring-groove trench (*30*, where two successive ring-grooves are present). Rideout interpreted the ring-groove as a foundation trench for a wall at least 2m high defining a building around 15m in diameter, with the outer post-ring a device for securing the rafters of the roof. Assuming a 45-degree pitch to the roof, he estimated the buildings as 11m high at the apex.

The Field School excavations at Ironshill East detected poorly preserved evidence that a house utilising ring-groove techniques occupied the site on which a larger post-ring roundhouse, that discussed above, was subsequently erected (*31*). This ring-groove structure measured around 8m in diameter (less than half that of its successor) and a single radiocarbon date suggests that it was probably occupied somewhere between the fourth and second centuries BC.

Whilst there are reasonable grounds for dating the few houses of ring-groove type hitherto excavated in Angus to the earlier part of the pre-Roman Iron Age, there is a growing body of evidence from recent excavations from as far apart as Dumfriesshire and Buchan to suggest that the ring-groove construction technique was in use between at least the mid second millennium BC and the early centuries AD. We should therefore avoid dating ring-groove houses to the pre-Roman Iron Age simply on the basis of the presence of this structural element, still less on cropmark evidence, unless there is compelling contextual evidence to do so.

RING-DITCH HOUSES

Ring-ditch houses form the greatest proportion of timber roundhouses known in Angus, with recorded examples numbering in hundreds; they are also the most distinctive and often too the most distinct in cropmark terms. On aerial photographs their trademark ring-ditches appear as horseshoe-shaped or crescentic cropmarks. Ring-ditch houses also survive as low earthwork remains in unimproved ground. The examples at the White Caterthun hillfort have been referred to in the previous chapter and a few hundred metres west of the fort there are a further three large examples set within an apparently associated field system now located in rough grassland.

A convenient starting point for identifying many of the key structural characteristics of ring-ditch houses is the upstanding example located close to the summit of Culhawk Hill, north-west of Kirriemuir, which was investigated by Thomas Rees in 1996. This building (*33*) lies at the upper end of the size range recorded for such structures. Its interior is over 15m across and was divided into two annular zones – a central floor area containing a hearth but otherwise featureless, surrounded by an irregular and shallow ditch at most nearly 4m wide by half a metre deep, its circuit interrupted at the entrance to the structure. The innermost level area accounts for only around a third of the floor space within this building. A closely spaced post-ring running around the inner lip of the ring-ditch is identifiable as the foundation of a timber roof support network. Rees proposed that the rafters may have reached their apex 10m or so above the ground surface and that they had been founded in an earthen bank (in places with an external stone revetment) at most 4.5m wide and 0.75m high, which ran concentrically with and external to the ring-ditch. An apparently secondary ring-groove running around the outer edge of the ring-ditch, but cutting its fill in places, defines the approximate position of the wall of the house.

Rees inferred from the lack of both occupation debris and artefacts, and the absence of evidence for the replacement of structural posts, that this building was kept clean and that it had had a short lifespan. Radiocarbon dates suggest the Culhawk building dates to some point between the second century BC and second century AD. At the time it was examined, this discovery appeared to extend the date range of ring-ditch houses into the last part of the first millennium BC, as until then ring-ditch houses had seemed from a handful of radiocarbon determinations for sites elsewhere in Scotland to be a

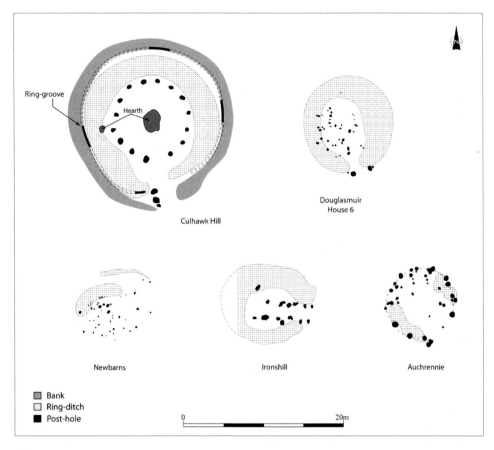

33 Plans of Angus ring-ditch houses as revealed by excavations. *Drawn by Leeanne Whitelaw after Rees 1998 (Culhawk Hill), Kendrick 1995 (Douglasmuir), McGill 2004 (Newbarns), Pollock 1997 (Ironshill) and Cameron et al. 2007 (Auchrennie)*

product of the centuries closer to the transition from the Late Bronze Age to the Iron Age. The likely span of Culhawk has since been corroborated by the first century BC to 1st century AD date obtained by Archie Dick from another Angus ring-ditch house located nearby at Auchlishie.

The characteristics of the Culhawk Hill ring-ditch house have been described at length since that structure retained features that have not survived in the more poorly preserved examples that have been excavated in arable areas. At Douglasmuir, Kendrick examined no fewer than six ring-ditch houses which, where dated by radiocarbon, belong to the Early Iron Age, between the eighth and fifth centuries BC – precisely the period that seemed to mark the floruit of such buildings when the first radiocarbon determinations for them became available. Features enabling the identification of these structures at Douglasmuir are the characteristic ring-ditch, here of variable depth, and in some cases an internal post-ring; no trace remained of any outer wall or bank (although Kendrick inferred the former presence of turf walls as a means of supporting the lower extremities of the rafters). These buildings ranged in internal diameter, based on their ring-ditch components, from 8m to 13m, and as at Culhawk Hill had sufficient capacity within the assumed roof-space for an upper floor possibly to have been inserted.

However, the Douglasmuir structures possessed various other characteristics not apparent at Culhawk Hill. The ring-ditches themselves had irregular, undulating bases that had been paved to varying degrees, and asymmetrical transversal profiles with gently ramped inner edges (that would have made access to the ring-ditch under the eaves of the buildings easier), combined with steep outer faces. Most were of similar scale to the Culhawk example, apart from that within the largest building, which was remarkably up to 1.8m deep. In two structures were found what may have been the burnt remains of hurdle fences that had lined the outer edges of the ring-ditches and may also have formed the internal facing of the wall of the house. The Douglasmuir structures also displayed greater evidence of secondary structural modifications, and quantities of apparently non-structural pits and post-holes within their central floor spaces (but no hearths, which may have been present once but subsequently removed as a result of past cultivation). Of course, in light of the problems of smoke evacuation mentioned above, it could also be suggested that the hearths were originally at first-floor level, although the present writers find this proposal unlikely!

Other excavated examples indicate further the variability evident in buildings of this type. At Ironshill a ring-ditch house examined by Pollock (*33*) was within the size range of the Douglasmuir houses but contained no evidence of an internal post-ring. Of interest was the discovery that the interior of this building had been cultivated soon after its demolition, with the hollow of the old house possibly being used as a kitchen-garden by the occupants of a successor house. A single radiocarbon date places this building between the sixth and third centuries BC.

Nearby, at Newbarns just inland of Lunan Bay itself, the Field School team investigated a heavily plough-truncated ring-ditch house, which formed the middle example of three closely spaced buildings visible on aerial photographs. This building was at the small end of the Douglasmuir range, with the extent of its floor defined by fragments of a heavily truncated ring-ditch, stake-holes and many pits and post-holes. Running just within the inner edge of the ring-ditch were up to three rows of stake-holes, possibly the foundations for perhaps successive, internal features such as wattle or hurdle screens which seem to have been intended to separate the central floor space from the ring-ditch. A curving slot recovered outside this ring-ditch may have related to a fenced compound originally set around this building.

There was nothing recovered during the excavation to date this Newbarns building. However, it would be dangerous to assume that its origins necessarily fall within the timespan of the other sites referred to above, since excavations elsewhere in north-east Scotland have recently traced the origin of ring-ditch constructions back into the second millennium BC, long before the 'end of Late Bronze Age' bracket suggested by the more precocious radiocarbon dates available until now. The most substantial evidence comes from Kintore, north-west of Aberdeen, where over the last decade upwards of 15 ring-ditch houses spanning much of the last two millennia BC have been excavated in advance of a range of developments, primarily by AOC Archaeology. Murray Cook's preliminary analysis of these buildings suggests that the earliest ring-ditch houses had post-rings outside the ring-ditch – in Angus one such example was excavated in 1999 within the A92 road upgrade corridor at Auchrennie, a little west of Muirdrum (*33*, see Chapter 3) and was itself dated by radiocarbon methods to the second millennium BC, corroborating Cook's proposal. From the Kintore evidence, Cook can not only demonstrate that ring-ditch houses with internal post-rings were present from the later second to the end of the first millennium BC, but that in addition, from around 400 BC until into the first millennium AD, ring-ditch houses without post-rings were also built. The Angus data could be squeezed into this model, but this could only be done at the risk of overlooking the potential for local variation in the development of vernacular house styles.

The ring-ditch is an element of the floor space – increasing the usable cubic capacity within the building, rather than relating to its superstructure. It is indisputable that the lowering of the ground level around the periphery of the floor increased the usable height below the sloping roof and no doubt permitted otherwise dead space to be more readily accessed (*32* C). Although some ring-ditches within such buildings have irregular pitted bases, the presence of basal paving in many examples suggests that their surfaces were intended for circulation – but by animals or humans? Some have interpreted the ring-ditches as semi-subterranean storage for crop, dairy and meat products and thus loosely similar in conception if not in shape to souterrains (although as we shall see interpretation of the potential functions of souterrains has been mired in similar controversies). Kendrick argued that the ring-ditch in the largest house at Douglasmuir, being 1.8m deep, was capable of having been covered and used as a full cellar, but that particular example is presently exceptional in scale and without ready parallel. Others have argued that the ring-ditches were for stalling livestock in what were effectively byre-houses (cattle are usually shown, though the exigencies of manoeuvring horned beasts into semi-sunken spaces on the peripheries of buildings are glossed over!) with the human occupants living either in the central floor space at ground level or on the posited first floor. These alternatives are reflected in ring-ditch house reconstruction drawings published variously by Jill Kendrick, Diana Reynolds and Ian Armit. What is currently lacking, despite repeated examination of the micro-structure and phosphate content of the soils filling the ring-ditches, and the charred plant and occasional animal bone recovered from the buildings, is any good contextual evidence of the activities that took place in these enigmatic features. As with so many categories of dryland site in lowland Scotland, the archaeologists' prayer must be to discover an example that suffered a catastrophic fire when in use, resulting in lots of in situ carbonised material. Elsewhere, however, copious sheep dung from the Oakbank crannog site suggests that at times a flock was housed in that structure.

CRANNOGS?

There are few indications of Iron Age lake dwellings in Angus. A stone foundation secured by oak piles discovered in the late eighteenth century during drainage works in the Loch of Kinnordy near Kirriemiur was probably a crannog. A similar structure, first exposed in 1781 during drainage works on a natural gravel ridge in Forfar Loch, was excavated by Lord Strathmore in 1868. The investigations revealed that the structure consisted of oak piles, logs and stones beneath midden material and that the neck of the ridge had been cut off by a ditch. Neither crannog is demonstrably of Iron Age origin, although as we have seen in the last chapter promontory locations were enclosed during that period. Some of the items recovered in 1781 from Forfar Loch – earrings, silver ornaments and chess pieces – are evidently of more recent origin, although where they were found in relation to the crannog is unknown, and elsewhere in Scotland Early Historic and medieval re-use of later prehistoric crannogs is attested.

The alleged site of an early medieval stronghold known as Barnsdale Castle within Rescobie Loch, east of Forfar, had been suggested as the possible site of a crannog. Exploratory diving by Nicholas Dixon of the Scottish Trust for Underwater Archaeology, under the auspices of the Field School, revealed no certain trace of any features that might be the remains of a crannog here, nor any other indications of crannogs in this body of water.

SCOOPED BUILDINGS

A further form of Iron Age dwelling, previously unrecognised in lowland Angus, was first discovered in 1999 during the examination of a series of indistinct cropmarks identified on a relict river terrace on the north side of the Lunan Water at Hawkhill. Excavations directed by Richard Strachan and Alastair Rees for the Field School demonstrated an atypical pattern of cropmarks comprising a sub-circular 'blob' and adjacent hook-shaped marks to represent a sunken-floored building and an adjacent souterrain. What may be the paving of a similar building was partly exposed nearby. The rather amorphous cropmark of the building effectively disguised its relatively good state of preservation within the arable zone.

The floor of this oval-shaped building, measuring 10m by 8m internally, had been terraced into a gentle south-facing slope, such that its upslope half was almost 1m below the present surface of the natural subsoil (*34, colour plate 17*). The sides of the scoop created by the excavation of the floor had been retained by a rough drystone wall, which may have projected little above the contemporary ground surface. The entrance on the south-eastern side of this structure had been disturbed by later constructions and its precise form remained elusive. In the absence of a post-ring within the building, a pitched roof may have been supported on a timber framework founded either on the wall-head or alternatively outside the scoop, although direct archaeological evidence for the latter suggestion was lacking, possibly as a result of plough-truncation.

Inside the building, one quadrant of the floor was paved, incorporating the upper stones of two rotary querns. Elsewhere there was no evidence for a laid floor and perhaps it had originally been of organic materials, such as timber planking, straw, or even bare earth. A raised hearth was present in the centre; wood charcoal probably relating

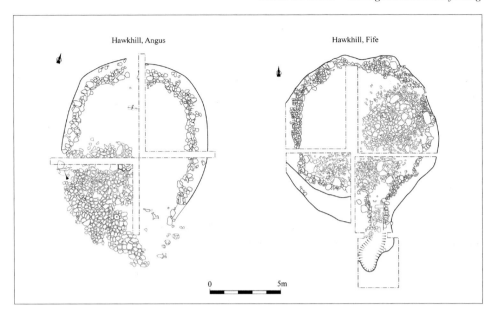

34 Scooped buildings at Hawkhill, Angus and Hawkhill, Fife. *Drawn by Leeanne Whitelaw after Rees forthcoming and Driscoll 1997*

to its last firing produced a radiocarbon date spanning the second century BC to the first century AD. Further radiocarbon dates spanning the second century BC to second century AD were obtained from cereal grains recovered from the building's internal deposits and are sufficient taken together to date the occupation of this new style of building with confidence.

There seems little reason to doubt that the Hawkhill structure was a domestic building, its size lying comfortably within the range known for timber-built roundhouses in Angus. We can be much less than certain that this style of structure was capable of supporting an upper storey; the presence of the central hearth suggests that, at most, this might have taken the form of a peripheral gallery. Whilst the Hawkhill building finds no ready excavated parallels in Angus, there are plenty of cropmarks comparable in size and rather indefinite character on aerial photographs that could betray the presence of similar structures — with the added bonus that the recessed nature of the remains means that original floor levels have much enhanced chances of survival compared with the degree of plough attrition that often accompanies clear examples of ring-groove or ring-ditch houses in the cropmark record. However, we should be careful to avoid a simplistic connection between cropmark morphology and buried structure, since the ring-ditch house investigated by Pollock at Ironshill (*33*) produced (albeit under substantial colluvial deposits) very similar cropmark imagery to that noted at the Hawkhill house.

Yet the Hawkhill building is not entirely without excavated parallels. A decade earlier, another Field School (the Scottish Field School for Archaeology) explored the prehistoric and medieval settlement systems of north-east Fife through their cropmark traces. They discovered by excavation at, serendipitously, another Hawkhill — this time near Wormit – that a cluster of similar 'splodges' (as the report's author evocatively described the cropmarks) related to at least three buildings of the same general type. The building most fully examined at the Fife site (*34*) bears a remarkable similarity to its Angus counterpart in size and structural detail, albeit being more sub-rectangular than oval in plan. The internal deposits contained no recognisable occupation debris or hearth deposits, which suggested that the sunken area may therefore have been a cellar beneath a raised living space. The entrance to the Fife structure was better preserved and consisted of a walled passage containing a threshold stone that indicated the position of a doorway. Unlike the Angus structure, this Hawkhill building produced nothing that could be radiocarbon dated and the Fife structures were proposed as Pictish dwellings of the mid first millennium AD, based upon morphological similarities with a securely dated scooped structure excavated the previous year at nearby Easter Kinnear. The Hawkhill site was thus interpreted as a hamlet of Pictish peasants, its apparently lowly status reflected in the poverty of the restricted range of artefacts recovered from the buildings, despite the fact that they are amongst the earliest buildings in Scotland seemingly to make extensive provision for storage capacity entirely within the buildings.

The Angus Field School results from Hawkhill have now provided a much closer and well-dated parallel for its Fife namesake than the Easter Kinnear building, and we can be reasonably confident in suggesting both Hawkhills as Iron Age structures. The chronologically sensitive artefacts from the Fife structures – querns, pottery and a stone lamp – are all of types conventionally dated as Iron Age *sensu lato*, and there would be no need to explain them away as ancient tools reused or residually occurring in later, Pictish buildings, if the Fife series were redated on the basis of the Lunan Water example. The structural similarities between these Fife and Angus buildings suggest a deliberate, meaningful design, rather than them representing one-off responses to installing buildings in sloping topographic settings. However, as we have seen, other structural forms were used over long periods in later prehistory and it would be inadvisable to set in stone the Angus Hawkhill structure as a type-site that also fixes the chronological range appropriate for all buildings of this type – one swallow does not a summer make.

STONE-WALLED ROUNDHOUSES

Stone-walled roundhouses (also known as hut-circles) and associated remains have traditionally been regarded as primarily a phenomenon of the Bronze Age in upland areas of Scotland, generally preceding a climatic decline that occurred earlier in the first millennium BC (Chapter 3). Whilst none of the Angus sites have been examined, excavations of groups of hut-circles in Perthshire, Aberdeenshire, Moray and Sutherland have all provided unequivocal evidence of some Iron Age structures occurring within settlement evidence that seems preponderantly to date to the later second millennium BC or the early part of its successor. These Iron Age structures are not distinguishable from their earlier counterparts by surface traces alone, presenting very real problems in interpreting the extent and permanence of Iron Age occupation in particular along the glens of northern Angus. We must also countenance the former presence of timber roundhouses in such areas, not readily detectable from the air due to the nature of the soils, the grazing regime and related factors in what is now improved or semi-improved land along the lower slopes.

COMPLEX ATLANTIC ROUNDHOUSES

There are a handful of massive stone-walled roundhouses in Angus that can be confidently identified as Iron Age constructions and these are examples of the so-called 'southern brochs'. These buildings, which display many of the architectural characteristics of the remarkable series of towers and related constructions of the Atlantic west and north, are scattered across southern and eastern Scotland, although with a noticeable concentration in the Upper Forth Valley. Where they have been examined in the past, most appear to have been occupied at some point during the first two centuries AD, to judge from the dating of the quantities of artefacts of Roman origin recovered from them. Due to the evident links between their occupants and the Roman world on the one hand and the use of alien architectural styles on the other, the appearance and subsequent demise of the southern brochs were for a long time interpreted as being intimately tied up with the ebb and flow of Roman military campaigns in Scotland. They have been proposed as the homes of broch-dwelling northerners, who either moved south to capitalise on a power vacuum after the first Roman withdrawal from Scotland in the late first century AD or who were deliberately set up by the Roman commanders as puppets to keep in check the troublesome local populations. Such interpretations have lately fallen from favour and the southern brochs are now widely regarded as having been put up for indigenous local elites, whose taste in monumental architecture extended beyond massive timber roundhouses. Instead, their desire for monumental scale was satisfied by adapting broch architecture to their own tastes. Whether all the known examples were erected at the same time, in response to specific events or pressures possibly associated with the Roman presence, or over a longer period of time, is a moot point; the vagaries of existing archaeological evidence do not allow us to be certain either way.

There are three confirmed 'southern brochs' in our area, all built – in a manner not shared with all the southern outliers of the type – within earlier fortified sites at Hurly Hawkin, Craig Hill and Laws of Monifieth. All have been investigated to varying standards in the past, but Hurly Hawkin is the best understood as a result of the extensive excavations directed there by David Taylor (*28*). It was constructed no later than the late first century AD (around the time of the Flavian advance into the North East) and was built over much of the interior and the decayed rampart of an earlier promontory fort, in a location that provided extensive views across the Carse of Gowrie. Its massive wall was over 5m wide, although surviving at most 1m high, incorporating chambers and what may have been the base of a stairway within its thickness. As is common among the southern brochs, it is unlikely that Hurly Hawkin had ever been a high tower comparable to the celebrated Shetland example of Mousa, and Taylor suggested its original height was 4m.

The central space, entered through the wall along a passage that had once been furnished with a door, was *c*.12.5m across (and thus within the range of timber roundhouse interiors). It contained a near-central hearth and patches of paving overlain by what the excavator interpreted as the burnt remains of its collapsed roof. He interpreted a series of post-holes and lines of upright slabs around the periphery of the enclosed court as the foundations of a set of lean-to huts that had sheltered in the lee of the wall. They may alternatively be suggested as relating to a series of radial partitions within a single living space.

From in and around the broch came a considerable quantity of artefacts, a sizeable proportion being items of Roman origin or inspiration, such as fragments of pottery and glass vessels, bronze pans and personal ornaments. Fraser Hunter observed that the personal decorative items were found mainly within the broch, in contrast to the more utilitarian items which were more commonly recovered outside it, and suggested that the ornaments had been deliberately and selectively placed within the abandoned building by later occupants of the site as a means of commemorating their ancestry.

Next to the broch, and set within the inner ditch of the promontory fort, was a large stone-walled souterrain with a paved forecourt of uncertain purpose. David Taylor believed that the souterrain had been built using stone robbed from the broch – and here we may have a potential indication of when a range of quality metalwork was deliberately discarded and 'sacrificed' in the ruined building. Whilst this is undoubtedly a reasonable inference, the supporting evidence does not prove this sequence beyond all doubt and it is possible to speculate that the broch and souterrain could have co-existed. Perhaps surprisingly, none of the other southern brochs seem to be associated with a substantial souterrain of the 'Southern Pictland' type.

There are a few other large stone-walled annular structures that could belong to the same period as the southern brochs, but as yet positive evidence for their date is lacking. In particular there are no definite signs of any of the technical details associated with Complex Atlantic Roundhouse architecture in their tumbled and overgrown remains. These include the 'dun' known as St Bride's Ring near Drumsturdy, a stone-walled structure *c*. 20m in diameter, and the more massively walled structures measuring over 30m across on Turin Hill that post-date the hillfort fortifications of Kemp's Castle (*21*) as well as a similar structure named Rob's Reed located at the west end of the same ridge. The Turin Hill structures, like others in Angus, have been compared since Childe's time to the circular homesteads that concentrate in north-west Perthshire, but it is not impossible that one could be a robbed-out broch. Until recently these Angus examples of 'ring-forts' had been assumed to date to late in the first millennium AD, but doubt has been cast on this by the discovery that two neighbouring structures of this general type excavated at Aldclune, near Blair Atholl in Perthshire, instead belonged in the early centuries AD. In this case the stray find of a beautiful and highly decorated Early Historic pin turned out not to be closely related in date to the derelict structure from which it was recovered. In terms of defining the chronological bracket for heavily walled circular structures in Tayside, the jury is still out. It may be so for some time yet, although some examples are clearly of the earlier part of the first millennium AD.

VARIATIONS ON A THEME

The foregoing review has identified many common themes relating to Iron Age housing in the lowlands of Angus – of the inland glens and hills, in the absence of excavations we know virtually nothing other than what can be inferred from sites in other parts of the Scottish countryside. The timber roundhouses of the lowlands incorporated subtly different foundation plans and construction methods, but the same basic engineering principle underlay all – an earth-fast timber framework supporting a thatched roof. In geometric terms, all are essentially cones placed over cylinders (*32*). These buildings ranged considerably in scale, the larger ones at least being capable in structural terms of supporting a first floor, even if this might have occasioned practical problems with evacuating smoke. Despite such reservations, we may note however, that hearths were successfully built over wooden floors within crannogs and that scarcement ledges and other structural details within Complex Atlantic Roundhouses demonstrate that these were undoubtedly multi-storey structures. There appears to have been a repeated desire to provide the Angus timber buildings with imposing entrances, possibly for a combination of symbolic and practical reasons. Such entrances would on the one hand serve to impress visitors and on the other provide well-lit sheltered areas where a range of practical tasks could be carried out; it is usually assumed that the low walls of timber roundhouses lacked any windows, although it should be pointed out that the toolkit necessary to construct moveable wooden shutters certainly existed at this time. The apparent differences in their architecture for the most part relate to the use of varying structural devices and raw materials for raising the walls and supporting the roofs of these roundhouses. Whether these variations are best explained in terms of chronological, functional or social diversity will be considered later.

Where archaeological evidence has been found of the activities that took place in and around these buildings, it suggests that they were the domestic residences of farming communities. The discovery of hearths within buildings provides a good proxy indicator for a domestic function, but in the lowland zone these have rarely survived the attentions of the plough. We require the better-preserved evidence of the Culhawk Hill and Hawkhill buildings as reassurance that these buildings did contain heating and cooking facilities. The repeated recovery during the excavation of these buildings of quernstones and other worked stones (including whetstones – good indicators of the iron tools that have long since rusted away), occasional fragments of handmade pottery, iron implements and the occasional exotic piece of Roman tableware or jewellery point to a range of domestic, craft and agricultural activities. These were discarded once broken, reused in stonework, or as suggested above in some cases deliberately sacrificed. With very rare exceptions, notably the Hurly Hawkin broch, artefact assemblages recovered from roundhouses are limited in quantity and range, and are predominantly utilitarian in character. This might suggest the relative material poverty of the occupants, but could also relate to the careful recycling of broken or redundant implements, not to mention the effects of dispersal and destruction by the plough. Inevitably the range of activities represented by the finds is skewed in favour of those not primarily represented by wooden and other organic equipment, since these dryland sites have preservation conditions wholly different from crannogs, for instance, where such material survives. Nonetheless, various domestic activities – polishing things, making clothes, eating, toiletry – are apparent from the objects recovered.

We of course cannot be absolutely sure that every timber roundhouse was a residence, given the variations in their scale and the limitations of archaeological evidence. However, as yet we cannot point to a timber roundhouse in Angus that we can definitively identify on archaeological grounds as having been non-residential. This may seem at first sight surprising, given the range of functions more recent farming communities often install in more dilapidated buildings no longer considered fit for human occupation. In theory, it is the last use of such buildings that ought generally to be the most identifiable to the excavating archaeologist. It is through the study of the building remains within their landscape and settlement context that we might begin to speculate as to whether there might have been, for example, communal buildings – the 'village halls' or shrines. As we shall see in the next section, Iron Age settlements were accompanied by non-residential structures, but none of these were round.

What is also evident from the excavation record is that no two timber roundhouses are identical – in Iron Age Angus there were no roving professional house-builders constructing timber roundhouses from standard components, although there is reason to believe that the approximately matched timbers needed to put these buildings up, as well as the quantities of withies required and other timber resources, may have come from managed woodlands. These were bespoke houses undoubtedly constructed and rebuilt by their occupiers using long-established technical know-how passed down through the generations, their particular scale and constructional details potentially determined by one or a combination of functional necessities, social conventions and, more prosaically, the local availability of raw materials. This latter of course may have been as much socially controlled as determined by pure presence or absence of resource – those who had ownership of woodland could have determined how and when such materials were expended.

As yet we are unable to trace from their surviving foundation plans any major transformations through time in the various Iron Age timber roundhouse styles in Angus. This contrasts with the well-documented evidence of very considerable changes to the scale and architecture of better-preserved stone-walled roundhouses in Atlantic Scotland over the same period, which resulted in the appearance of complex Atlantic roundhouses (brochs and duns). The apparent inertia in the east is at least partly the result of a preservation bias, since various attributes visible to a greater extent in the western houses – their above-ground appearance and the way they were furnished – are almost wholly archaeologically intangible in lowland Angus roundhouses. These and other factors – the organisation of the use of space, the social and familial relationships of the occupants – could have changed over time but, unlike in the west of Scotland, the basic range of ground plans of timber roundhouses apparently did not. As far as we can presently tell it is only towards the end of our period that novel forms of architecture appear in the lowlands, in the shape of the stone-walled 'southern brochs' and the series of scooped buildings.

IRON AGE ECONOMIES – SUBSISTENCE OR BREADBASKET?

Agriculture formed the key means of food production for the Iron Age inhabitants of Angus. Food could still be gathered from wild plants, hunted, fished and fowled, but it was the produce of crop-growing and stock-rearing that sustained communities. On the whole, non-agricultural activities seem to have contributed only modestly to the diet; there is little sign that deer hunting on horseback was by this stage the prestige sport it was to become some centuries later, when it is often shown on Pictish stones. Then, as today, many parts of lowland Angus were blessed with extremely fertile soils. Was this then a land of plenty, or was putting food on the table much more of a struggle? Further, how were the upland areas exploited? In this section we review the archaeological evidence, both direct and indirect, for the economic basis of Iron Age society in Angus.

By direct evidence we mean the physical residues of agricultural production, be they the tools used for cultivating and processing crops, plant remains, or the bones of animals. We have already referred to agricultural tools found during settlement excavations (*35*).

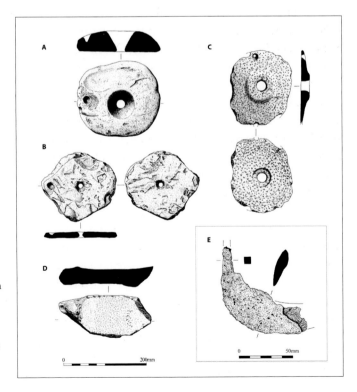

35 Artefacts related to food production recovered during Field School excavations: rotary (A-C) and saddle (D) querns from Hawkhill; iron reaping hook from Redcastle souterrain (E). *Drawn by Alan Braby and Kevin Hicks. Crown Copyright: Historic Scotland*

Harvesting tools include an iron sickle found at Hurly Hawkin and an iron reaping hook found in the souterrain at Redcastle (see below). Iron shares for simple ploughs (ards) although found further south in Britain by this time have yet to be found in Angus. The most common artefacts indicating crop processing are quernstones. Either whole or broken, these are recovered sometimes simply discarded but more often found reused, perhaps symbolically, in the walls and paving of roundhouses and souterrains. These querns were used primarily for turning cereals into flour and the rotary-action hand querns introduced into Scotland perhaps around 200 BC arguably represent the great labour-saving devices of later prehistory. They are far more effective in producing flour than the laborious back-and-forth actions and manual removal of the product required for saddle querns and rubbing stones. Rotary querns can take a number of forms, but function best with metal fitments; the flat disc-like form was preferred in eastern Scotland.

Palaeobotanical remains recovered during excavations allow insights into the range of crops and other plant resources, the cultivation methods employed, as well as crop processing methods. This evidence normally consists of charred cereal grains and crop processing debris, sometimes mixed with weeds of cultivation and wild plants. Found within archaeological deposits, these are mostly scattered but some deliberate deposits of dumped material, perhaps accidentally charred on domestic hearths, are recovered. Such contexts also produce wood charcoal, which can provide information on local woodland character (although the selection of wood brought onto archaeological sites is clearly deliberate and some species may have been avoided) and the methods used to manage and exploit it. The range of material surviving on dryland sites is inevitably restricted by preservation conditions, as is clear by comparison to the range of burnt and unburnt charred plant material that can survive on waterlogged sites. Jennifer Miller's exploration of the wide range of plant components recovered from Oakbank Crannog, Loch Tay, and her consideration of their likely uses, demonstrate vividly the limitations of the lowland Angus resource.

Analyses by Mike Church and Mhairi Hastie of the generally small assemblages of Iron Age charred plant remains recovered from Field School and certain other recent Angus excavations provide a consistent indication of barley having been the most significant crop. Wheat, both emmer and winter-sown spelt, and oats generally occur in smaller quantities and were either secondary crops or in some cases possibly little more than weeds within the barley crop. However, Iron Age farmers only rarely grew 'pure' crops in the way that we understand them today. Church noted that there are variations within the range of crops recovered from different locations, which suggests some sophistication in the way different portions of the arable landscape were exploited. At Hawkhill, he identified (in addition to cultivars) a wide range of woodland and moorland resources that must have been brought some distance to this near-coastal location in the lower valley of the Lunan Water. The assemblage from Ardownie souterrain (see below) examined by Hastie, contained a range of perennial weeds. The occurrence of these, rather than annuals, indicates larger-scale plough cultivation of regularly used and perhaps manured fields, rather than small-scale horticulture.

Of stock-rearing we know very little. The generally acidic soils of Angus do not favour the preservation of animal bone. Where fragments of animal bone have been found, as at Hawkhill, they are from cattle, sheep and possibly goat, and pig. However, finds are very sparse and nowhere in the recently examined sites has an assemblage been found from which statistically significant results could be obtained on such matters as species representation, or herd or flock composition, which would indicate whether cattle were kept for dairy or meat, sheep for wool or meat, and so forth. By the Iron Age, sheep were in general woolly animals (their earlier progenitors were distinctly hairy in appearance) but proxy evidence for this is rare in Angus. There are no known iron shears, for example, tools that survive in some areas with kinder soils and become relatively common in the last centuries BC. Nor is there direct evidence for weaving in the form of loom-weights. Spindle whorls, as found at Finavon and Hurly Hawkin for example, do however indicate spinning, and the existence in the native repertory during the Roman period of relatively delicate copper-alloy brooches indicate that some of the garments worn were fine enough weaves to be held in place by these flashy imports.

Archaeologists of the most recent generation have been critical of Stuart Piggott's influential view of Iron Age farming in north Britain, famously being dominated by '… Celtic cow-boys and shepherds, footloose and unpredictable, moving with their animals over rough pasture and moorland …'. That said, stock-raising will undoubtedly have been important, with some animals being kept close to the farmsteads for milk, dung, blood, meat and muscle power. Transhumance, the seasonal movement of livestock through the landscape to suitable pastures, is also likely. As well as allowing the beasts to profit from differing growing seasons back from the coast, such activities also facilitate contacts – perhaps especially for the young – between different human communities. Animals, perhaps cattle particularly, were doubtless too a way of demonstrating their owner's status literally 'on the hoof', but the meagre tally of skeletal evidence from Angus does not allow the detection of any particularly fine specimens.

We have little or no direct evidence for either horses or wheeled vehicles in Iron Age Angus, although these are known elsewhere. The assumption must be that small ponies, maybe 12 hands at the withers, would have been available and – too small to have been ridden any distance by a grown man – could have pulled spoke-wheeled carts, for which we have a little evidence, both literary and archaeological, from eastern Scotland. Other proxy evidence in the form of harness fittings and a horse-bit is present, for example, at Hurly Hawkin.

We can speculate further that, if the easier production of flour entailed by the adoption of rotary querns led to greater cereal production, this would increase the amount of arable land, perhaps making further inroads too on the woodland cover. Sadly, because of the poor survival of animal bone, it is impossible to be sure such an upswing in the output of flour might be matched by the keeping of more dairy cows. However the availability of milk-and-mush would have enabled more children to be raised, thus providing more hands for agricultural work.

Can we detect the fields of the Iron Age farmers? In the uplands we can see discrete plots of land, often small, defined by low stone banks and/or containing small heaps

36 Undated field boundary cropmarks and natural ice wedges at Newbarns, near Lunan Bay. *Courtesy RCAHMS: Crown Copyright*

of cleared stone, in some cases associated with stone-walled roundhouses and, as near White Caterthun, ring-ditch houses. Banks may have served to define stock enclosures, but the clearance of stones suggests that cultivation was attempted at higher altitudes than at present. As yet we sadly lack any reliable information on the date of these field systems in Angus, although other Scottish evidence of this kind is later prehistoric in date. Field School participants also detected evidence of near-level cultivation terraces, again undated, on the southern slopes of the White Caterthun, within the area enclosed by the outer hillfort ramparts but in proximity to ring-ditch houses. Again this style of ground preparation for cultivation seems to have started elsewhere in Scotland within the Iron Age.

In the lowlands the evidence is even more elusive, since later prehistoric banks no longer survive and we must rely on cropmark evidence. Certain areas, such as around Lunan Bay, or near Boysack, show linear ditched features, very possibly land boundaries, running across prehistoric and Pictish settlement areas (*36*). Without any secure means of dating them in the absence of excavation, they as yet are not readily interpretable. What Angus and eastern Scotland (with the arguable exception of East Lothian) more generally lacks is the evidence for extensive subdivision of the arable landscape and the creation of large field systems. Elsewhere in the Angus lowlands, such as around Friockheim, fragments of pitted boundaries, referred to by archaeologists unimaginatively as 'pit alignments', have been recorded from the air (*colour plate 18*). Particularly in the Lothians, extensive networks of pit alignments, for example around the Garleton Hills, demarcate what appear to be later prehistoric field systems, in some cases attached to hillforts or enclosed settlements. However, the Angus evidence is much more fragmentary and some more elaborate enclosures formed of such alignments are indubitably Neolithic, a situation which cannot be blamed simply upon differing quality of aerial photographic coverage. Therefore we are forced to accept the possibility that pit alignments in Angus may have had a differing function (ritual or ceremonial perhaps, rather than as agricultural boundaries) and may belong to a different timespan from the Lothian cases.

Another important component of the landscape must have been woodland, although this is likely to have been very substantially reduced in area from preceding millennia. The widespread presence of timber roundhouses necessitated different kinds of wood – withies, straight-growing poles and more substantial load-bearing timber uprights – for their construction. Timber is heavy and this, along with the roughly matched pieces of wood entailed in these buildings, suggests that it would have been obtained more readily from managed woodland than from the 'wildwood' – natural unaltered woodland. In managed woods, the cycle of planting, coppicing, pollarding and felling is controlled. Some of the charred hurdles found within one of the Brown Caterthun ramparts are likely to have derived from coppiced woodland. Overall, however, formal evidence for the form of Scotland's surviving woodlands by the Iron Age remains rare. This is especially the case for improved lowlands as in Angus, where surviving pollen evidence that would assist is rarely present. Wood was also essential as a fuel for cooking, heating and for industrial processes (notably the smelting and smithing of iron). Elsewhere turf or peat was used, and surface-gathered coal, from the shoreline of the Forth Estuary for example, makes a first appearance in south-east Scottish settlements later in the Iron Age. However, in lowland Angus, wood seems to have dominated for such purposes.

UNDERGROUND, OVERGROUND – THE STORAGE OF SURPLUS AGRICULTURAL PRODUCE

In the pre-modern past, Angus was capable of producing an agricultural surplus, as is made clear by the ministers who compiled parish descriptions for the *Statistical Account of Scotland* in the 1790s. There is plentiful archaeological evidence that this was the case in prehistory too, assuming the many souterrains that formed part of the typical settlement layout, at least in the early centuries AD, were indeed for storing agricultural surpluses. However, there are other, more enigmatic timber-framed structures found during settlement excavations that may also relate to storage. All this evidence relating to Iron Age economy is indirect; the association of these features with agriculture can only be inferred.

Souterrains are one of the characteristic Iron Age structural features of several areas of Scotland, but they have been noted far more commonly between the Tay and the Grampian foothills than anywhere else (*37*). Popular interest in them stems from a fascination with the subterranean and complex nature of their construction (the most

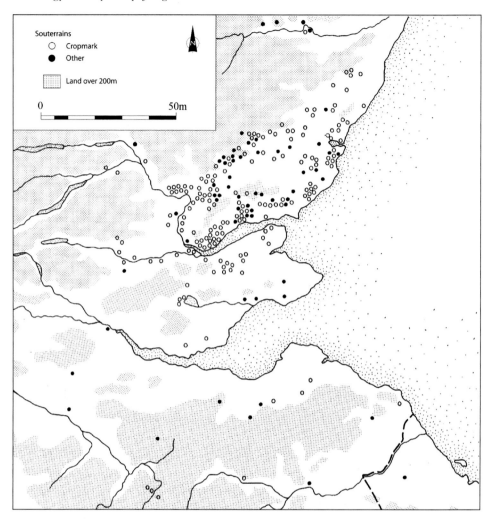

37 The distribution of souterrains in east-central Scotland, showing the impact of aerial photography. *Courtesy: Ian Armit*

elaborate examples incorporate side passages and multiple entrances, and in plan view have the appearance of giant-sized rabbit warrens) and the continuing debate over their function. In Angus sites such as Carlungie and Ardestie draw visitors and students keen to understand these enigmatic features. They have attracted repeated academic consideration in recent decades, famously in F.T. Wainwright's study and most recently in papers by Ian Armit and Roger Miket, to which the following summary owes a considerable debt.

Wainwright's *The Souterrains of Southern Pictland*, published in 1963, drew together the disparate evidence from Angus and Perthshire for the first time. He catalogued 57 previous discoveries of large stone-lined 'Southern Pictland' souterrains, published the results from his excavations during the previous decade of examples at Carlungie and Ardestie, and presented a view of the chronology, function and associations of souterrains. Wainwright's field projects, along with Taylor's research at Hurly Hawkin also underway in the 1960s, were the first scientific investigations of these souterrains and provided solid evidence that they were associated with above-ground buildings. The chronological association between that at Hurly Hawkin and the neighbouring broch is contentious, as we have already signalled.

All but six of the souterrains considered by Wainwright had been discovered accidently over 50 years earlier. They had often been emptied out very crudely, so that the quality of information about some of even well-known souterrains such as Pitcur II is actually very poor. Some antiquarian investigations were better than others, and in particular we may point to the researches of Andrew Jervise, who investigated several souterrains in and around the 1860s. One of these, at West Grange of Conon, was found by accident in 1859 when a large stone was dislodged during agricultural operations. Jervise emptied the souterrain passage and a distinctive corbelled side chamber, and located what he believed to be the stone floor of a building close to the ground surface and within the curve of the gallery. He also found a group of long cist burials (see Chapter 8, *52*). The souterrain was back-filled during the 1860s to protect it from damage at 'the hands of the mischievous' and by intrigued visitors. Limited reinvestigation of the souterrain by the Field School, under the direction of Kirsty Cameron, proved the worth of Jervise's actions since, despite modern cultivation, the below-ground structure survives in much the same condition as it was nearly a century and a half ago. Only the claimed above-ground building now seems dubious, for what Jervise had seen may have been outcropping bedrock.

For a while after Wainwright's overview there was little advance in the study of these structures. Occasional newly discovered structures were subject to rescue excavations, such as the magnificent example at Newmill, Perthshire and the (at the time) enigmatic timber-lined structures at Dalladies, just into former Kincardineshire. However, from the mid 1970s aerial photography had a massive impact on the state of knowledge, as it for the first time enabled souterrains to be identified independent of Clydesdale horse or Ferguson tractor. Gordon Barclay, writing in 1980, recognised the potential of this new source of information, identifying the first handful of potential cropmark sites in Angus. There have been many more recognised since, such that there are now in the order of 200 examples in Angus alone, a radical change since Wainwright put together his corpus. In fact, so numerous are souterrains that they can now be considered as standard features of many lowland settlements in the county. Through examination of some of these cropmarks, the recent archaeological projects that are the focus here have considerably increased our knowledge of the range of structural forms and capacities of souterrains.

The function of souterrains has been hotly debated over the years. Arguments have been put forward for their use variously as subterranean dwellings or refuges, animal shelters or ritual loci. The suggestion that they were dwellings has become unsustainable through the discovery of associated surface structures. An explanation as bolt-holes in times of trouble is also very improbable for these examples; the structures themselves could not be defended and, as the roofs of souterrains would have been visible above the ground and they were positioned in many cases in close proximity to houses, hostile detection of them would have been straightforward. Their narrow, dark passages, sometimes with stepped entrance passages, render souterrains unlikely places into which to drive livestock, although Wainwright himself preferred this hypothesis based upon his analysis of the soils from Carlungie. The interpretation of souterrains as purely religious or ceremonial structures now seems highly unlikely given the sheer number of structures, although as will be apparent this is not to say that the construction, use and closure of the structures did not include ritualised acts. However, this might also be true of much other Iron Age architecture.

The currently favoured explanation of souterrain function is that these dark, underground passages were constructed primarily as cellars for storage of surplus agricultural produce. Such a function may help to explain the common orientation of the entrance passage (oblique) to the main gallery of the souterrain – this device may have been designed to keep the main storage space free from natural light and especially sunlight, although some souterrains had doors in their entrance passages that would also have served to keep the interior dark and cool. Some archaeologists have proposed that grain was stored within them; this is supported to some extent by the concentration of Angus souterrains in good arable land and the repeated discovery of quernstones in souterrains. Others have argued that the cool conditions and even temperatures would be better suited for the storage of meats and dairy produce. The recently excavated Ardownie souterrain described below has provided perhaps the best indication to date of the nature of the goods stored within a souterrain.

To a considerable degree the suitability of souterrains for storing different kinds of perishables depends on providing a cool, even-temperature, probably low-humidity atmosphere (although the occasional provision of a drain in the floor of a souterrain, as at Ardestie, suggests dampness may sometimes have been a problem). The provision of a watertight roof was crucial in this regard, but regrettably the roof is the one structural element that, with few exceptions, does not survive. In many cases this appears to have been the result of their deliberate removal.

Recent investigations have provided useful information on the dating of souterrains. For the most part these indicate a date before which they could not have been abandoned or filled in, since datable artefacts (usually of Roman origin or inspiration) and carbonised material suitable for radiocarbon dating almost invariably derive from soils either on the floor when the structure was initially abandoned or from the infill deposits inserted above this. The dates obtained repeatedly indicate that the use of souterrains did not extend beyond the fourth century AD, with radiocarbon determinations, rather than Roman material, indicating this cut point. Indeed, Ian Armit has argued for a 'souterrain abandonment horizon' between the late second and early third century AD as a direct result of socio-political changes argued to follow from the withdrawal of the Roman army from the Antonine Frontier. We consider that it is difficult from the available evidence to support such a narrow date range for the demise of these structures.

Dating the origins of souterrains is less straightforward. A date in the late centuries BC is often assumed; this is based on a single radiocarbon date obtained from the floor of one of the small Dalladies souterrains. Whilst this determination might accurately reflect the date of closure of that souterrain, the taphonomy and the mixed nature of the dated sample should give us cause for concern as to its accuracy. As we have seen, some have regarded souterrains as developing from ring-ditches within roundhouses, features which also provide enhanced storage capacity. There may be some truth in this, but it was nevertheless not simply a case of sudden replacement, since the latest ring-ditch houses (such as Culhawk Hill) may well have been occupied at the same time as souterrains elsewhere were already in use. In that the two kinds of structures – annular semi-sunken spaces below the eaves of houses, or curving passages extending beyond domestic buildings – effectively represent alternatives, wholesale replacement might not be anticipated. It would be difficult to be categorical from an examination of the many cropmark traces, but no excavated ring-ditch house also has a souterrain springing from within it.

The following recently excavated examples showcase the range of structural forms and illustrate some of the interpretative issues that have dogged souterrain studies for decades.

A 'SOUTHERN PICTLAND' SOUTERRAIN AT ARDOWNIE

A striking and well-preserved 'Southern Pictland' souterrain was discovered in 2001 at Ardownie Farm Cottages, on the new line of the A92 Dundee–Arbroath road, less than 1km south-west of Ardestie. As the road alignment could not be moved, the souterrain and associated features were excavated by CFA Archaeology (*38*) and the results published by Sue Anderson and Alastair Rees.

A large stone-lined souterrain with two passages was unearthed (*colour plate 19*). Any associated above-ground house must have lain outside the area available for excavation,

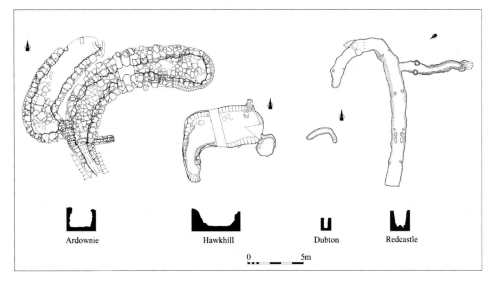

38 Comparative plans and profiles of recently excavated souterrains in Angus at the same scale. *Modified by Leeanne Whitelaw after Anderson and Rees 2006 (Ardownie), Rees forthcoming (Hawkhill), Cameron 2002 (Dubton) and Alexander 2005 (Redcastle)*

39 The main passage of the Ardownie souterrain. The 'creep' connecting this passage with its neighbour is visible in the right foreground, with the door-jambs and beam slot in the middle distance

although paved areas, one incorporating a rotary quern, were revealed on either side of the souterrain entrance. The main passage was 19m long and up to 2.2m wide; it corbelled inwards to 0.6m wide at roof level about 2.2m above the carefully paved floor. The subsidiary, western passage measured approximately 10m long by 2m wide and was entered through a narrow lintelled passage or 'creep' that led from the main chamber (*39*). Together these chambers form one of the most capacious of the 'Southern Pictland' souterrains, with a combined floor space in excess of 60 square metres. The excavators suggest that the larger passage could have been a secondary addition to its neighbour, but this was not demonstrable by close inspection of the masonry. Animal bone found beneath the paving of the main chamber provided a radiocarbon date spanning the first to fouth centuries AD. This material was certainly deposited during the period of use of the souterrain, but it does not necessarily indicate the construction date as it cannot be demonstrated that the paving was not a secondary addition to the souterrain.

The roof of the souterrain had been removed in antiquity. The method of roofing of these souterrains has proved a contentious subject. Although some, such as Hurly Hawkin and Pitcur II, have surviving stone lintels spanning them and others collapsed within them (the latter along a third of its length), Watkins and others have argued that some structures could never have been fully roofed in stone, since it would have proved impossible to engineer the removal of all the lintel stones without damaging the corbels. A timber-framed roof has been suggested in some instances, with either logs laid flat on the corbelled wall-head or a pitched construction erected over the passage like those topping roundhouses; stone lintels may have been used for weak spots such

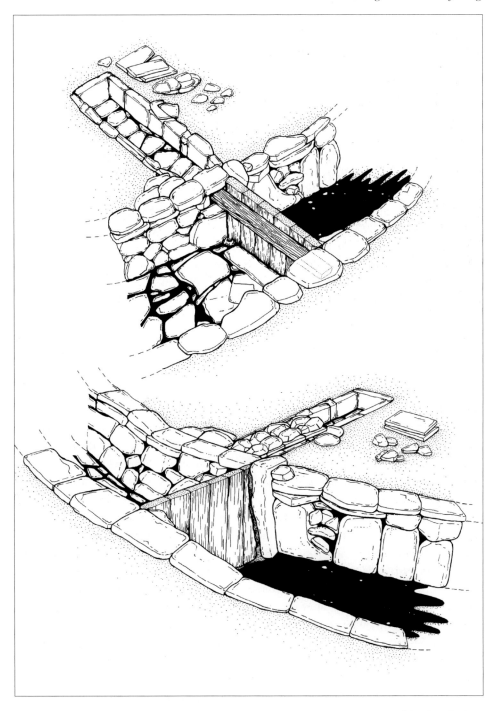

40 Oblique views (upper: interior; lower: exterior) of the suggested reconstruction of the door locking mechanism at the Ardownie souterrain, based on excavation data published by Anderson and Rees 2006. *Drawn by Leeanne Whitelaw*

as junctions between main and side passages. Roger Miket has argued recently that whatever the precise form of the roof, it must have been capped with earth (perhaps the material excavated to create the souterrain) to provide a watertight seal and to allow the creation of a dry storage space beneath. Turf would certainly have been preferable to thatch which, without benefit of a smoke-producing fire below, would rapidly have been infested by insects and suffered related problems.

The sloping entrance passage displayed, 3.5m from its outside end, two door jambs projecting slightly into it. The excavations revealed an ingenious door-locking mechanism, possibly paralleled at Carlungie but not recognised as such by Wainwright. A slab-covered slot buried in the ground beside the souterrain appears to have contained a sliding beam that slotted through opposing bar-holes behind the door jambs (*40, colour plate 19*). The effect was that the door of the souterrain could be barred on the inside by someone outside, with the locking mechanism capable of being hidden out of sight. Clearly, whoever built this souterrain wanted to keep others out, suggesting that valuable items were stored within. It must have presented a conundrum to unwanted visitors trying to gain entry and suggests that, in this case, unlike Newmill, the entrance was not set within a roundhouse.

Analysis of pollen from sediments deposited whilst the souterrain was in use indicate the former presence of cereals, grasses for fuel fodder or flooring, heather for bedding or tinder, sphagnum moss for personal or medical needs as well as dandelions and thistles with diuretic properties, in different parts of the chambers. A few animal bone fragments were recovered also, but it is less than certain that they reflect the storage of meat products on the bone. Ardownie souterrain was interpreted on this basis as used for the general storage of both wild and cultivated produce required by an Iron Age household.

Both of the souterrain passages appear to have been deliberately backfilled with dumps of charcoal-rich topsoil-derived material, but not immediately after the final use of the souterrain since water-borne sediments had first accumulated over the floor, possibly entering the souterrain through a hole in the roof. A rare enamelled and decorated bronze skillet (saucepan) handle and a sherd of samian pottery, both of Roman origin, were recovered from backfill and post-abandonment deposits respectively, and a rotary quern was retrieved from a rubble accumulation blocking the entrance, which must have been placed there after the final use of the souterrain. These broken Roman fragments, combined with radiocarbon dates, suggest abandonment did not occur here before the second half of the second century AD.

A PARTLY STONE-LINED SOUTERRAIN AT HAWKHILL

The Field School examined a much smaller souterrain adjacent to the scooped building at Hawkhill. This boot-shaped souterrain was entered through a steeply sloping corridor 0.6m wide, which led down to a level, unpaved and square-ended passage 6m long and up to 3.6m wide (*38*). This provided a floor space of 22 square metres, around a third of that available within Ardownie. Walling survived within the entrance section, but elsewhere had been almost entirely robbed out, if indeed it was ever present. What we may have found at Hawkhill is a partly stone-lined, partly timber-lined, souterrain of a type first recognised in smaller structures at Dalladies, although if so, the absence of the foundations for a timber framework in the unwalled section at Hawkhill is perplexing. From the deepest part of the chamber, on the floor of the souterrain, part of a millstone grit rotary quern was recovered. Two further fragments of rotary quern and a broken saddle quern were found in the backfill deposits in the souterrain. As with Ardownie, this souterrain appears to have been backfilled deliberately, although it was still visible as a slight surface depression several hundred years later when metalworking debris was deposited there. Dating for this souterrain is provided by its association with the adjacent scooped building, suggested above as occupied somewhere between the second century BC and the second century AD. The Hawkhill structure produced no further useful material better to fix its function.

A TIMBER-LINED SOUTERRAIN AT REDCASTLE

Within a square barrow cemetery (see Chapter 8) a wholly timber-lined souterrain was fully excavated by the Field School, under the direction of Derek Alexander. This souterrain was most probably associated with an unenclosed settlement of roundhouses and at least two further unexcavated souterrains recorded as cropmarks a little to the west in the same field. The souterrain itself survived 0.9-1.3m deep suggesting that, had it been constructed to provide access for adults walking upright, up to 1m or more of the original height of the structure must have been truncated by ploughing and wind erosion, a not-impossible figure given the light soils around Lunan Bay. This is sufficient to have removed any traces of a timber roundhouse that might have stood immediately beside it; certainly none survived.

From a narrow entrance, the souterrain curved gently downwards, passing the former position of a doorway, where there was a sharp drop in the floor level. Having turned through almost 180 degrees a slightly curving square-ended passage was reached, into which a narrow side entrance provided an alternative access (*38*). The main passage was around 12m long by 0.9m wide at the base; it thus contains about 11 square metres of floor space. Four opposing pairs of post-holes spaced at 3-3.5m intervals along the length of the main passage represent the earth-fast components of an internal timber framework (*41*). Timber lining of the walls would have been necessary to prevent the soft subsoil from collapsing inwards – the unconsolidated nature of the sandy subsoil (as observed during the excavations) would have rendered this souterrain rapidly unusable without such a lining. Patches of clay identified in the entrance passages may have been remains of collapsed wattle and daub walling. The pairings of posts along the passage suggested to the excavator that the vertical timbers were joined by transversal braces either at the top, bottom or both, to form a framework that would support a turf roof. Given that the timber uprights were earth-fast, however, a cross-brace at ground level

41 Redcastle souterrain fully excavated; ranging rods mark the positions of the vertical posts of the timber framework. *Crown Copyright: Historic Scotland*

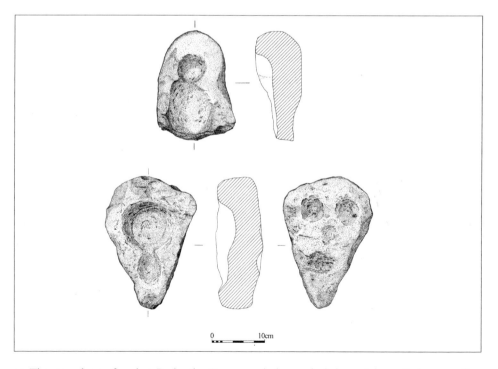

42 The stone lamps found at Redcastle. One example has pecked decoration on its lower surface. *Drawn by Kevin Hicks. Crown Copyright: Historic Scotland*

would have been redundant other than possibly to support a plank-built floor. The basal sand of the souterrain provided no indication of dishing to suggest that it had been walked on much, and either original timber or possibly straw flooring should be envisaged.

There were no deposits within the souterrain that could certainly be related to its use and there was nothing found by which its construction could be dated. Unlike the examples mentioned above, however, this souterrain appears to have been left to fill in gradually following its disuse and the deliberate removal of its roof. Datable Roman glass and pottery, and radiocarbon dates, suggest that abandonment occurred no later than the fourth century AD and possibly much earlier within the first millennium. Perhaps the most striking finds from the excavation came from a pit adjacent to the side entrance. Two stone lamps were found here, consisting of figure-of-eight depressions pecked into triangular-shaped stones. These can be envisaged as having been equipped with an organic wick, perhaps of twisted dried moss, with the dished area of the lamp holding tallow or possibly seabird or similar oil that would have fuelled a flame. One of the lamps is broken, but the other is complete and has four circular impressions on the underside, forming what looks uncannily like a skull or a face (*42*). These lamps evoke well the need for lighting within these dark and shadowy underground spaces, and act as a salutary reminder that many Iron Age activities, other than immediately around the hearth within roundhouses, must have been largely confined to daylight hours.

MINIATURE SOUTERRAINS AT DUBTON, BRECHIN

At the opposite end of the spectrum from Ardownie are the four miniature souterrains, two laid out end-to-end forming a distinctive reverse S-shape, associated with the vestigial remains of small circular timber buildings and areas of paving excavated at Dubton, Brechin, by Kirsty Cameron in 1998. They had the characteristic hook shape in plan and, in the absence of stonework, some form of timber-lining must have been inserted to prevent the subsoil from eroding from the edges of the passage (as it did rapidly during the excavations).

The largest of the Dubton examples was 7m long and up to 1.3m wide, and the smallest only 4m long and 0.4m wide (thus providing only about one square metre of usable floor space). There did not appear to be any obvious means of accessing the smallest example from the ground surface, with uniformly vertical sides present (*43*). Perhaps a small child was simply lowered in by hand, as might be suggested by the narrow necks of well-preserved Iron Age storage pits further south in Britain. Child labour may be difficult to recognise archaeologically, but it was certainly a feature of the Iron Age; one of the most direct and gruelling testimonies is the small size of some of the leather footwear in Austrian rock-salt mines. In any case the passage was surely too narrow to have been walked along except by a child. Perhaps these small souterrains were only accessed from above, effectively consisting of hanging storage using a timber framework

43 One of the micro-souterrains excavated at Dubton, Brechin; both scales are 1m

set below a movable cover. Hanging items from an overhead framework, or from the roof, would mean that any stored foodstuffs would benefit from the cool temperature whilst avoiding contact with damp surfaces; contact with rodents (house mice were a new pest of the Iron Age in Britain) and creeping insects would be curtailed too.

A single radiocarbon date from one of the souterrains spanned the first two centuries AD, indicating the broad contemporaneity of its abandonment with that of the other, larger souterrains considered here. The only artefacts from these features were two fragments of rotary quern that had been deposited during the early stages of the backfilling of two separate features.

MORE VARIATIONS ON A THEME

These examples demonstrate that not only did the structures we group together as souterrains vary in their construction materials, but they also differed greatly in their capacity. The 'Southern Pictland' souterrain at Ardownie had a floor space six times that of the timber-lined structure at Redcastle (*44*) and 60 times that of the Dubton micro-souterrain. We cannot overlook the implications these huge differences in size have for how much – and what – could be stored. Anderson and Rees have painted a picture of the Ardownie souterrain as a store-house for a range of seasonally available goods to provide for an extended household over the yearly cycle, warning sagely that although capacious we should not regard these structures as having been filled to the brim, since

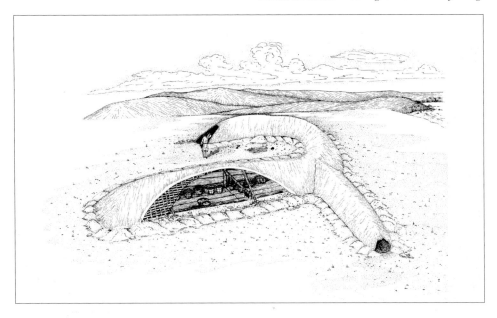

44 Artist's impression, based on Redcastle, of how a timber-lined souterrain may originally have looked. A cutaway exposes the internal arrangements. *Drawn by Leeanne Whitelaw*

open space would have been needed for movement and the circulation of air. Then how much could have been stored in a micro-souterrain? In terms of scale might they best be regarded as the equivalents of fridges or bread-bins for short-term storage of perishables?

Does this mean simply that these subterranean structures served households or communities of varying size, with the largest – or perhaps those not obviously linked to particular households, as at Ardownie – being communal storage spaces? Or are these hugely different capabilities to store surplus produce the result of social distinctions otherwise difficult to detect archaeologically in the Angus Iron Age, except perhaps by proxy from different house sizes? In the absence of accompanied inhumations, so key to estimates of social differentiation elsewhere in Iron Age Europe, we cannot offer a reply to these questions. Perhaps local land-holding elites were able to invest their resources and the time and labour of slaves or peasant farmers in building large souterrains capable of storing goods produced by those who owed labour dues or rendered by subservient tenant farmers. Calling in labour as a social obligation is probably how hillforts were built and maintained, so maybe here we are seeing a thread through time. Or can we invoke yet another potential explanation, suggested by Ian Armit, that these structures were at least latterly used as storehouses for produce, to trade with or be paid as tribute to, the Romans? Whatever the explanation, there was a substantially local dimension to it; nowhere else in eastern Scotland are souterrains known in such numbers and nowhere else has aerial photography provoked such a dramatic increase in their discovery.

There seems little doubt that souterrains formed a common component of farming settlements in Angus, at least in the early centuries AD. Cropmarks indicate that some were clearly entered from within or stood adjacent to roundhouses, but we need not get overly concerned as to whether this was universally the case. Whether the move away from souterrain usage was over a relatively short time frame and tied up with changing relations with the Roman world, as Armit's 'souterrain abandonment hypothesis' contends, or a more gradual process, has been addressed by others. What we can say with reasonable confidence is that by around AD 400 souterrains were disused and in many cases, but by no means all, had been carefully filled in with little ceremony. After this date, to judge from the Easter Kinnear (Fife) structures, where an individual house had a clear additional storage capacity, this effectively took the form of a semi-sunken cellar within the building.

RAISED GRANARIES?

Souterrains are not the only types of structure that could have functioned as storage space for agricultural produce. Excavations at Ironshill and at Douglasmuir revealed patterns of post-holes that represent the foundations of small timber structures framed upon rectangular or sub-rectangular arrangements of anything between four and nine usually closely set posts, and between 3m and 6m across. A possible example of a nine-post structure is visible as a cropmark south of the Ironshill palisaded enclosure (*45*). Similar structures have been detected in small numbers in settlement contexts elsewhere in south-east and central Scotland, but they are more characteristic of southern Britain and nearer areas of the continent, where they occur in sometimes considerable numbers in hillforts and both enclosed and unenclosed settlements.

Kendrick concluded that the most likely explanation of the Douglasmuir structures was as raised granaries, to store produce in dry conditions in a raised environment where it was easy to access and not susceptible to damage by rodents, weevils and other pests. It is generally assumed that the superstructure of these little buildings was separated from the earth-fast posts by overhanging flat stones on top of the latter; these would have stopped mice and rats accessing the grain. Kendrick argued that this interpretation derived some support from the recovery of charred cereals from the post-holes of one structure. However, it is not clear how this material supports the preferred granary interpretation, since the presence of a granary implies the storage of surplus crops, whereas charred cereal remains – unless the granary burnt down – generally reflect primarily crop processing activities. Whilst raised granaries are a reasonable interpretation, others have hypothesised a range of other potential functions for what are in archaeological terms morphologically simple foundations (as watch-towers, shrines, exposure platforms for the corpses of the dead, or the substantial entrance porches to roundhouses where the remainder of the structure – perhaps originally stake-built – has been ploughed away).

None of the Angus structures has been independently dated, but by association the Douglasmuir examples appear to belong to the earlier Iron Age (the Ironshill examples are in proximity to excavated buildings of different dates and so their

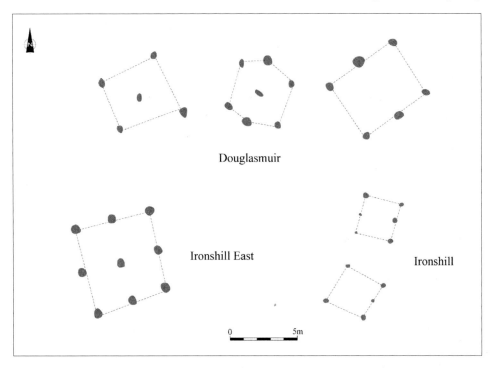

Douglasmuir

Ironshill East

Ironshill

0   5m

45 Comparative plans of small rectangular structures, sometimes interpreted as footings for raised granaries. *Drawn by Leeanne Whitelaw after Kendrick 1995 (Douglasmuir), Pollock 1997 (Ironshill) and transcribed from RCAHMS aerial photographs (Ironshill East)*

chronological associations are uncertain). Perhaps they were a form of specialised storage facility that was later superseded by souterrains. We are still a long way from understanding these enigmatic structures, but it is clear in Angus, as elsewhere in Scotland where sizeable Iron Age settlement excavations have been carried out, that these features are never present in the quantities encountered on some southern British sites.

One telling piece of evidence for Stuart Piggott as he elaborated his stock-raising hypothesis, was the absence of substantial below-ground storage pits for grain in Scotland. These have been encountered in considerable numbers on some southern British and continental sites, and the method for using them has been tested experimentally at 'Iron Age farms' like the celebrated example at Butser in Hampshire. Capable individually of storing one to six tonnes of grain, these features would have required to be emptied immediately once the clay bung sealing them was broken open. They are certainly an indication of substantial grain production, but their continuing absence from Scotland is a reflection that this storage technology is largely confined to limestone and chalk environments and is likely not to have worked successfully in the colder and moister conditions of Scottish subsoils. Absence of evidence for storage pits is thus very definitely not evidence of the absence of cereal cultivation.

FROM STRUCTURES TO SETTLEMENTS

Having reviewed the principal structural evidence for Iron Age settlement, it is necessary to consider what can be gleaned as regards settlement form and variability, and its change over time. Can we model patterns and hierarchies of Iron Age settlement and, beyond that, landholdings across Angus, or at least in those cropmark-producing parts of the lowlands where there is more (and perhaps more reliable) data? The answer is that we can make a start, but there remain three difficult, at present seemingly intractable, hurdles that result from the limitations of the cropmark evidence and the excavated data so far gathered.

Firstly, for how long could a timber roundhouse stand before it needed major repair or replacement? Some have argued that the timber frameworks of roundhouses would decay relatively quickly at ground level due to constant fluctuations in the water table and thus moisture levels, such that replacement would be required every generation. Others contend that these same buildings could in fact have remained upright for up to a century, or indeed longer, and that decay would not have seriously affected their stability. Important evidence in this regard is likely to come from reconstructed timber roundhouses, of which the Pimperne house (built at Butser in the 1970s and demolished when it was less than 20 years old) already provides instructive evidence. Here, internal timbers had rotted through at ground level, but without any deleterious effect on the cone-on-cylinder structure.

Timber supply would also have been important. It is of course reasonable to expect that the timber species and thickness were directly related to its use-life as load-bearing elements in any given environment. These issues are not mere semantics, but have a fundamental relationship with how we model longevity of occupation in what are thus far relatively sparsely dated settlements. As in more recent times, maintenance in practical terms is likely to have been central to the long-term viability of buildings; in Scotland, that has always meant maintaining roofs and thus keeping structures watertight. It is also likely that keeping a fire burning in the central hearth was critical, not so much because the building was heated, as because the smoke filtering through the roof would have fumigated the thatch and thus helped prolong its effectiveness. Given too the evidence now being provided by experimental reconstructions of timber buildings from Archaeolink in Aberdeenshire southwards, it is easy to be seduced into thinking that such practical considerations largely determine building longevity. However, these have always been melded with social considerations and some archaeologists, drawing on anthropological considerations, have felt that houses may very much be 'generational', replaced when the head of the household died. In such cases, houses may have been deliberately destroyed, but they may equally have simply been downgraded and used, for example, to hold livestock. Specialist buildings for this purpose are seemingly absent in mainland Scotland before the 'byre-houses' represented by the Pitcarmick series in the later first millennium AD (see Chapter 7). That roundhouses were used in this way is graphically illustrated by the quantities of sheep dung associated with the Oakbank crannog building. In Angus evidence is as yet lacking (see p. 108).

Do the four superimposed post-ring houses at Dalladies, referred to above, thus together potentially represent 100 years of occupation on that spot or four centuries? Were these Iron Age settlements long-lived elements of the Angus landscape, the basic framework of which in terms of landholding and the like may have been relatively unchanging over extended periods of time, or is there the possibility that they reflect more temporary patterns of settlement and agriculture? The truth is that we have no simple answer, but we should be wary of seeing these settlements as the products of a kind of 'timeless' Iron Age, in which rural change was so slow as to be almost imperceptible. In better-dated areas further south in Britain, where tighter chronologies are possible, there are frequent indications of widescale changes, sometimes in matters of decades, frequently within a couple of centuries.

Secondly, how do we demonstrate the contemporaneity or otherwise of roundhouses, between or within settlement units? The inertia of, and the recurrence of similar, timber roundhouse foundation plans indicate that we cannot date them closely from cropmark traces alone, although a close association of a building with a souterrain at least allows its likely chronological context to be narrowed. For our most precise dating technique (dendrochronology) really to be of service on a dry-land site we would need preserved timbers in quantity. Even this would not be unproblematic, given the distortions charring can entail. Nor do the varieties of architecture appear any more to be neatly sequential; we cannot read off the chronological sequence on the basis of buildings of different ground plan any more than we can presume that those same buildings were contemporary and had different functions or social status. Cropmarks on aerial photographs provide a palimpsest of all that happens to have been visible when the image was recorded and, as surely as a Cubist painting, flatten the chronological dimension in what is represented. Excavation data provides more detail, but the limitations of dating are such that even with this we are rarely on terra firma. For example, can we say whether the six ring-ditch houses at Douglasmuir were standing and occupied at the same time, or do they represent the gradual drift of a smaller settlement unit? The same principle applies at Dalladies. These issues are and will remain crucial to modelling the size and potential populations of settlements as households, hamlets or villages. In Scotland the fine chronologies that rapidly evolving artefact types can sometimes elsewhere provide in Iron Age settings remain an unattainable goal, so that we need to content ourselves with asking rather broader questions about what the patterns in our evidence may indicate.

Thirdly, how do we define the boundaries of settlements? There are few, if any, readily identifiable land boundaries that might demarcate the properties of communities or estates, such that Pollock argued that subsidiary watercourses may have formed the major land boundaries along the Lunan Valley. Archaeologists must classify settlement forms by morphological characteristics, and in our area the distinction most evident in the cropmark record is between enclosed and unenclosed settlement. Enclosed settlements, the small examples often termed homesteads, include sites where one or two roundhouses are known or assumed to be contained within a fenced or ditched-and-embanked compound. In some instances, potentially both styles of enclosure are present in sequence. To date, only one fenced and no single-ditched enclosures have

46 The complexity of a cropmark landscape extending over several fields inland from Lunan Bay. Many of the smaller circles, crescents and 'blobs' may correspond to later prehistoric roundhouses; the linear traces may be field boundaries or, in some instances, ice wedge casts. The paler tone indicates areas where cropmarks are particularly susceptible to develop. Modified by Leeanne Whitelaw from Pollock 1997

been excavated in Angus. Unenclosed settlements, on the other hand, comprise various seemingly isolated roundhouses, discrete groups of structures or extensive spreads of buildings. In this latter case, such as around Inverkeilor in the Lunan Valley, it is not possible to estimate from cropmark evidence alone where one settlement might end and another begin, or indeed whether at any time all the inhabitants of the buildings in the area may have regarded themselves as a single community (*46*).

However, there is a real risk that attempting to define settlements purely on spatial grounds might in any case be misleading. For example, was the large roundhouse set within a palisaded enclosure at Ironshill East a self-sufficient homestead in its own right or a functionally distinct element of a larger settlement (*47*)? There has been a perfectly understandable tendency in light of ethnographic parallels to interpret sites such as these as the private residences of the local chiefs and landowners. The large roundhouse at Ironshill East is of a scale that Richard Hingley has determined as 'substantial' and

47 Aerial photograph of the palisaded enclosure, bisected by the modern fence line, at Ironshill East. Also apparent amongst rather diffuse marks is a penannular ring-ditch, potentially a house. *Courtesy RCAHMS: Crown Copyright*

is comparable in terms of internal floor space to the Hurly Hawkin broch. There are several similar-looking cropmarks of apparently substantial, isolated roundhouses along the Lunan Valley that might thus relate to a series of local chieftains, but the evidence advanced above warns that we should not assume that all are of the same date.

Yet it may not be that straightforward. There are other potential non-domestic explanations for the Ironshill East building, as rehearsed by Rideout in relation to the morphologically similar building and enclosure he excavated at Bannockburn. One suggestion might be as communal meeting places. Catherine McGill's excavations at Ironshill East demonstrated that this building and enclosure date to no earlier than the last centuries BC and are likely to have been abandoned within the first three centuries AD. This latter period represents the floruit of souterrain usage, yet, despite the relatively imposing character of the architecture compared to buildings in its general surroundings, the combined cropmark and excavation evidence does not indicate a recognisable souterrain within this enclosure. A chiefly residence without a food store would seem at odds with the foregoing discussion of the function and widespread distribution of souterrains. There are cropmarks of souterrains in the vicinity and a previously unrecognised example was found during trial trenching around 40m north of the enclosure, its broad contemporaneity with the enclosure indicated by the recovery of a Romano-British trumpet brooch from it. Perhaps then there was such a store, but positioned outside the enclosure; this suggestion, however, seems to be special pleading. This does not preclude the possibility of Ironshill East as an elite residence, but if so it might suggest that the property continued 'beyond the pale'. The palisade, whether intended to display status and privacy and/or to protect from animals or assailants, may thus not have been a settlement boundary in the sense of enclosing all the elements needed for the routines of daily domestic life.

Whilst the results of the Field School in Angus and other projects in eastern Scotland have contributed significantly to clarifying numbers of issues to do with domestic living in roundhouses in the later prehistory of the Scottish lowlands, the foregoing discussion will have made it plain that many issues remain unresolved. With these major caveats in mind and the certainty that future excavations will fill in the gaps and occasion our views to be revisited, what broader trends can be observed in the settlement record? We offer a tentative overview in our final chapter.

7

Where are the houses?
Early Historic settlement

There is a striking contrast between what we now know of the wealth of archaeological evidence for Iron Age settlement and the poverty of information relating to the houses and farms of the population of Angus following the abandonment of timber roundhouses and souterrains by the middle of the first millennium AD. Aerial photography has now provided images that populate the landscape of Iron Age Angus with farms, enclosed and unenclosed, when a generation ago Herbert Coutts believed that a good proportion of the area's Iron Age inhabitants dwelt in forts. However, the same technique has not led to the identification of the settlements of what became a key part of 'Southern Pictland'.

There is plentiful archaeological, and some documentary and thus historical, evidence for the presence of the Picts in Angus. The most striking evidence is that provided by the symbol stones (*colour plate 20*). Their date of origin can be disputed but probably lies for the earliest examples, with incised decoration, around the middle of the first millennium AD. Angus contains numbers of both Class I and Class II sculptures, but this important material is not considered in detail here since none of the Field School exercises touched directly on this remarkable legacy. That said, there is reason to believe that the positioning of stones in the landscape – near boundaries or, where little clusters of stones are encountered, at significant intersections in the topography – could be informative, in those cases for which we are sure the stones have not been subsequently displaced. Distinctive place-name elements are also important, with the prefix 'pit-' taken to indicate a significant landholding such as an estate. Most occur on the better soils, precisely the places where defining and naming places would have been very important. It is generally accepted that such place names were attributed in eastern Scotland towards the end of the first millennium AD, as the second elements of them are invariably Gaelic in character. When an influential survey of the Picts was undertaken half a century ago, the absence of both graves and houses were identified as significant components of 'The Problem of the Picts'. To some extent, the issue of burial has been addressed by the discovery of square barrow cemeteries amongst the cropmarks, especially in the Lunan Valley (Chapter 8).

Contrastingly, recognising domestic settlement for the Picts of Angus has proved a more enduring problem. Other pioneering approaches have been tried over the last 50 years. In the absence of much credible archaeological evidence for houses, there have been attempts to model settlement patterns using the proxy evidence of forts, symbol stones and pit-prefix place names, most notably in the thoughtful but problematic research undertaken by Barry Cottam and Alan Small in the 1970s. These are interesting lines of enquiry that have been addressed by others; however, our focus here, reflecting that of the Field School, is on the archaeological evidence for settlement (*48*).

In this chapter we necessarily cover a period that extends both before the formation and after the fall of the Pictish kingdoms as they are historically documented. We have not retained the ungainly term 'proto-Pictish' for first millennium AD material believed to predate the sixth century AD, when use of the label 'Pictish' can be justified on rather more solid grounds. We have therefore elected, in considering the archaeological evidence for settlement and bearing in mind the imprecision with which some of this material can be fixed chronologically, to use the generic term 'Early Historic' to describe

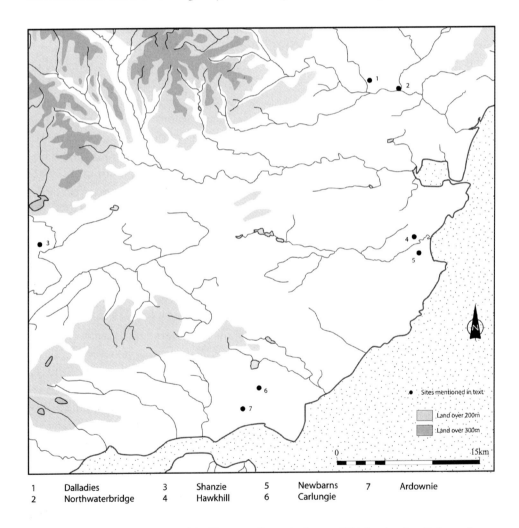

| 1 | Dalladies | 3 | Shanzie | 5 | Newbarns | 7 | Ardownie |
| 2 | Northwaterbridge | 4 | Hawkhill | 6 | Carlungie | | |

48 Locations of key sites mentioned in Chapter 7. *Drawn by Leeanne Whitelaw, based on Ordnance Survey mapping: kind permission, 2003, Ordnance Survey*

the structures of this period. Moreover, the buildings (and burials) that have been detected are in many cases far from uniquely Pictish in character, but reflect styles more widely represented across northern Britain. This is unsurprising in a period when new population aggregates were effectively being forged – the process that anthropologists and historians term ethnogenesis was underway.

CONTINUITY OF OCCUPATION AT IRON AGE SETTLEMENT SITES?

Until fairly recently the search for the physical remains of Early Historic settlements in Angus and neighbouring counties focused on its hillforts, the few visible circular homesteads and duns, and, in light of Early Historic evidence from sites like Loch Glashan in Argyll, on crannogs too. Another approach was to seek to identify post-souterrain activity on Iron Age settlements. It has long been understood that many souterrains were deliberately filled in and that the fills could contain small quantities of datable Roman material. The implication was that these structures were backfilled by the inhabitants, who intended to continue in occupation in the vicinity.

In the 1980s Trevor Watkins published a thoughtful review of the state of knowledge as regards post-souterrain settlement at that time. The most coherent evidence had been found by F.T. Wainwright at Carlungie, where two adjacent sub-oval stone-floored buildings about 6m by 4m in extent had been built after the demolition of the souterrain, and at Ardestie. Of less value was the discovery of a fragment of Pictish cross-slab in the paving of a disturbed building of no earlier than medieval date, located close to a souterrain discovered during road construction at Northwaterbridge, now in Aberdeenshire. Watkins also drew attention to discoveries made during his own excavations in neighbouring counties, at Dalladies and Newmill. At Dalladies a probable fire-pit for roasting cereals, partly cut into an infilled souterrain, contained charred barley that produced a radiocarbon date spanning the fifth to seventh centuries AD. At the latter site a fire-pit connected with iron-working provided a radiocarbon date covering the later eighth through to the early eleventh century AD. Finally, he remarked on the juxtaposition of souterrains and long cist graves (examined in the next chapter) as discovered at West Grange of Conon (discussed in the previous chapter) and possibly also at Carlungie.

Watkins used this meagre evidence of activity to propose continuous occupation of settlements for centuries after the disuse of souterrains, at least at some locations. He rejected an alternative explanation of the Dalladies and Newmill evidence as indicating reoccupation after a period of site abandonment, on the fragile basis that the surviving nature of the post-souterrain settlement was sufficiently vestigial that demonstrating continuity was not realistically achievable. Making inferences from an absence of evidence is always dangerous, but his hypothesis is not without its merits.

Some recent investigations have provided further examples of Early Historic activity in and around abandoned souterrains. At Shanzie near Alyth, excavations by Headland Archaeology detected evidence of secondary activity within the main passage of a large stone-lined souterrain (in this instance also demonstrating that the souterrain had not been deliberately infilled when its use ceased). Here, carbonised barley found on paving laid over deposits that accumulated after the souterrain's initial abandonment, was radiocarbon dated to the later ninth or tenth centuries. Russell Coleman and Fraser Hunter interpreted this evidence as opportunistic, temporary reuse of a rediscovered structure rather than as continuous post-souterrain occupation. In this case, their conclusion appears inescapable.

CFA Archaeology's excavations at Ardownie souterrain, on the upgraded A92 just outside Dundee, led to the identification, a few metres to the west, of a substantial sunken stone-lined hearth beside an area of paving, interpreted as places for cooking and working respectively. Charred material from this hearth provided radiocarbon dates that suggested its use at some point between the mid seventh and mid tenth centuries AD, again distinctly later than the souterrain.

Finally, the Field School excavations at Hawkhill near Inverkeilor revealed more extensive evidence of later first millennium AD activity around the Iron Age scooped building and nearby souterrain. This included small paved areas suggested as open-air working platforms, an iron-working forge and an unusual multiple burial considered further in Chapter 8. Radiocarbon dating suggests that activity at these features centred on the eighth or ninth centuries AD.

These additional discoveries still do not allow the issue of whether there is a post-souterrain hiatus in occupation before subsequent Early Historic use of these locations to be resolved. As more evidence of Early Historic activity at Iron Age souterrain settlements accrues, however, it becomes less easy to explain it away as purely coincidental reuse of long-abandoned sites. Nonetheless, the existing information suggests considerable diversity in the chronological relationship between souterrain and subsequent uses; structures at Carlungie may have been built very soon after the souterrain was decommissioned, whereas the datable activities nearby occurred probably several centuries after the infilling of the Newmill souterrain. What these new discoveries noticeably have in common with Dalladies and Newmill is that none consists of, or is accompanied by, a recognisable Early Historic building. This begs the questions as to what sort of activities are represented at these locations – are they to be understood as indications of 'off-site' agricultural and industrial activities, simply practised at a convenient spot? Alternatively, are they suggesting a more important occupation in the vicinity, but one marked by buildings which have simply been eliminated by subsequent ploughing, or constructed in styles that no longer depended on earth-fast elements (post-holes and the like) which make them archaeologically recognisable?

RECTANGULAR BUILDINGS

One of the main characteristics of the settlement record over many areas of north Britain is that during the first millennium AD, more especially around its third quarter, the predominant forms of buildings encountered shifted from circular forms to rectilinear ones. The change starts in a significant way in southern Britain at the end of the pre-Roman Iron Age.

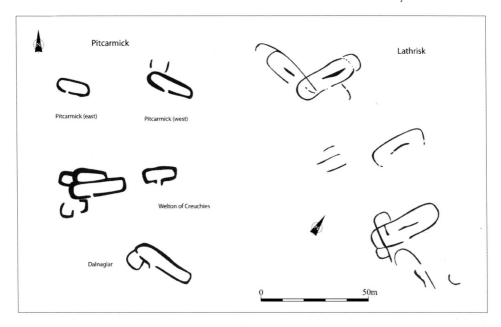

49 A selection of upstanding Pitcarmick-type houses from upland Perthshire and the probable timber halls known as cropmarks at Lathrisk, Fife, drawn to the same scale. *Drawn by Leeanne Whitelaw after Alcock 2003 / RCAHMS and Maxwell 1987*

Within those areas impacted most by Rome, it is largely a product of the centuries when Britannia was part of the Empire. Further north and west, the timing of this change seems delayed, and numbers of influences and causes can be suggested for the adoption of rectilinear architecture here. In no particular order, these might include the association of rectangular buildings with the prestige of Rome or with the chapels of the new religion, Christianity. Stalling cattle or horses indoors may also have been significant; the first buildings specifically built for this purpose in Scotland (as far north as Pool on Orkney) belong to this period. On the high moors and in the valleys on the southern skirts of the Grampians, particularly in Perthshire, but also in Angus valleys, especially Glens Prosen and Clova, a particular form of stone-footed longhouse is central to this argument.

These 'Pitcarmick' houses (named after the Perthshire site where the first excavation on the type occurred) are of considerable scale, being up to 30m long, with stone wall footings or low banks defining slightly bowed sides and more rounded ends; they are often associated with what might be stock enclosures or yards (*49*). Excavations of two buildings at North Pitcarmick in 1993-4 by John Barrett and Jane Downes demonstrated that the earlier, and larger, structure was occupied perhaps as early as the eighth century. It measured 26m by 6m internally, with an entrance approximately mid way along the long side. An internal hearth was recovered to one side of this entrance, suggesting domestic occupation, whereas a soakaway drain running along the centre of the building to the other side of the doorway indicates use as a byre. Leslie Alcock suggested from their distribution above the 300m contour that Pitcarmick houses may have been summer shielings rather than permanently occupied farmsteads and it is noteworthy that in some areas their distributions overlap markedly with earlier hut-circles. Be that as it may, a key conclusion to draw from these major structures is that big buildings that would leave few archaeologically discernable traces in areas with more intensive land-use – effectively components that penetrated the subsoil – were built at this time. Had examples of the Pitcarmick type been erected in the lowlands, in landscapes that have been ploughed perhaps several hundred times since, the chances of recovering coherent archaeological traces of them would be slight indeed.

In fact, examination of the record for domestic buildings of first millennium AD date across Pictland highlights two issues. One is the very considerable diversity in plans and building styles that seem to have been employed, so that there is no standard Pictish building type. Second, a wide range of evidence indicates that many buildings were by this stage no longer generally reliant on earth-fast timbers (chocked into post-holes and thus highly visible to the excavating archaeologist) for their structural integrity. Once one allows for buildings springing from horizontal sleeper beams, built on post-pads, with walls incorporating crucks, perhaps even erected in log-cabin style (not likely for the best Scottish hardwoods) as well as sophisticated carpentry joints of the kinds evidenced on some first millennium AD crannogs and in some contemporary timber-framed fortifications, it is not surprising that the excavator's task in identifying the former presence of such buildings is in many circumstances much more difficult. Ironically, for timber buildings at least, it is the case that the more sophisticated the elevations of a building, the fewer below-ground archaeological traces it may leave. In the first millennium AD, the elements of some buildings that leave the clearest archaeological traces may less frequently be structural elements like post-holes, but rather indications of semi-sunken storage capacity, as at the Fife site of Easter Kinnear, discussed previously.

It therefore follows that some rather unimpressive traces may be all that survive of rather grander timber buildings. By way of example, is it possible that the Early Historic paving and hearth identified at Ardownie are not simply isolated features or related to settlement outside the area available for excavation, as the excavators suggested, but instead are all that survive of a rectangular building? The suggestion has already been made for rectangular hearths and more ephemeral remains inside the great Early Historic fort of Clatchard Craig, which formerly lay above Newburgh in Fife. The absence of contemporary domestic debris would still require an explanation.

It has long been appreciated that there are other series of rectangular buildings in the first millennium AD record from eastern Scotland. Initially, it was aerial photography that gave rise to the detection of such buildings, now known to extend between the Anglo-Scottish Borders and the Moray Firth. Excavation of the cropmarks of large rectilinear timber buildings started south of the Cheviots in the 1950s and some of the varieties noted on Anglian sites such as Yeavering, near Wooler in Northumberland, can be paralleled in Scotland. In some cases we may follow Gordon Maxwell in suggesting the Scottish examples are Early Historic timber halls, although other plans, as we have seen, are more usually Neolithic and in some instances somewhat similar patterns of post-holes do not suggest roofed structures.

One of the handful of examples detected in Angus, at Newbarns beside Lunan Bay, was investigated by the Field School in 1999. The excavations directed by Catherine McGill

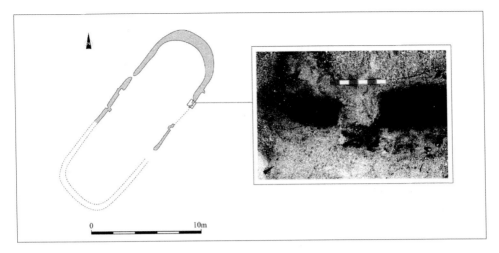

50 The suggested plan of the Newbarns building, extrapolated from the excavated end, with an inset showing one of the offsets on the wall line. *Plan drawn by Leeanne Whitelaw after McGill 2004*

exposed over half of this sub-rectangular structure, which was straight-sided with an apsidal end (*50*) measuring around 18m long and 6m wide. Its wall line was defined by a shallow ditch up to 0.5m deep, within the base of which rectilinear and oval slots of varying dimensions might represent the settings of individual timbers that framed the building. Two entrances were detected on the long east wall, a feature that is characteristic of some other first millennium substantial buildings. Along the long walls were spaced opposing pairs of rectangular post-holes off-set from the wall line, both externally and internally. The internal examples may represent the foundation slots of crucks, forming roof supports, their external equivalents were perhaps buttresses providing support for the wall-head. Alternatively, they too may have been cruck slots. Radiocarbon dates spanning the eighth to eleventh centuries AD were obtained from charred grains recovered from the wall slot and provide a broad chronological span within which this building was occupied.

The floor space within the building was almost devoid of archaeological remains. This might indicate that only the last vestiges of occupation traces had survived the plough, and indeed much of the wall slot was markedly shallow. Had internal posts, say along the main axial line of the structure and thus supporting the ridge-pole of the roof, been set on stone post-pads there is every likelihood that, once dislodged by the plough, any sizeable flat stones fit for this purpose would have been removed from the field. If there were crucks set into the walls, of course, additional internal roof supports would not have been required. It is also possible to envisage that the building had been provided with a raised timber floor, such that we would not expect features such as hearths – perhaps set at a relatively elevated level – to have survived in the archaeological record.

A little west of this building cropmarks revealed a distinct ring of at least six pits defining an area over 25m in diameter. Excavation of two of these demonstrated that they were contemporary with the building, on the basis of radiocarbon evidence, and that they contained successive deposits of crop-processing waste. Perhaps the peculiar circular arrangement of the pits in itself was not important – it may be that what was once present within the area they defined had been significant, but has itself left no archaeological trace.

The constructional details and size of the Newbarns building find general parallels in Early Historic timber halls and Anglian buildings found elsewhere in northern Britain, albeit numbers of these date earlier, to around the sixth and seventh centuries. In north-east Scotland perhaps the best excavated parallel is the rectangular stone-footed building (but assumed to have had a timber superstructure) excavated by Ian Ralston at Green Castle, Portknockie, Banffshire. That building, as it survived, was over 7m long and 4m wide, with a rounded end and containing an internal post-pad for a roof support. It is not independently dated, but ran parallel to, and within, the elaborate Pictish timber-framed wall that edged this tiny promontory. Elsewhere, the cropmark record indicates that such major timber buildings can occur either singly or grouped. A cluster of broadly similar looking, albeit larger, buildings has been recorded at Lathrisk, in Fife (*49*) although they have not been excavated or dated. These examples may have extra internal storage capacity, to judge from dark marks placed axially within them, and are very visible on the air photographs. Individual examples of rather grander timber halls also appear in the cropmark record: one of the clearest, apparently placed in this instance within a palisaded enclosure, is at Monboddo in Aberdeenshire. Finally, the general similarity of the elongate rounded form of the Newbarns example bears comparison to those of Pitcarmick houses of comparable date.

Who lived in this building at Newbarns, if indeed it was a residence? The scarcity of timber structures of this scale and form in the cropmark record, compared to the greater quantity of Iron Age ring-ditch houses, for example, suggests – with reservations that many may have been lost to ploughing – that the former were not the vernacular housing of the Angus farmer at the end of the first millennium AD. Perhaps then it would be more advisable to interpret the Newbarns structure as the home of a local worthy, although whether Pictish or Gaelic-speaker we cannot say, given its dating bracket. Size alone could not be used to define the likely status of this building since its floor space is smaller than that of some of the Pitcarmick houses; neither did it produce any finds that would have assisted its interpretation. It does not, however, show any modification of the kind that might have arisen had livestock also been kept within it. Perhaps this was not considered necessary in the lowlands.

This brief review indicates that our knowledge of the physical remains of Early Historic settlement is accumulating steadily, though gradually. We are forced to countenance the depressing possibility that vernacular farming units were constructed by methods that have survived very poorly in the ground, such that greater sophistication in the archaeological approach to them will be required if they are to be identified in the arable lowlands of Angus. However, the discovery at Easter Kinnear in north-east Fife of a scooped building, its semi-sunken interior forming a kind of parallel for the Grubenhauser used as workshops and weaving sheds in the Germanic areas of Britain, gives cause for optimism. Rebuilt on several occasions, with a concave cross-section and dating to the sixth or seventh centuries AD, the physical characteristics of this building give a marked, but rather informal, cropmark signature. Similar structures, later in date than Hawkhill, may thus be lurking within the unprepossessing cropmark 'splodges' of Angus.

8

Burial traditions in the
first millennia

This round-up of recent archaeological discoveries in Angus ends with a consideration of the archaeological evidence for the disposal of the dead. We concentrate on the first millennium AD, since little is known about pre-Roman Iron Age funerary practices in Angus and, indeed, that is true in Scotland as a whole – with a few exceptions such as in the Lothian plain to the south of the Forth, discussed briefly below. Iron Age burial traditions, whatever they may have been, were not ones that normally left archaeologically detectable traces, as either inhumations or cremation deposits. Perhaps the dead were left out for the birds to peck, or even cast into rivers or the sea. The few burials that have been identified seem to reflect very much an abnormal Iron Age burial rite and thus we should be careful to avoid creating 'typical' burial traditions from what may have been exceptional or even on occasion deviant graves, on the basis that this is the only evidence that survives.

Other parts of Scotland, particularly the Lothians, did have a more established and recognisable tradition of burying the dead earlier in the Iron Age. Interment occurred either in small pit grave cemeteries or in isolated, sometimes elaborate and monumental cists, but it would be unwise to generalise from this evidence; different communities, perhaps tribes, may well have adopted different practices (as is seen later in the adoption of barrow cemeteries only in certain parts of Scotland). Occasional burials from the Lothians and nearby reflect more general Iron Age funerary practices, found from place to place across temperate Europe; these include two instances of inhumations of warriors with panoplies of sword and spear and even one burial with a two-wheeled vehicle, representing a variant on a practice with good parallels in the Belgian Ardennes and also seen as far afield as Austria and the Czech Republic. All these last are recent finds, suggesting very firmly that archaeologists are far from knowing the full range of Iron Age practices in the country.

Attitudes to the treatment of the dead were to change considerably during the first millennium AD, with the result that in Angus, as in other areas of north-east Scotland, at least some sectors of society were interred thereafter in an archaeologically detectable manner. The typical recognisable grave of the first millennium AD in northern Britain consisted of an individual laid out full length on his or her back, in either a stone-lined long cist or simply a dug grave (into which a coffin may also have been inserted,

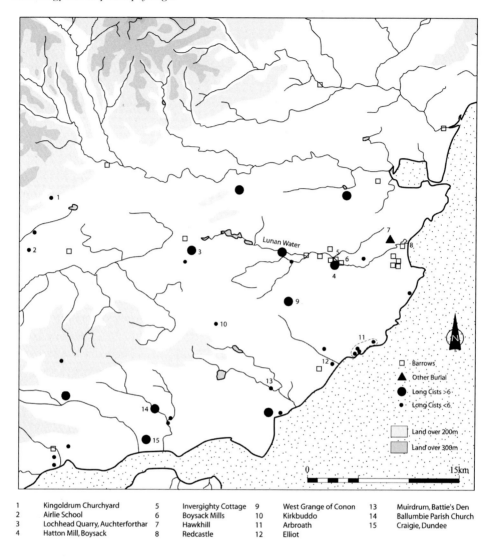

1	Kingoldrum Churchyard	5	Invergighty Cottage	9	West Grange of Conon	13	Muirdrum, Battie's Den
2	Airlie School	6	Boysack Mills	10	Kirkbuddo	14	Ballumbie Parish Church
3	Lochhead Quarry, Auchterforthar	7	Hawkhill	11	Arbroath	15	Craigie, Dundee
4	Hatton Mill, Boysack	8	Redcastle	12	Elliot		

51 Locations of key sites mentioned in Chapter 8, and the distribution of long cists and barrow cemeteries in Angus. *Drawn by Leeanne Whitelaw, based on Ordnance Survey mapping: kind permission, 2003, Ordnance Survey*

although the archaeological evidence for this may be less than distinctive) (*colour plate 21*). Such graves have been found either singly, in small groups or in larger cemeteries. These inhumations are found in what are called 'long cist cemeteries', under cairns or earthen mounds, or within ditched enclosures. Across lowland Scotland, there are some regional differences in the character of these burial structures, but these variations are not clear-cut and there is considerable overlap in their distributions.

In Angus, two forms of first millennium AD burial structure recur – simple long cist burials and more elaborate structures in which long cist burials lie within ditched square or round enclosures (and often referred to as square or circular barrows) (*51*). In fact, the former presence of a barrow mound can only be suggested for Angus, as all the examples examined to date have been within the arable zone and have thus been ploughed flat. Whereas almost all the long cist burials have been discovered by chance during ground-disturbing works, be it ploughing or house or road construction, the known barrows are mostly (but not entirely) the result of detection during aerial reconnaissance. The distribution of both types concentrates on the lower-lying and better agricultural land, and may provide proxy evidence for the distribution of contemporary settlement which, as discussed in the previous chapter, is difficult to find on the ground. However, the distribution of these burials as they are known so far seems to be geographically considerably more restricted within Angus than that of Bronze Age short cists. Since the same processes have led to the discovery of short cists and long cists, the evidence seems to point to a real distinction in the distribution of these burial forms. It would thus seem a reasonable conjecture that the distribution of Early Historic long cists in Angus is not merely a product of recovery bias, since in general the dislodging of skeletal material and the stones in long cists during ploughing ought to be as identifiable as when their Bronze Age precursors were disturbed in similar circumstances. Of course, there are differences – the slabs in short cists are generally more sizeable and short cists may often be sited on natural knolls more susceptible to disturbance from the erosive impact of ploughing, but these factors do not seem sufficient to explain the distributional differences noted. It is also true that in other parts of eastern Scotland the distribution of long cist cemeteries seems narrower than the known spread of primarily Bronze Age short cists.

LONG CIST GRAVES

Audrey Henshall's classic survey of the long cist cemeteries of Scotland, published in 1956, identified six such sites in Angus where six or more graves had been found together – at Aberlemno, Carlungie, Carnoustie, Craigie, Pitmuies and West Grange of Conon. To these can be added two further pre-twentieth-century discoveries at Farnell Church and Templeton. The typical characteristics of long cist cemeteries are closely spaced graves, often set in rows, with the graves orientated broadly east–west and containing the body laid out with the head to the west. Cemeteries typically contain both adults and children, and as a whole, based upon the calibration of available radiocarbon dates, they appear to have origins in the first half of the first millennium AD and to have fallen out of use by the end of the ninth century AD, if not before.

However, for most of these pre-twentieth-century Angus discoveries, very little detail is known of the cemetery layout and dating, and there are no graphic records of the discoveries. Typical is the case of the Carlungie cemetery, where the excavator of several graves, Alexander Hutcheson, recorded that a local inhabitant informed him that a great many burials at the same location had been disturbed in the past by farmers searching for stones to build fireplaces. The exception in terms of the quality of the record is the group of six long cist graves examined in 1860-1 by Andrew

Jervise adjacent to the souterrain at West Grange of Conon, near Colliston (*52*). The fact that they were discovered during fieldwork at the souterrain – already an object of archaeological interest and well-recorded at this date – accounts for the fuller record of these burials.

In the past few years, three further long cist cemeteries have been discovered and excavated to modern standards. Twenty graves of fouth- to seventh-century AD date, all containing adult burials where identifiable, were excavated by AOC Scotland in 2004 after their discovery during gravel quarrying at Auchterforthar, near Forfar; these probably formed part of a larger cemetery. Within what was exposed of this cemetery there were distinct clusters of graves that the excavator speculated might define family groupings. In 2005 an as yet undated long cist cemetery containing at least 41 graves and enclosed by a ditch was excavated in advance of a housing development by SUAT at Ballumbie, Dundee, when it was discovered beneath the medieval church and graveyard (*53*). Near Hatton Mill in the Lunan Valley at least 15 graves forming part of a larger cemetery, which included barrows, were identified by CFA Archaeology during trial trenching in 2004, but were not fully investigated (*54*).

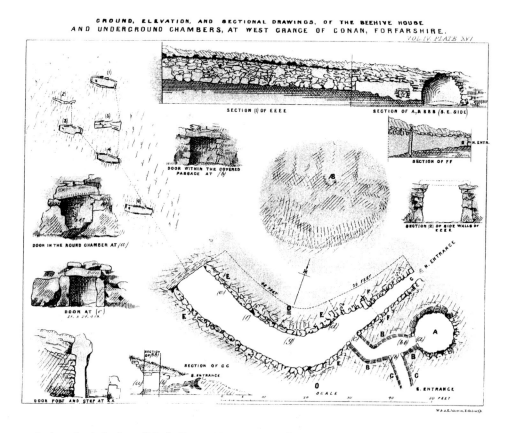

GROUND, ELEVATION, AND SECTIONAL DRAWINGS, OF THE BEEHIVE HOUSE AND UNDERGROUND CHAMBERS, AT WEST GRANGE OF CONAN, FORFARSHIRE.

52 Andrew Jervise's plan of his findings at West Grange of Conon, 1860-1. The long cists are shown top left. *Courtesy: Society of Antiquaries of Scotland*

As yet, there have been no discoveries on a scale to compare with the largest cemeteries south of the Tay. In Fife and in Lothian, cemeteries containing well over 100 graves have been identified. Despite this, the Carlungie evidence considered above at least hints that major cemeteries of this type may yet be located in Angus.

53 The long cist cemetery at Ballumbie under excavation. *Courtesy: SUAT Ltd*

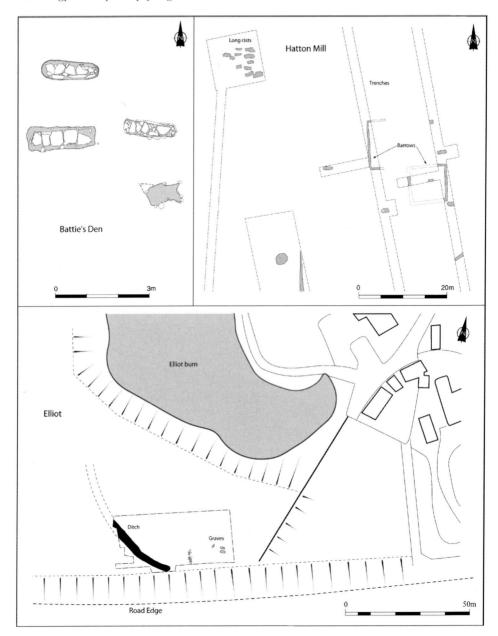

54 Recent discoveries of long cist burials and square barrows at Elliot, Battie's Den near Muirdrum, and in trial trenches at Hatton Mill in the Lunan Valley. *Drawn by Leeanne Whitelaw after Cameron et al. 2007 (Elliot) and unpublished CFA reports*

However, to concentrate upon the cemeteries alone is to underestimate the distribution and frequency of the discovery of long cist burials and potentially also the varieties of burial site in use during the first millennium AD. Over 20 further finds of certain or probable long cists are known from the antiquarian literature; in each case five or fewer graves

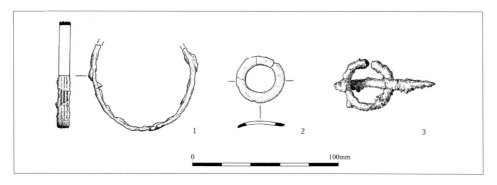

55 The iron bracelet (1) and bronze ring (2) from Elliot (*drawn by Alan Braby*) and the Craigie brooch as published by Hutcheson (3). *Courtesy: Society of Antiquaries of Scotland*

were noted and the majority of cases are singletons (*51*). Many are nineteenth-century discoveries, but some recent finds have been made. Since there are many eighteenth- and nineteenth-century accounts of discoveries of 'stone coffins', where it cannot now be established whether the structures described are long cists, Bronze Age short cists or medieval graves, the probability that long cists have more frequently been found is great.

A key issue is whether the single long cists and the small groups represent elements of larger cemeteries, as opposed to smaller burial plots or even isolated burials. Discoveries made in recent years within the corridor of the A92 road upgrade demonstrate that both circumstances may apply (*54*). At Battie's Den, near Muirdrum, a cluster of at least three long cists aligned east to west was identified by CFA Archaeology on the boundary of a proposed quarry, on the upper margin of sloping ground. The size of the cists indicates that all contained adults, but neither human remains nor artefacts were recovered. These burials are likely to form part of a larger group that extended beyond the area available for evaluation. Conversely, two adjacent long cist burials and a dug grave were found on a promontory beside the Elliot Water, south-west of Arbroath close to the North Sea shoreline. Here excavations by CFA were sufficiently extensive to confirm that the discoveries were isolated, since ploughing seems not to have been sufficiently damaging to have obliterated all evidence of other interments had they been present. The promontory appears to have been cut off by a substantial ditch, along the inner margin of which a dry-stone wall or rampart had stood. The date of the enclosing work and its chronological relationship to the burials were not established, although a later prehistoric or Early Historic date best fits the character of the earthwork. The only other features encountered were a number of pits and a fragmentary wall foundation, and neither these nor the enclosure features need be contemporary with any of these graves.

These long cists were in poor condition and the skeletal remains, both of adults, were fragmentary; neither contained any grave goods. They were orientated east–west, with the heads placed to the west. They have been dated by radiocarbon and calibrated to the sixth to seventh centuries AD. The dug grave was set on a different (north-east–south-west) alignment. There was no body preserved within it but a small bronze ring, probably a fastener for a belt or for clothing, and an iron penannular bracelet found lying on its base, were probably grave goods that accompanied the corpse (*55*). The date of the dug grave at Elliot is not known, although the zinc content of the ring indicates brass rather than another copper alloy, which Fraser Hunter has argued to indicate re-use of Roman alloy. This ring is thus of Roman Iron Age or later date.

BARROW CEMETERIES

Barrow cemeteries containing square and round barrows are not unique to Angus, but they are certainly common in the cropmark record here. Available dating evidence suggests they belong to the Early Historic period and certainly a more recent period than the celebrated square barrows of eastern Yorkshire. Such barrows have been identified in at least 20 locations in Angus with all – apart from a couple of exceptions considered below – detected by aerial reconnaissance since the advent of systematic aerial survey in the mid 1970s. These sites, as far as the cropmarks reveal, generally contain fewer than 10 barrows, with the structures typically less than 10m across and containing a grave centrally placed within the square or annular ditched enclosure that delimited the barrow. The cemetery at Invergighty Cottage near Hatton Mill in the middle reach of the Lunan Valley stands out amongst the Angus examples in that it consists of over 20 barrows, both round and square. Only a few such cemeteries in Scotland still remain as upstanding, earthwork monuments – two of the classic examples are at Garbeg and Whitebridge in the county of Inverness. Here the barrows consist of square or annular ditches with external banks that surround central low mounds or stony cairns. These upstanding survivors indicate what may have been lost from the Angus examples as a result of ploughing, although it is possible that some may not have included internal mounds, as is suggested for burials of Grabgarten type on the continent.

Whilst the known distribution of barrow cemeteries reflects the varying responsiveness of different soil types to producing cropmarks and the propensity of aerial surveyors to revisit areas known to produce good quality cropmarks, there is a notable concentration of barrow cemeteries along the Lunan Valley (*51*). Several examples have been identified along the 10km between Friockheim and Lunan Bay, and include sites at Newbarns and Redcastle towards the coast, and Hatton Mill, Boysack and Invergighty further inland. Dave Pollock has argued that the latter two, lying opposite each other on relict river terraces beside tributary burns of the Lunan Water, might have been placed beside major prehistoric land boundaries defined by these stream courses.

The Field School excavations of the barrow cemetery at Redcastle represent the most comprehensive examination of such a site yet undertaken. Prior to the Field School only two barrow cemeteries in Scotland north of the Tay had been subject to any systematic excavation. In 1977 two square-ditched barrows were excavated in advance of quarrying operations at Boysack Mills. One of these contained a deeply set burial placed in a wooden coffin below substantial boulders; it was attributed to the first to second centuries AD, as this was the most likely date for an iron ring-headed pin recovered from the grave. Further afield, excavations in Garbeg (near Drumnadrochit in Inverness-shire) in the mid 1970s revealed that in two of the excavated cases the central low mounds within the barrows covered grave-pits. The penannular ditch of Cairn 1 covered a round mound, below which was found a linear U-sectioned grave pit in which skeletal material did not survive. This 1.6m long pit could not be related to the fragments of Pictish carved stone recovered earlier from the overlying cairn material. The architecture of Cairn 3 was more elaborate. This was defined by a square arrangement consisting of four detached lengths of ditching, with conspicuous schist boulders occupying the undug angles between the ditches. The interior was occupied by a low peaty mound, over which had been placed a rectangular kerbed setting of stones. Beneath both these features Laurie Wedderburn and Dorothy Grime identified a grave pit a little over half a metre deep and some 1.7m long which contained the shaft of a human femur and a poorly preserved skull. More recently, two square barrows and a nearby round barrow immediately adjacent to, if not within, a long cist cemetery were discovered during trial trenching in 2004 near Hatton Mill (*54*).

THE BARROW CEMETERY AT REDCASTLE

Many of the general characteristics of barrow cemeteries are demonstrated by the cropmark example investigated by the Field School under the direction of Derek Alexander at Redcastle, located at the mouth of the Lunan Water and perched on a raised beach overlooking the sandy expanse of Lunan Bay, between an old stream channel and the edge of the raised beach (*56*).

Five square barrows, two round barrows and nine unenclosed graves were examined, with at least one round barrow (outwith the excavation area) remaining unexcavated. The graves were generally orientated south-west to north-east. Of the interments recovered, only ten individuals could be aged, all of whom were adult; of the six which could be sexed, five were certainly or probably female and one was male. It was not, however, possible to indicate any definite correlation between the sex of the deceased and the form of grave constructed.

The square barrows were similar in character, albeit varying in size between 6.5m and 10m across over ditches that survived up to 1m wide and 0.3m deep (*colour plate 22*). There were distinctive breaks at the corners of the ditched enclosures leaving causeways at the angles, each slightly over 1m wide. The purpose of these gaps is unknown and they may once have been occupied by upright stones as at Garbeg. Based upon the evidence of some of the barrows still visible at Garbeg and Whitebridge, it is more likely that at Redcastle originally there would have been low banks present outside the ditches and a central mound or cairn over the grave – the considerable quantity of pebbles found in the ditches, no doubt brought up from the beach, could be all that remain of such features since being eradicated by ploughing. There is no indication here, nor at Boysack Mills, that the ditches had ever held any timber feature, such as a fence. The two round barrows were *c.*8-8.5m in overall diameter and were bounded by apparently unbroken but narrow ditches.

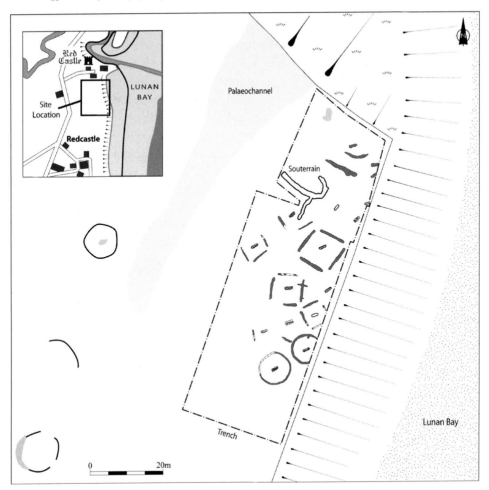

56 Redcastle: barrow cemetery, other graves and souterrain in excavation area, with cropmarks of further traces in the vicinity. *Drawn by Leeanne Whitelaw, modified from Alexander 2005*

With one exception, the graves present within the barrows were of extended inhumations laid out in long cists (*57*). The central grave in the largest square barrow was more deeply cut than the others and, unusually, its alignment was not square to that of the enclosing ditches; this grave-pit was 1m deep and the long cist set within it had been covered by more massive capstones. In fact everything about this barrow was bigger than its neighbours, which may tell us something about the status of the individual buried there. The grave within the smallest square barrow was unusual in that the body had been interred within a wooden coffin visible as a dark organic stain (as at Boysack Mills) and had been packed in place with beach pebbles. The curving profile of the stain suggested to the excavator that the body had been interred in a halved and hollowed out tree trunk rather than placed in a plank-built coffin. Although rare, tree-trunk coffins have been found at Whithorn, Dumfries and Galloway. Alexander noted that one of the few references we have to Pictish burial practices is in an Irish elegy which states that

57 Grave pit containing the extended inhumation in a long cist within the largest square barrow excavated at Redcastle. *Crown Copyright: Historic Scotland*

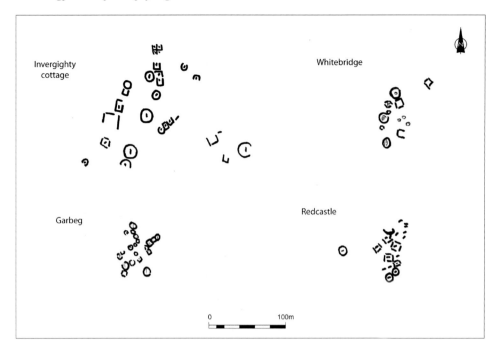

58 Comparative plans of barrow cemeteries. The Inverness-shire examples at Whitebridge and Garbeg are upstanding sites, whereas the lowland Angus examples are cropmarks. *Courtesy: Derek Alexander*

King Bridei, the victor of Nechtansmere in AD 685, was buried in a 'block of hollow withered oak'.

The nine apparently unenclosed graves displayed the same range of structural charac-teristics as those present within the barrows. All were orientated broadly south-west to north-east, with the bodies in seven cases laid in slab-defined long cists and the remainder in simple dug graves. The graves were relatively evenly spaced across the site, with only two unenclosed graves being in close proximity to each other. This may mean that where no barrows were present, the graves had been marked out on the surface, perhaps with a certain sized grave plot, which allowed subsequent burials to be placed at a discrete distance. However, it is possible that some originally may have been under barrows, of which the shallow ditches and banks had subsequently been entirely erased by ploughing. Two such possibilities lie at the southern end of the cemetery; the graves here are aligned with that within the square barrow to the north-east and may thus have formed a group of three contiguous barrows similar to arrangements within other cemeteries, such as at Garbeg or Invergighty Cottage (*58*).

Radiocarbon dates obtained from nine burials demonstrate on calibration that the cemetery at Redcastle was most probably founded no later than the early fourth century AD and grew organically (rather than in a linear fashion) until at least the later ninth century (although, given the nature of radiocarbon determinations a longer timespan is possible, with a maximum range between the first and twelfth centuries). There was no evidence that the preferred form of burial changed through time.

59 Artist's impression of a burial party approaching a barrow cemetery, based on Redcastle. The ditches that now reveal such cemeteries as cropmarks are highlighted in black. *Drawn by Leeanne Whitelaw*

The cemetery was therefore in use before, during and slightly after the period of the Pictish kingdom. Taking into account the likelihood of further graves not excavated, the excavator calculated that only around 20 people had been buried in the cemetery over a period of 500-700 years. It is evident thus that only a very limited sector of the local adult population was buried (at approximately one individual per generation) in this cemetery. It is difficult in this light to avoid interpreting Redcastle as the burial ground of the local landowning aristocracy – the elite family who were perhaps the equivalent of the Mormaers or another tier of the Pictish hierarchy, recorded elsewhere in near-contemporary documents. It might be suggested that the cemetery was located on the seaward periphery of their landholding. Perhaps in the distribution of barrow cemeteries along the Lunan Valley we have a relic of the patterns of Pictish landholding (59). Alternatively, the dead represented in these cemeteries may have been the spiritual leaders of society, although the mix of sexes represented at Redcastle might make such an interpretation problematic.

The highly selective burial practice at Redcastle appears to contrast with the patterns of burial in the contemporary long cist cemeteries, where a wider range of the population is represented, as evidenced most clearly by the inclusion of children amongst those buried. The rate of expansion of the Redcastle cemetery also appears to contrast with that encountered within the larger long cist cemeteries. At Hallow Hill, St Andrews in Fife, for example, excavations in the 1970s revealed that almost 150 adults and children had been interred (and quite probably more since the full extent of the site was not determined) over a similar time period. Could the different burial types reflect social divisions, with the barrow cemeteries being burial grounds for the landowning classes (at least in those areas where they occur) and the long cist cemeteries or smaller groupings used to inter those of less-elevated status? There may be something in this, but the truth is probably more complex and lies in the origins of the widespread adoption of the long cist as a burial structure in the first millennium AD in Scotland and its relationship to the arrival of Christianity. What is of course clear for this period – really the first since earlier prehistory when numbers of the dead can be identified archaeologically – is that it is still only a tiny proportion of the likely population who appear in the burial record at all.

PAGAN OR CHRISTIAN?

The advent of the new eastern religion – Christianity – in the area is an obvious candidate for causing changes in perceptions as to the proper treatment of the dead. So when did Christianity first reach Angus? Ninian is claimed to have evangelised the Southern Picts from his base at Whithorn in Galloway in the fifth century, but the nature and impact of his reputed activities remain uncertain; his influence may well not have spread as far north as Angus. In the second half of the sixth century, Columba is similarly described as travelling among and probably converting at least some of the Northern Picts, from the monastery he established on Iona, but again it is not known whether the influence of the Irish Church in the west did not take some time to reach Angus. Some simple incised crosses from the county, as on Turin Hill, may bear witness to this early activity. In due course, it is more certain, however, that the influence of the Northumbrian Church extended northwards across eastern Scotland during the later seventh and eighth centuries. Much of the early history of Christianity in the area involves the interpretation of the documents of the period, alongside the study of surviving place names (notably those containing the 'Egles' place name element), the recognition of further stones incised with the Cross and the dating of the iconography depicted on the Class I and II Pictish symbol stones. This is properly a specialist study, the details of which cannot be rehearsed here.

Can we detect the adoption of Christianity in the burial record? The view has been commonly expressed in the past that long cist cemeteries provide evidence of the adoption of Christian beliefs, Charles Thomas and the late Leslie Alcock, for example, suggesting that they may reflect the Ninianic conversion of local populations. Certainly, the ordered and regular east–west alignment of graves with the head to the west, the absence of grave goods and the occasional association of long cist cemeteries with Early Christian monuments (such as the Catstane, now languishing close to the main runway within Edinburgh Airport in Lothian) would tend to support an interpretation of these cemeteries as the burial grounds of Early Christian communities. Some of the Angus long cist cemeteries – at Ballumbie, Kingoldrum and Farnell for example – have been discovered at or close to sites later occupied by parish churches and burial grounds. Whilst these examples might indicate the continuity of Christian belief and practice at these locations, they appear to be the exception rather than the norm and other commentators such as Audrey Henshall have identified the lack of coincidence in the siting of long cist cemeteries and churches as a regular occurrence. Long cist cemeteries do not generally appear to have been associated with any contemporary buildings, such as chapels, in eastern Scotland.

Edwina Proudfoot and Christopher Aliaga-Kelly have suggested that the bigger long cist cemeteries might be the burial grounds of several settlements and thus a token of the developing structure of society, reflecting the 'multiple estates' postulated on other grounds. In southern Scotland, as at Sprouston near Roxburgh, however, certain large cemeteries can have major first millennium AD settlements marked by timber halls in their vicinities. Proudfoot and Aliaga-Kelly postulate that cemeteries that served several settlements were not in their view generally initially accompanied by chapels or other forms of religious architecture. The evidence for associations of such cemeteries with later parishes is ambiguous; it seems reasonably clear for the Lothians, according to Proudfoot and Aliaga-Kelly, but does not hold true for Fife, where the distribution is both substantially coastal and locally clustered, as around St Andrews itself.

Yet there is growing evidence from across Scotland that the beginnings of the long cist burial tradition occurred before either the Ninianic or Columban missions. Radiocarbon dates and other indications make it clear that at least some long cists and dug graves are pre-Christian, but this comment refers almost exclusively to single graves or, at most, small clusters. For example, the long cist cemetery at Hallow Hill appears to have developed out of a small pagan burial site represented by a richly furnished primary cist burial containing exotic Roman artefacts amongst other items.

Burials accompanied by grave goods are often regarded as being of pagan, although not necessarily pre-Christian, origin. There is some supporting evidence from Angus. A burial accompanied by a pennanular iron brooch with textile adhering, discovered in long cist at Craigie, Dundee at the turn of the twentieth century (55) was recently dated by radiocarbon methods, indicating that this person had died at some stage between the late first and early fourth centuries AD. In 1885, a cist disturbed when a drain was being dug at Airlie School, close to an earlier findspot of long cists, was found to contain a Roman glass cup which has been re-dated by Dominic Ingemark of Lund University to the period AD 160-260 (a third- or fourth-century date had previously been ascribed to it). A similar find of a Roman glass cup is recorded as having been discovered around 1843 when several cists were found in the vicinity of Kingoldrum churchyard. However, there are conflicting accounts of this discovery, one stating that the glass cup was found with a bronze chalice inside an Early Christian hand-bell, and not necessarily from within one of the cists, and so this discovery is best treated with considerable caution.

There are other examples of artefacts being recovered from long cist graves. One of the burials at Lochhead Quarry, Auchterforthar, was associated with an amber bead, and one of the skeletons at Ballumbie was wearing a bracelet on its right arm. The graves at West Grange of Conon (close to the souterrain) included burials accompanied by coloured pebbles and a fragment of a black cannel-coal ring. According to Fraser Hunter, at sites such as Conon the artefacts seem commonly to have been broken before having been deliberately incorporated into the burial. Their personal nature suggests they may have been valued items deliberately reduced to fragments as part of the burial rite and included as tokens, perhaps of the deceased's possessions, perhaps from those of a mourning relative.

On this basis how are we to interpret the limited evidence from Elliot? Could the dug grave there with its associated finds have been a pagan, possibly pre-Christian, burial placed on a site added to by Christian cist graves set on a different alignment?

Whilst opinion has tended towards viewing long cist cemeteries as an expression of Christian belief, the reverse has generally been the case for barrow cemeteries. There are good grounds for this, not least through the pre-Christian date inferred for the Boysack Mills barrow and now confirmed by the date of the earliest burials from Redcastle. Moreover, there is a repeated association of early, perhaps fifth- to seventh-century, Class I Pictish symbol stones with barrows, such as at Garbeg, or used as side-slabs or capstones of burial cists. Much ink has been spilt in interpreting these stones, but it is reasonably clear that not all of the iconography on them is Christian, even if some of the symbols may reflect knowledge of Christian schemes. Yet we should not be blind to the fact that many of the characteristics of the Redcastle graves themselves – their structure and general orientations (some definitely have heads at the west, although others are aligned south-west–north-east) and lack of grave goods accompanying the bodies – could have been argued as evidence of Christian burials in another context.

Another key discovery is the immediate juxtaposition of barrows and a long cist cemetery discovered at Hatton Mill – would the two be placed together if one was Christian and the other pagan? In 1996 two square-ditched burials similar to those at Boysack Mills were found in a long cist cemetery at Thornybank, Midlothian, reinforcing the view that these burial forms were not mutually exclusive.

Ultimately, if we cannot be sure that all long cists were Christian burials, or that all square barrow cemeteries and long cist graves with burials accompanied by artefacts were necessarily pagan, it is necessary to interpret all new discoveries on their own merits, rather than by making simplistic interpretations based upon universal explanatory models of dubious validity. Rather than viewing the adoption of Christianity as being accompanied by a sudden change in burial practices, is it possible that the percolation of Roman burial traditions throughout and beyond the Roman province may have influenced the funerary rites beyond the frontier, even if only indirectly, before Ninian and his successors ventured northwards? That said, for eastern Scotland either side of the great estuaries of Forth and Tay, the correlation between areas with long cist cemeteries and those displaying early 'Egles' place names – indicative of early Christian communities – remains very marked. Perhaps the adoption of isolated graves and small burial grounds had taken place prior to the arrival of Christianity, with the appearance of later, more substantial cemeteries a result of the new religion.

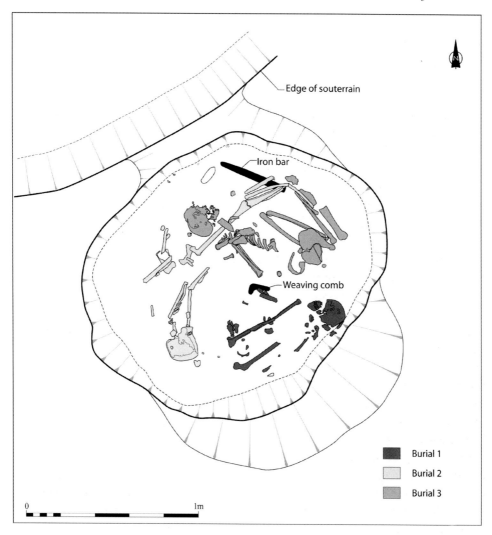

60 The 'deviant' burial of three women at Hawkhill. *Drawn by Leeanne Whitelaw after Rees forthcoming*

POST-MORTEM — AN UNUSUAL MULTIPLE BURIAL AT HAWKHILL

If Redcastle provides an example of an ordered cemetery for the local landowning class, used over several hundred years, then an unexpected discovery during the Field School excavations at Hawkhill lies at the other end of the spectrum in terms of its likely interpretation. Here was something altogether more puzzling and, in a sense, more intimate. In about the seventh or eighth century AD, based on calibrated radiocarbon dates, three women of whom two at least were over 30 years old, and the eldest probably considerably older, were interred together in an unlined and irregular pit at the precise end of the largely infilled souterrain associated with the earlier Iron Age settlement (*60*). A nearby setting of posts may be related to this burial pit.

The first body (Burial 2) had been placed extended on its right side facing into the centre of the grave. The second (Burial 3) had been arranged in a crouched position, with its head lying in the lap of the first. The third (Burial 1) was put higher up in the grave-pit, on her back with the knees drawn up tightly to the chest. It is unlikely that these positions were natural and at least two of the bodies must have been tied or otherwise restrained to account for their disposition. The deposit within which the bodies had been interred was extremely rich in charcoal, with much burnt animal bone and teeth. Beneath the bodies lay an iron weaving comb and an iron bar. Iron-working activities had been undertaken nearby and there were other fragmentary remains to suggest that this was an industrial site around the same time as the burial took place (Chapter 7).

These three females had evidently not been treated with the same respect afforded to those laid to rest in nearby cemeteries. In the absence of any pathology to suggest how or why they may have died, we can only speculate as to their identity and the reasons for their burial together here. Were they slaves, a mistress and her slaves, outsiders, heretics or witches, or even murder victims? The form of the burial has no ready parallel in the northern British archaeological record for this period and is an example of what archaeologists now like to call a 'deviant' burial. Whilst some aspects of the burial have resonances in the Anglo-Saxon or Norse worlds, details – sometimes major details – differ. For example, pagan Norse graves sometimes include what appear to be female servants, but in such instances the primary burial is male. The multiple interment and contracted nature of some of the bodies in fact is more reminiscent of prehistoric burial practices than Pictish ones. Was then the location of the burial pit at the end of a prehistoric souterrain accidental, as logic would suggest, or deliberate?

9

Celts, Romans, Picts and Scots in Angus

Archaeologists working on Scottish material have rather different views as to how complex Iron Age societies in eastern Scotland were. On the one hand, they note that, compared to the Late Bronze Age with its evidence for a range of status goods being hoarded, many Iron Age objects are relatively prosaic and many settlement sites produce few objects. They are also sceptical as to the extent that the Heroic Tales and other literature written down at more recent dates in Ireland but based on earlier oral traditions can really be used to throw light on the character of Iron Age societies at other times and in other places. They thus have doubts about whether the traditional, generally androcentric, model of a 'Celtic society' captured in that literature, with small-scale kingdoms headed by a king surrounded by his elite retinue, and dominating free farmers and craftsmen and below them bondsmen, was typical of other times and other places, such as pre-Roman Iron Age Scotland. They also note that, while some Iron Age houses are certainly bigger and grander than others, detecting hierarchies in the settlement record is not problem-free; the nature of the occupation of the supposedly dominant hillforts is often not noticeably different from that found on physically lesser sites. There is little convincing evidence that the biggest of the Scottish hillforts were 'hilltop towns', as Gordon Childe believed, on analogy with sites further south in temperate Europe, as he wrote his synthesis on Scottish archaeology three-quarters of a century ago. Overall, then, the pre-Roman Iron Age societies of Scotland may have been distinctly less hierarchical than is often imagined.

Of course, as is often the case with the archaeological and early historical records, all the evidence does not point in the same direction, making the judgement of it less than clear-cut. Various pieces of information can be brought together to make the contrary case. On the other hand, the written information we have needs to be taken into account and whilst it is reasonable to have reservations about the information conveyed by classical authors and it is sensible to consider, for example, the speech made by the Caledonian war-leader Calgacus, just before the battle of Mons Graupius, as what an educated Roman – Tacitus – *thought* he ought to have said rather than a straight piece of journalism, we cannot simply dismiss all this evidence. Little in the brief classical testimonies suggests societies or practices very different from what the Roman Army had encountered elsewhere as they marched northward. Ptolemy of Alexandria's map, put together in the second century using intelligence gained in the previous one, names the tribe of Angus as the Uacomagi. Wherever, and whatever scale, the battle of Mons Graupius was – whether south in the Earn Valley or Perthshire, or north in Aberdeenshire – it indicates natives able to coalesce in numbers around a war leader to organise resistance. Even if one takes the view that northern Scotland was too politically different from Rome and too economically poor to make its incorporation into the Empire worth the candle, these reservations cannot apply to Angus. As discussed below, a Roman legionary fortress was commissioned at nearby Inchtuthil and Roman forts intended to be permanent extended northwards through the county. It is reasonable to infer that such forts were imposed across a zone that was, even in defeat, relatively politically stable.

At an earlier date, simply building the major hillforts would have required substantial amounts of labour, which would have needed to be organised. Whilst the anthropological record suggests to us that there are numerous ways of getting people to work together at least temporarily – work feasts, for example, accompanied by copious amounts of alcohol – the completion of a major engineering task like the erection of the innermost enclosure at the White Caterthun implies the existence of a leader or leaders, however shadowy they may be in the archaeological record at other times. Although eastern Scotland mostly lacks the extensive field systems that characterise several parts of Iron Age England, the indications of the scale of settlement in the countryside and the opening-up of the landscape for cultivation and stock-raising again imply means of control and, behind these, power relations amongst people. It is likely that land was owned, even perhaps privately owned, by this time.

The Iron Age of Angus had lasted for some 800 years before it was obviously disrupted by the arrival of the Roman Army. It would, however, be unreasonable to consider it as timeless and unchanging across the preceding centuries, and at least some of the evidence at our disposal suggests it was – from time to time at least – hierarchically organised. Archaeological distribution maps of course conceal chronological variation. Although emphasising some of the same portions of the Lunan Valley as does Roy's map of the mid eighteenth century, the distribution of cropmarks does not imply all those sites were in use at the same time – as Roy's map does (*61*).

We can perhaps point, for the Lunan Valley, to an Early Iron Age landscape, around the middle of the first millennium BC, dotted with unenclosed farmsteads such as Douglasmuir and composed primarily – at least in terms of its major buildings – of ring-ditch houses. Such buildings by that time may have been part of the landscape for almost a millennium, to judge from the outcome of Murray Cook's work further north at Kintore. At Douglasmuir there was one building of greater size than the others, which might suggest (amongst other possibilities) some ranking within the settlement, if it is assumed that other structures were contemporary with it. Looked at in two dimensional plans, the difference appears perhaps not very significant, but whoever built the biggest house was able to obtain more substantial lengths of straight-growing timber and, crowned with a steeply pitched conical roof, that building – allowing for its neighbours to have

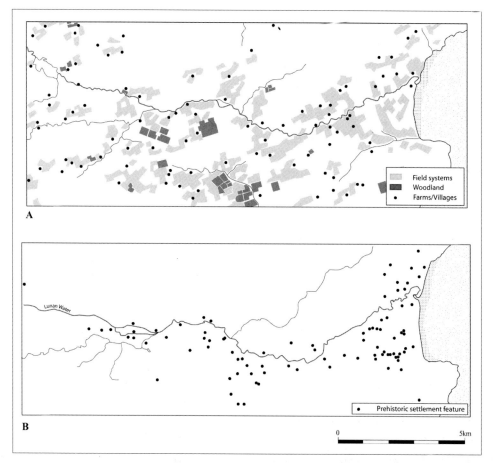

61 Two views of land-use and settlement in the lower valley of the Lunan Water: a 'snapshot' as surveyed for General William Roy in the mid eighteenth century; a palimpsest of later prehistoric settlement features of different dates and types as indicated by the cropmark record

been standing then – would have signalled a significant and very obvious difference. If the internal ring-ditches were storage features, akin to prototype souterrains, then another emphasis signalled by the bigger structure may have been to do with agricultural production and storage at a household level. Some of the four-poster 'granaries' may also relate to these Early Iron Age settlements, based on dating from elsewhere.

Once we move beyond the relatively subtle differences noted here in relation to Douglasmuir, more substantial variability in the social order can be recognised. Even if built over extended periods and making use of work feasts and similar mechanisms, the appearance and development of hillforts across some parts of the county implies the existence of authorities able to mobilise labour. We cannot rule out the possibility that these elites may have resided in the main hillforts or smaller forts such as Mains of Edzell, but positive structural or artefactual evidence from their interiors that support indications of social differentiation and the use of these places as seats of power, remains elusive.

We can contrast this with how the landscape might have looked early in the following millennium. The picture by then appears to be one of greater diversity. Farmsteads – the primary units of agricultural production – remained principally unenclosed clusters of roundhouses. However, by that time post-ring buildings without ring-ditches and scooped buildings (whatever their frequency) were being built. These farming units were routinely accompanied by souterrains of varying capacities and constructional details, which may well suggest unequal access to perishable resources. However, it appears that ring-ditch houses were still being built and, therefore, it seems unwise to propose souterrains as a simple or sudden functional replacement for ring-ditches. It seems to be the case that some people with access to resources to erect a new roundhouse continued to build in a long-established tradition. There were probably also present at this time large timber buildings set within their own enclosures, as at Ironshill East, and occasional large stone-walled 'southern brochs' built over the decayed ramparts of earlier forts. Both these latter settlement forms may have been elite residences (although other explanations are possible). Since the enclosing works of hillforts (but not necessarily the coastal promontory forts) appear from the still-small dating evidence to have been abandoned by this time, could we be seeing in these new forms of settlements a different expression of authority?

It has to be admitted that the processes by which settlement characteristics evolved between the middle of the first millennium BC and the early centuries of our era still cannot be mapped out with any confidence from the limited data presently available. However, there presently seems no case to evoke a sudden transformation of settlement pattern at any particular point, or to seek an external stimulus for the changes that are apparent. Whilst the appearance of the 'southern brochs' might have been related to the waxing and waning of Rome's north-west frontier in the first two centuries AD, some of the other developments had begun before the army of Claudius, and probably even that of Julius Caesar, landed on Britain's shores.

With some archaeological evidence and a healthy dose of speculation it has been possible to provide an impression of the settlement features present within the landscape at say 500 BC and AD 100. By no later than the fourth century AD, if not well before, the character of settlement had changed again, more fundamentally, with the probable abandonment of timber roundhouses and particularly souterrains as elements of vernacular settlement units. At the most basic level, what had gone into a rapid decline was earth-fast timber-work as a major component of buildings and the banana-shaped cropmarks that reliably indicate souterrains.

In terms of the basic economy, it is now possible to move away from Stuart Piggott's view on Scottish Iron Age agriculture. This was, in any case, markedly at odds with his predecessor Gordon Childe's opinion, expressed most forcibly in his *Scotland before the Scots* of 1946. In sum, and as suggested by the still-limited evidence furnished by sites within Angus, this advocated a much more prosperous agricultural basis for the country, albeit one where – in Childe's Marxist views – the development of a class-based society and new arrivals often contributed to instability and war. Whatever else the Iron Age evidence from Angus may now be taken to suggest, it does not support this last contention.

THE ROMANS IN ANGUS

In the late first century AD the Roman Empire expanded into northern Britain, marking the beginning of over three centuries of contact, sometimes peaceable and on other occasions far from it, between the inhabitants of Angus and the Roman world. On three occasions Roman military campaigns north of the Firth of Forth led to the establishment of garrisons intended to be permanent. These were in the late first, mid second and early third centuries and are known respectively (after the family name of the emperors who ruled from Rome at the time) as the Flavian, Antonine and Severan occupations, the longest (Antonine) being for no more than 25 years. Only during the first incursion was Angus permanently garrisoned.

Here we will not consider the archaeological and textual evidence for the Roman military presence in our area in any detail, not least since the nature of Roman military occupation was not a research aim of the Field School. David Woolliscroft and Birgitta Hoffmann have recently ably reviewed the archaeological evidence for Roman military constructions north of the Forth-Clyde isthmus in the light of their researches conducted under the auspices of the Roman Gask Project, and Lawrence Keppie's *Scotland's Roman Remains* provides a valuable guide to what little is still visible in Angus.

In the late first century AD auxiliary forts and fortlets were constructed along Strathmore at strategic locations beside or near the confluence points of major watercourses, at each location generally south of the major river there (*62*) – at Cargill (Rivers Tay and Isla) Cardean (River Isla and Dean Water) Inverquharity (River South Esk and Glen Prosen) and Stracathro (River North Esk and West Water). Near Meikleour in Perthshire, construction was begun of a much larger legionary fortress beside the River Tay at Inchtuthil, but the job was never fully completed. Despite unsubstantiated claims for permanent Roman forts having been built as far north as the Beauly Firth, the Strathmore forts remain the most northerly confirmed examples known in Britain and at the time formed the furthest outposts of Roman occupation in Europe.

These constructions are commonly interpreted as having been built around AD 83 by Agricola's successor as provincial governor after Agicola's defeat of the Caledonian forces at the battle of Mons Graupius. Its location is hotly disputed but perhaps was most likely located north of the Mounth; others, however, have argued that it lies south of Angus, near the River Earn in Perthshire. Archaeological evidence from closely datable pottery and coins found during excavations at Cardean, Stracathro and elsewhere suggest that the forts were abandoned shortly thereafter, around AD 86 or 87. Based primarily upon their reading of the archaeological data and textual evidence provided by Tacitus' *Agricola*, Woolliscroft and Hoffmann have challenged this accepted chronology and, somewhat controversially, proposed an earlier move north and thus a longer period of Roman military occupation of these northern outposts beginning under one of Agricola's precursors in the AD 70s, allowing for perhaps 15 years of occupation. Whilst the intricacies of the arguments for and against need not concern us here, the impact of a 15-year occupation on the psyche of the Angus folk would surely have been different from that resulting from a three-year stint, for as Woolliscroft and Hoffmann point out,

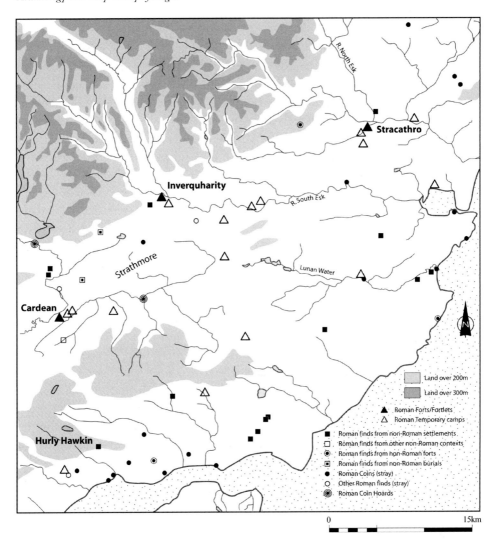

62 The Roman presence in Angus, as indicated by the distribution of Roman forts and temporary camps. Findspots of Roman artefacts from non-Roman contexts are also shown. *Drawn by Leeanne Whitelaw, based on Ordnance Survey mapping: kind permission, 2003, Ordnance Survey*

the longer span was sufficient for a generation to have grown up knowing nothing but Roman rule.

The withdrawal of the Roman forces southwards by the late AD 80s marked only one stage in a period of considerable fluidity in the physical extent of Roman military involvement in northern Britain. Following a period of consolidation along the Tyne–Solway isthmus, which culminated in the construction of Hadrian's Wall from the early AD 120s onwards, the Roman military again expanded northwards; this second advance was at the behest of Emperor Antoninus Pius. This renewed campaigning, in the years around AD 140, led to the military resettlement of southern Scotland and the construction of the Antonine Wall between Forth and Clyde. A line of Flavian forts set up between the Forth and Tay was rebuilt, and Woolliscroft and Hoffmann have also recently suggested occupation at Cargill fort at this time on the basis of surface finds they made there of Trajanic and Hadrianic coins. To the best of current knowledge, however, the Antonine military occupation did not extend further along Strathmore into Angus and so far none of the other forts in the line to Stracathro have produced any datable finds attributable to this span. The Antonine occupation of central Scotland came to an end in the mid 160s, when the Roman forces again withdrew south of the Forth-Clyde.

Notwithstanding the military nature of Roman settlement, the interaction between Roman military units and local tribes in our area appears to have been generally peaceful for the first 100 years or so. There were occasional conflicts, however – the construction of Hadrian's Wall appears to have been preceded by some degree of disturbance, and a commemorative coin issue of AD 154-5 may relate to a Roman campaign north of the Antonine Wall. From the later second century onwards, however, the relationship between the Roman province and those living beyond the Forth appears to have descended into, at best, an uneasy coexistence maintained on the Roman part through treaties, diplomacy, monetary payments, patrolling and espionage; but punctuated increasingly, and particularly so during the fourth century, by unrest and raiding by the Picts and punitive campaigns undertaken by Roman field armies that would increasingly have been manned by Germanic-speaking mercenaries. There was to be no further sustained military occupation north of the Forth, beyond the brief stay by the army of Emperor Septimius Severus around AD 210. He appears to have campaigned through Strathmore and north of the Mounth, and also constructed a legionary vexillation-fortress on the south side of the Tay at Carpow. Severus was probably the first Roman Emperor to set foot in Angus. This occupation, although doubtless intended to be permanent, was aborted with his death at York and Roman forces once again drew back to the Tyne–Solway line for, as was often the case, his successor Caracalla had very different plans.

Almost all of what we know of the history and chronology of the fourth-century conflicts derives from an array of Roman commentators. These sources refer to at least eight separate instances of hostility involving Picts and Romans, spanning Constantius Chlorus' campaigns in AD 305-6 and the Pictish attacks on the Roman province in AD 396-8. If the lack of literary reference to third-century conflict is taken at face value, those hostilities seem to have followed a period of relative calm succeeding the Severan campaigns. These literary sources also together appear, perhaps unwittingly, to document the coalescence of Iron Age tribes into a more cohesive unit, in due course termed by those sources as Picti – to us the Picts. The earliest certain reference to the Picts was in AD 297 by Eumenius although, as noted by Gordon Maxwell, he was referring to an already established grouping.

What can archaeological evidence tell us about the nature of the contact of Rome with the farming communities of Angus and how this may have changed over time? There is very little to suggest that what Hanson has termed the 'brief interludes' of Roman occupation directly led to the adoption by local communities of Roman ways of living in any major way. Unlike circumstances within the Roman province south of Hadrian's Wall, in Angus no towns or rural villas were established, no monetary economy grew (although Roman coins were certainly present) and there is no evidence for the development of literacy. The inhabitants did not imitate Roman architectural styles for their buildings, preferring to continue to live in roundhouses, and did not in the early centuries AD adopt Roman religious or burial practices, such as erecting gravestones. As discussed in Chapter 6, some members of the upper echelons of society may have profited from the disruption that undoubtedly occurred. However, they did this by building massive stone-built roundhouses ('southern brochs') as a means of signifying their elevated social status, although whether this occurred before or after the appearance of the Romans on the scene is a moot point. There is emphatically nothing Roman in this architecture.

At its most immediate, the campaigning of Roman armies would likely have led to loss of life, either as a result of fighting or, in modern parlance, as 'collateral damage'. If in the past it has been suggested that the burning of native forts that produced vitrification, or the existence of unfinished circuits in other cases, were the outcomes of Roman military activity, such a view is now entirely unsustainable. We should, however, envisage that the construction of temporary camps to accommodate armies on the march or to house soldiers constructing forts, and the establishment of permanent auxiliary garrison points in the late first century AD, led to the destruction of crops and pastureland and the displacement of communities. The need for rapid construction of the temporary encampments, typically defended by a single rampart and external ditch (*colour plate 23*) indicates that tracts of open ground – most likely arable fields and pasture larger than the sites themselves, to allow for a reasonable field of vision beyond them – would have been selected by Roman scouts and surveyors.

At both the Cardean fort and the Inverquharity fortlet, evidence has been found for roundhouses cut across by Roman defensive ditches, the former revealed by excavations between 1966 and 1975 and the latter visible as cropmark traces. At both locations, as well as at Cargill, settlements of roundhouses (and at Cargill and Inverquharity souterrains also) have been detected either within the area occupied by the forts or in their immediate vicinity. This might indicate the presence of settlements cleared to make way for the Roman forts, but while not an unreasonable interpretation it is not in all cases possible to confirm such a direct connection from the archaeological evidence alone. It is alternatively possible that at least some of these structures had been abandoned before the Romans arrived; others may have been established after the Romans dismantled their forts and left. At Cardean, excavations detected a roundhouse built over the demolished remains of a Roman granary. Woolliscroft and Hoffmann speculated that some of the structures might even relate to settlement present while the Roman garrisons were in residence, representing a local variant of the more obviously Roman civilian settlements that grew up outside longer established Roman forts further south, for example at several of the garrison points along the Antonine Wall. However, we find this unlikely because civilian settlements tend to be established after forts have come into being, and the form of structures and the material culture they contain is 'provincial Roman' in character. No accepted civilian settlement in Britain to our knowledge consists entirely of 'unreformed natives' (at least to judge them in terms of their domestic architecture) building new roundhouses in the lee of the fort.

Once established in a base, either through trade, taxation or requisition, the Roman occupiers would have needed as far as possible to source a range of goods and services from the surrounding environment – certain foodstuffs, fodder for animals, leather, building materials, and labour. For the inhabitants of Angus this requirement may have been felt most acutely during the Flavian occupation of the area, but the county also most probably fell within the Roman zone of resource exploitation during the Antonine occupation. The nature of these transactions has been the subject of much general discussion over the last century or more, not least because the archaeological evidence is scarce and open to more than one interpretation.

In Angus the most direct evidence of contact between the Romans and local society is provided by the artefacts of principally first- and second-century origin, although including some of third century date, that have been found with some frequency during the excavations of Iron Age settlements (*62*). The majority have been found in the backfill of abandoned souterrains (as was the rare skillet handle at Ardownie, see Chapter 6) where it has been argued by Ian Armit that most were deliberately deposited as part of a ritualised closure of those structures. As we have seen in Chapter 6, a similar argument has been propounded by Fraser Hunter to explain the concentration of Roman items found during Taylor's excavations within the remains of the Hurly Hawkin broch. Hunter has recently made considerable advances in examining the meaning of Roman material from non-Roman contexts in Scotland.

These Roman goods are mainly good-quality items associated with eating and drinking (fine pottery, glassware, wine-drinking paraphernalia) and dress and personal decorations (brooches) although an occasional toiletry implement has turned up. However, these discoveries, individually or in small quantities, are not sufficient to suggest that a Romanised toga-clad wine-drinking county set developed in Angus, merely that exotic items were being acquired that fitted existing tastes and reinforced existing forms of social display.

The currently preferred explanation is that most of these items reached native hands not as a result of direct trade between the Angus farmers and Roman merchants, but through trade or gift-giving between the Roman administration and local elites, who may have been responsible for collecting from their followers tribute payable to the Roman administration. In the absence of a monetary economy and thus coinage, it is to be assumed that taxes were paid in kind, through supply of goods and services. The source of the Roman goods is believed to be the local Roman community, since with few exceptions they are of types that were used by the Roman military and have been found during excavations of Roman forts in lowland Scotland. The local elites are believed to have redistributed such items amongst their followers as one means of maintaining and emphasising their own power and status. The archaeological basis for this 'prestige goods economy' model is that a greater number and wider range of Roman goods are found at a few high-status sites in central and southern Scotland, contrasting with the more limited quantity and range found at the majority of native settlements. In

Angus this differential is apparent in the much wider range of Roman artefacts found by Taylor during his excavations of the Hurly Hawkin broch and souterrain than at any other settlement excavated to date.

With less direct evidence to draw on, Armit has argued that the Antonine occupation of lowland Scotland stimulated the demand for agricultural produce, leading to a rise in the production of grain. In Angus, he argues that a concomitant rise in the number of souterrains constructed and used to store that surplus was the outcome. This is at face value an appealing 'pax Romana' model, underpinned by a synergistic relationship between the Romans and Angus farmers, at least for this one short period. The new power in the locality would have thus directly influenced a reorganisation of the agricultural system. Its drawbacks are that there is very little evidence to date the construction of souterrains other than in a very few examples, the difficulties of providing good evidence that souterrains were primarily grain stores, and further why this native response should have been so localised within eastern Scotland (see Chapter 6). There is also an apparent disjuncture between the Roman military preference for wheat as the staple cereal for producing bread and other foodstuffs and the preponderance of albeit restricted palaeobotanical evidence to suggest that barley, used by the Roman army as punishment rations, was the primary crop in Angus.

Whatever the nature of Roman–native contacts in the later first and second centuries AD, archaeological evidence suggests that by the fourth century the relationship between the Roman Province and the inhabitants of Angus had changed fundamentally. A first sign of the change may be the discovery in the north-east of a number of third-century AD hoards of Roman coins, suggesting that local leaders were being influenced in new ways – there are two reported coin hoards from Angus (*62*), both found long ago and of which we know very little detail. There were by then very few Roman goods circulating within our area, and the settlements of roundhouses and souterrains that had been occupied two centuries earlier may already have been largely abandoned, to be replaced by new vernacular building types of which we know very little (see Chapter 7). Uncertainties over the dating of Roman artefacts recovered from backfilled souterrains currently do not allow us to be as categorical about the end date for souterrains as Ian Armit was some years ago. That said, a fundamental change in storage technologies is clear by the middle of the first millennium AD. Perhaps significant land-use change at this time is implied, but the only certainty is that the technological solution offered by below-ground storage in specially constructed passages had fallen out of favour.

The archaeological evidence suggests that the significant shift in the nature of indigenous societies occurred broadly over the same period that Roman sources refer to an increase in the frequency of hostilities in northern Britain. This phase is marked, at least in the minds of the Roman commentators whose testimony we have, by the emergence of the Picts as a distinct political and military entity, and one capable of entering into alliances with others of the named barbarian groups coming to the fore around, and increasingly within, the fringes of the Empire. It is reasonable to suggest that Roman campaigns may have brought soldiers back to Angus on one or more occasion during the fourth century, but solid evidence for this is lacking. There are several Roman temporary camps recorded in Angus (*62*) but where they are datable, either from Roman artefacts discovered within their ditches or through possessing distinctive shapes, sizes or entrance morphologies, they are of Severan or earlier date. However, the absence of fourth-century AD camps is far more widespread and what we may be witnessing is rather that the late Imperial field armies, bolstered by Germanic mercenaries, may have campaigned rather differently than their predecessors.

A much-debated question has therefore been 'did the Romans create the Picts?' The conventional view in recent decades, following John Mann's interpretation of the literary evidence, has been that the Iron Age tribes of north-east Scotland coalesced ultimately to form the Picts in response to the presence nearby of, and the military threat posed by, Rome. It was this proximity that underscored this particular ethnogenesis, causing previously disparate groups increasingly to meld themselves into a bigger, single group, both politically and militarily. Fraser Hunter recently reviewed this model in light of the archaeological evidence for the third and fourth centuries in north-east Scotland and suggested that this material pointed to political and social developments being more complex than this. Hunter suggested that the archaeological evidence, rehearsed above for Angus, points to a 'major political and social change' in the third and fourth centuries AD that disrupted settlement patterns and access to material goods, and pressures arising from these circumstances led to the emergence of new power groups. He suggested that these changes did not come entirely from internal sources, but instead were a result of Roman influence, either directly through Roman interference in internal politics that created a 'dependency culture', or indirectly through the destabilising effects of Roman wealth entering local society.

It is reasonable to say that the sparse archaeological evidence from this period that is available from Angus is susceptible to different interpretations. What seems to be clear, however, is that long-established settlement types, especially the open settlements of roundhouses, go out of use at broadly the same period as the supply of Roman products appears seriously to falter. These apparently concurrent changes affecting settlement forms and access to Roman goods were not restricted to Angus, but occur, albeit with local variations, much more broadly across Britain north of Hadrian's Wall, from the Lothians to the Western Isles. The apparent decline in the number of open settlements in use and in the availability of certain kinds of material culture is perhaps testament to widespread social and political changes during what must have been difficult and uncertain times north of Hadrian's Wall. Opposition to Rome may have held together larger coalitions in this area, but fissiparous tendencies may have become more difficult to resist as the apparent threat receded. Like all times of change, there would have been winners as there would have been losers and the emerging elites would have sought out new means to mark their importance.

THE PICTS AND THE SCOTS IN THE FIRST MILLENNIUM AD

In most discussions of the prehistory and early history of Angus, the second half of the first millennium AD plays a major part. This is the period in which three at least of the recorded peoples of Early Historic Scotland can be documented in the area. In each case, of course, it is the kings and aristocracies who are mentioned; whether the mass of the population labelled themselves in this way seems doubtful. Foremost amongst these groups are the Picts. From the later ninth century, however, they are assumed to decline rapidly in importance, as a result of successful dynastic and other manipulations, at the point of swords and doubtless by other means, at the hands of the Scots. The elite of the Scoti, with their retinue, had by this time expanded their territorial sway from their heartland west of Drumalban.

History records that key events took place in the 840s AD and saw Cinaed mac Alpín (Kenneth I) become King of the Picts and Scots, following the death of the last Pictish monarch, Drust. This apparently momentous event may have appeared less so at the time, since the indications are that this was far from the first occasion the Scotic and Pictish elites had measured each other up as allies, as advantageous bloodstock to marry, or as targets for subjugation or annihilation. The fact that Cinaed himself was to die at Forteviot in 858 indicates that the Pictish royal centre there was still in use and is another pointer that the impact of the dynastic change may initially have been rather muted. Whilst the only contemporary obituary of Cinaed called him simply 'rex Pictorum', from this stage the Picts, as a significant political power, go into marked decline around AD 900 and disappear from the few documentary records that do survive. There was only a brief mention of Picts as being amongst the former peoples of Scotland in the fourteenth-century Declaration of Arbroath, that central statement of Scotland's nationhood. It is nonetheless likely that considerable numbers of the lesser ranks on the land may still have considered themselves as Picts for some time after the mid ninth century, perhaps until there was patently no point in continuing to do so. In linguistic terms, the prime concomitant of the Scotic takeover was the establishment of a form of Gaelic as the language for naming places that mattered, and arguably as the tongue of command.

At an earlier date it is likely that a Germanic language was first heard anew in Angus, following the departure of the continental mercenaries who had bolstered the field armies of the late Roman Empire. In the seventh century the Northumbrian Angles began their expansion up the eastern seaboard of Scotland, from strongholds such as Bamburgh and palace complexes such as at Yeavering, establishing themselves in Lothian before mid century. Excavation evidence notably from the Dunbar area and metal-detected finds, fit reasonably with the chronology provided primarily by the Venerable Bede in his *History of the English Church and People*. A bishopric was established just south of the Forth at Abercorn, and from that area further expansion northwards is indicated.

This northward expansion by the Angles faltered definitively in AD 685, at the battle of Dun Nechtan, alternatively called Nechtanesmere or Lin Garan – the 'pool of the herons' (first recorded in considerably later sources). Here in May of that year the army of King Ecgfrith of Northumbria was decisively checked by King Bruide mac Bili's Picts; the 40-year-old Anglian king died in the fighting. For long the preferred location of the conflict has been placed firmly within Angus and near Dunnichen ('Nechtan's fort', south-east of Forfar). Many consider that, although carved perhaps two or three generations later, the battlefield scene on the great Class II Pictish slab in the kirkyard at

Aberlemno (*colour plate 24*) only a few miles away, depicts this event: long-haired Picts in tunics and pointed-toed shoes, on foot or on horse, manifestly get the upper hand over helmeted Angles; an English corpse is pecked by a raptor in the final scene.

Yet there have always been problems with this interpretation, Bede's description indicates topography ('inaccessible mountains') much more rugged than Angus can provide. The historian Alex Woolf has recently argued that the battle was actually located much further north near another 'Dun Nechtan' – Dunachton in Badenoch. At the same time he argues that the key Pictish kingdom of Fortriu (Bruide mac Bili's territory) – long positioned by historians in central Scotland north of the Forth–Clyde isthmus on what transpire to be very flimsy grounds – was equally north of the Central Highlands. There were to be further battles between Picts and Angles into the eighth century which the unknown patron of the Aberlemno stone may have wished his sculptor to commemorate, if indeed that remarkable stone does turn the 'reporting of near contemporary events into art', which the Hendersons have suggested would be very unusual at that time. If Woolf's research has produced a credible alternative to the Dunnichen area as a site for Ecgfrith and his household's calamitous defeat, it nonetheless requires the Anglian warband to have ventured surprisingly far into the Highland massif. Angus may thus still be kept in the frame for this event.

Another key Angus site long given a place in early Anglian-Pictish relations is at Restenneth (*colour plate 25*). The late Douglas Simpson, amongst others, saw in the lower courses of the tower of the church at Restenneth the physical confirmation of another key event. In the early eighth century, the Pictish king Nechtan mac Der-Ilei, sent emissaries to Ceolfrith (latterly abbot of the great Northumbrian monastic community at Wearmouth-Jarrow) to ask for builders to erect a stone church 'in the Roman manner' for him. These stonemasons would assuredly have discussed the construction among themselves in an early form of English, but subsequent stylistic analyses by Eric Fernie and then Neil Cameron indicate that the oldest surviving structural elements in the basal part of the tower at Restenneth are too late, although by how long is contentious, to allow structural and historical evidence to be married. Where in Pictland Nechtan's building was erected remains to be discovered, but candidates might include other Angus sites (such as St Vigeans, with its important collection of sculpture from a remarkable setting above the lower Brothock Water) as well as others beyond the county – Meigle or Forteviot, for example. At the latter, the surviving sculptured chancel or perhaps doorway arch (now in the Museum of Scotland in Edinburgh) is one of the few remaining elements of a stone church of this general vintage in eastern Scotland north of the Tay. Dated to the ninth or tenth century AD, it too cannot have been a component of Nechtan's early stone building. However, along with the suggested displacement of Fortriu northward, mentioned above, it is also possible that this church was put up north of the Mounth.

Neither of these central planks of Angus's Pictish celebrity – the location of Nechtanesmere and the stone-built church of King Nechtán – has thus survived unchallenged by recent generations of scholars. The same, however, is not true of the remarkable collection of Early Historic sculpture from the county, marvelously reassessed by the Hendersons in 2004. Angus contains noteworthy examples of both incised Class I stones, decorated with Pictish symbols, and even more so the Class II slabs, on which these symbols, now portrayed in relief, are mixed with avowedly Christian iconography. The latter include some of the most accomplished carvings of the Cross and, by extension, physical statements on the new religion in first millennium AD eastern Scotland, notably at Aberlemno Kirkyard, but even more spectacularly on the reverse of the Class I stone in the manse garden at Glamis. Allowing for the depredations at the Reformation or at other times, Angus and adjacent parts of Perthshire have more clusters of Class II sculpture – good indicators of early church or monastic sites – than any other county within Pictland. These often occur on the richer agricultural soils, as was noted a generation ago by Cottam and Small. On occasion too, substantial additions can be made to the corpus of such material, as at Kirriemuir in 1995, where Scotia Archaeology found a cross slab and 11 fragments of sculpture in the demolition of the late eighteenth-century churchyard wall. As well as the important collection of sculpture earlier recovered around the church on its conspicuous mound at St Vigeans (*colour plate 26*) there are series of stones still on display locally, notably at Glamis and Aberlemno. One of the areas within eastern Scotland where Early Christian sculpture seems to have been particularly important is thus Angus. Here, these monuments, described by Stephen Driscoll as 'manifestations of local aristocratic support for the church' seem to have been a significant means of bolstering the power of both the local aristocracy and of the Church, institutions which were hardly separate from each other at this time.

Space precludes us from considering in any detail much-discussed questions such as the dating and interpretation of this sophisticated sculpture, for the Class II stones in particular represent complex exercises in visual theology. It must be admitted that none of the projects conducted during the Field School threw any direct light on any of the contentious issues surrounding these carvings. For example, a certain amount of evidence indicates that some stones may originally have been set up over, or at least placed on or near, burial places, this being attested, for example, for the symbol stone from Dunrobin, Sutherland – apparently associated with a low stone cairn. Within Angus itself, five skeletons were discovered by Andrew Jervise in the nineteenth century in short cists close to St Orland's Stone at Cossans and a case was made that the nature of the upper fill of the central burial pit within the first square barrow to be dug at Boysack Mills intimated that it may originally have supported such a stone. However, no supporting evidence was found at Redcastle for the latter practice, nor is there any other indication that the Angus sculptured stones either still, or even once, were located at the positions of any of the known cropmark square barrow cemeteries. Nor have any of the recent discoveries of long cist cemeteries been accompanied by finds of sculptural work, even fragmentary. However, beyond that, it is perhaps worth noting that the long cists recovered above the Water of Elliot to the south of Arbroath add to the tally of such burials identified in and around 'Aberbrothick', and provide a wider context for the suite of early sculpture from St Vigeans. Meggen Gondek's recent consideration of the resource implications of what have traditionally been called the Class II and III Early Christian sculptures within southern Pictland perhaps supports the suggestion that the most likely location for the investment that Nechtan's stone church would have represented is one of the sculpture-rich locations of this period, whether coastal St Vigeans, one of the inland sites of Angus or indeed in Perth and Kinross.

Beyond the rich iconographic traditions, and – more dubiously – the burials, direct archaeological testimony of the early Church is however relatively rare. Early Christianity is likely to have become established in Angus under complex circumstances of external influence – from Iona and the Columban west as well as, perhaps primarily, from the south. Before the rising tide of the Northumbrian Church's importance, southern influences may have been driven from British sources and there is a story of St Ninian of Candida Casa – Whithorn in Galloway – being responsible for the conversion of the southern Picts. One indication of this may be the fact that the late Latin word for a church, *Eclesia*, was adopted into British speech and beyond that into the Pictish area. Angus and the Mearns (former Kincardineshire) – in one problematic source one of seven recognisable components within Pictland – include the most northerly examples of this place name element, as in Eglismonichto, to the north of Dundee.

Apart from the burials, the main contribution the archaeological results from the Field School and other recent archaeological projects within Angus make to the archaeology of the Picts is in regard to settlement. As has been discussed above, one of the less-expected outcomes in this regard has been that the excavated forts and enclosed sites failed to produce evidence of Early Historic construction or modification. This may be considered at first sight a disappointing outcome, given the arguments advanced by Cottam and Small a generation ago for a positive correlation in terms of distribution between forts and Class I sculptured stones, although these authors expressed their views with due caution. It is of course possible that the Field School selection was inadvertently biased against first millennium AD sites or components of them (it has to be remembered how restricted in scale many of the excavations were) but this seems hardly compelling as an excuse, given the diversity in both size and form of first millennium AD enclosed sites elsewhere in Pictland south of the Great Glen. It can be noted that none of the innermost, generally circular, features noted on the summit of the White Caterthun and also recorded (albeit as rather more massive constructions) on Turin Hill were tested; Perthshire evidence does suggest some such circular homesteads or 'ring-forts' to have been in use through the first millennium AD. Thus these locations may have been used in Pictish times, as might other, rather ruinous examples of heavily walled enclosures, like St Bride's Ring near Monifieth. Of course some sites that might have been pertinent – notably 'Dun Nechtan' itself – have been so reduced as to be unlikely to furnish useful evidence.

Equally, small-scale excavations on the vitrified fort on Dundee Law suggest that it was abandoned during Roman times, to judge from both the radiocarbon dates and the small finds including Roman sherds it produced. This is unlike, for example, another vitrified site, Craig Phadrig on the outskirts of Inverness, which was refurbished and used anew in Early Historic times. There is, however, the occasional older find that may suggest reuse of earlier enclosed hilltops in Angus in the first millennium AD, although not of Pictish refortification. Most remarkable amongst these is the copper-alloy plaque

– perhaps originally worn across the chest – from the Laws of Monifieth, an item well-drawn in 1796 (showing its double-sided decoration) but now sadly lost. This stray object is one of very few portable artefacts from mainland Scotland to have a Scandinavian runic inscription – albeit unintelligible – on it and is thus also one of the few known items from Angus that is demonstrably likely to have passed through the hands of a Viking.

The Field School has, however, contributed significant additions in terms of the lesser, unenclosed settlements of the Early Historic inhabitants, at Newbarns and their immediate predecessors, the latter both in terms of souterrain sites such as Ardownie and through the sequence of remains recovered from Hawkhill. None of these suggests other than settlements relatively low down, or middle-ranking within, the social scale, although it has to be admitted that the Newbarns building had been so reduced by ploughing by the time of its examination that its interpretation will always be difficult to calibrate finely. In light of what has been said previously about the early churches being of timber it should, however, be made explicit that the orientation of the Newbarns hall is such that it cannot have been a Christian establishment. Newbarns has a good claim to be the grandest Pictish building so far examined in Angus, although its date means that we cannot rule out the possibility that its builder was an incoming Gaelic speaker. That said, it is broadly comparable in size to the individual buildings of Pitcarmick type in the upland settlements and to the rather differently constructed 'hall' within the tiny Banffshire (now Moray) promontory fort of Green Castle, Portknockie.

If Angus lacks secure evidence for a major enclosed fort of Pictish/Scotic date, so too is there an absence of any sure equivalent of the complex of cropmarks at Forteviot on the Water of May, a tributary of the Earn in Perthshire, taken to represent a palace site. Likely candidates in locational terms might be around Brechin or St Vigeans, given the importance of these places as ecclesiastical centres, but so far the requisite cropmarks of large halls and the like seem to be absent there. Amongst the cropmark large 'halls', that at Boysack – 18m by 9m – within a rectilinear palisade and a further example noted by RCAHMS, just across the Lunan Water from Boysack Mills and Invergighty Cottage barrow cemeteries, might well represent a later first millennium AD centre of some significance, with, like Forteviot, evidence of significant Neolithic monuments in their vicinity. It is, however, debatable whether – given their types – these would still have been readily perceptible features of the Early Historic landscape, in contrast to the Forteviot examples. All in all, however, such major buildings seem to be rarely represented amongst the cropmarks of the county.

Overall, it would appear that in the decades before AD 1000 Angus formed a prosperous component of the Gaelic kingdom of Alba in which estates, thanages and important ecclesiastical centres – notably Brechin – became established. Like much of the east side of the country south of Kinnaird Head, it seems to have suffered far less at the hands of the Norse Vikings than the west and north of Scotland. If the work reported here has opened some new windows on the later prehistory and Early Historic centuries in Angus, from an archaeological perspective there remains much to research and that is more especially the case with the record of the centuries straddling AD 1000.

Appendix

A NOTE ON RADIOCARBON DATES AND THE BUILDING OF
CHRONOLOGIES FOR THE PREHISTORY AND EARLY HISTORY OF ANGUS

Establishing the timetable for events in the prehistory of Angus relies very heavily on radiocarbon dates. Noting the stratification on archaeological sites can allow structures to be put into relative order and, on occasions, particular artefacts recovered in archaeological contexts can provide helpful indications of the date of, for example, the accompanying burial. However in most instances in Angus, currently providing absolute 'calendrical' dates depends on interpreting the results of radiocarbon assays. As this is not an absolutely straightforward exercise, a few remarks on radiocarbon dates are appropriate, so that readers unfamiliar with this dating technique can appreciate something of the strengths and weaknesses associated with it.

A radiocarbon determination is essentially the outcome of a short-term observation of a long-term process – the decay of radioactive carbon in once-living materials after they are dead. It is thus expressed in statistical terms with a 'plus or minus' range associated with a central date; doubling the plus or minus range – the standard deviation – increases the likelihood that the date of death of the item concerned falls within the quoted range to about 95 per cent. A further problem is that the date of death of the item being measured – say carbon from a substantial tree-trunk used in building a house – may be some way removed from what the archaeologist is interested in dating; good oak timber for example, might have been salvaged from an older structure, so that the date when it was cut down might lie considerably before its reuse in the building for which a date is sought. For such reasons, archaeologists prefer to submit samples of short-lived materials (e.g. carbonised cereal grains) when they can be recovered from useful contexts on site – but this is not always the case.

It takes something less than 6000 years for the quantity of radiocarbon in a dead organism to halve. This timescale would be fixed and definite if the amount of accessible radiocarbon that living things could take up had always been constant – as was believed 60 years ago when the technique was first developed. Sadly it soon became clear that this was not the case – the impact of detonating nuclear bombs had a pronounced effect and it thereafter became plain that earlier emissions – including the widespread burning of forests by farmers in the Neolithic period – had also skewed the straight-forward correlation that would have been possible had the 'carbon reservoir' always been constant. The recognition of this problem caused a further round of measurements and recalculations, whereby the results of radiocarbon assays were calibrated with dates for organic materials dated by other methods which were not susceptible to the same problems. Tree-ring dating – dendrochronology – was a major element of this and the result is that it is now possible to calibrate the results produced by radiocarbon analyses with absolute historical dates initially obtained by other means.

Calibration works better for some periods than for others and we can be more sure of the results that are suggested if we are able to use advanced statistics to calibrate several radiocarbon dates from the same archaeological context. However, this is rarely possible as yet, and in many cases estimates of dates – say for a particular site – are still based on relatively few radiocarbon determinations. One of the worst periods for calibration exercises is the first millennium BC and so the chronological scheme for this appears 'fuzzy' and imprecise. However, it is so with good reason – this is the best estimate achievable given some of the uncertainties sketched above. Calibrated radiocarbon dates in text are often given with brackets that cover four centuries or thereabouts – say 800-400 BC. What this does not mean is that the building in question, for example, from which the calibrated radiocarbon assay is derived, lasted for 400 years. It simply means that, within the limits of the calibration and statistical exercises as presently understood, the best estimate (with 19 chances out of 20 of being right) is that the real date of the item under consideration falls within that span. Thus elements of the chronological discussions in this book may seem rather vague; they are a reflection of the availability of few clues apart from radiocarbon dates to construct our timeline for most of the periods at issue here.

New radiocarbon dates for Scottish archaeology are printed annually in *Discovery and Excavation in Scotland* (published by the Council for Scottish Archaeology; see below). Historic Scotland maintains an online radiocarbon dating database at www.historic-scotland.gov.uk/index/archaeology/archaeology_resources.htm

Further reading

The following guide aims to provide general introductions to the periods considered here and to identify the key sources used in writing this account. We hope that this selection of the literature allows readers to follow up on topics of interest to them.

Journal titles are:
PSAS   *Proceedings of the Society of Antiquaries of Scotland*
TAFAJ   *Tayside and Fife Archaeological Journal*

Annual reports on field archaeology undertaken in Angus are contained in:
Discovery and Excavation in Scotland, produced by the Council for Scottish Archaeology

The most recent introduction, which includes an extensive guide to the literature, on the archaeology of Scotland is:
Edwards, K.J. & Ralston, I.B.M. (eds) 2003, *Scotland after the Ice Age*, Edinburgh: Edinburgh University Press

I INTRODUCTION

Previous accounts of the archaeology and history of Angus include:
Coutts, H. 1970, *Ancient Monuments of Tayside*, Dundee: Dundee Museum and Art Gallery
Coutts, H. 1971, *Tayside Before History*, Dundee: Dundee Museum and Art Gallery
Oram, R. 1996, *Angus & the Mearns: a Historical Guide*, Edinburgh: Birlinn
Taylor, D. 1968, 'Prehistoric, Roman and Pictish settlement' in Jones, S.J. (ed.), *Dundee and District*, Dundee: David Winter & Son, 127-43
Warden, A.J. 1880-5, *Angus or Forfarshire: the Land and People, Descriptive and Historical*, Dundee: Charles Alexander. 5 vols

To get a flavour of the impact of aerial photography on the identification of archaeological remains in the wider region, and to compare the archaeological records in upland and lowland areas:
RCAHMS 1990, *North-East Perth: An Archaeological Landscape*, Edinburgh: HMSO
RCAHMS 1994, *South-East Perth: An Archaeological Landscape*, Edinburgh: HMSO

For a fuller explanation of the aims of the Field School:
Finlayson, B., Coles, G., Dunwell, A. & Ralston, I. 1999, 'The Angus and South Aberdeenshire Field School of the Department of Archaeology, University of Edinburgh – research design', *TAFAJ* 5, 28-35

2 HUNTER–GATHERERS IN ANGUS

Recent overviews of Mesolithic Scotland include:

Saville, A. (ed.) 2004, *Mesolithic Scotland and its Neighbours*, Edinburgh: Society of Antiquaries of Scotland

Warren, G. 2005, *Mesolithic Lives in Scotland*, Stroud: Tempus

For classic site-based evidence from Angus:

Hutcheson, A. 1886, 'Notice of the discovery of a stratum containing worked flints at Broughty-Ferry', *PSAS* 20, 166–9

Mathewson, A. 1879, 'Notes on stone cists and an ancient kitchen midden near Dundee', *PSAS* 13, 303–7

3 FARMING COMMUNITIES OF THE NEOLITHIC AND BRONZE AGES

Recent overviews of these periods include:

Ashmore, P.J. 1996, *Neolithic and Bronze Age Scotland*, London: Batsford

Hunt, D. 1987, *Early Farming Communities in Scotland*, Oxford: BAR British Series 159, 2 vols

Noble, G. 2006, *Neolithic Scotland: timber, stone, earth and fire*, Edinburgh: Edinburgh University Press

Shepherd, I.A.G. & Barclay, G.J. (eds) 2004, *Scotland in Ancient Europe*, Edinburgh: Society of Antiquaries of Scotland

Sheridan, A. (forthcoming) 'From Picardie to Pickering and Pencraig Hill? New information on the "Carinated Bowl Neolithic" in northern Britain'

For Neolithic sites in lowland Angus:

Barclay, G.J. 1999, 'A hidden landscape: the Neolithic of Tayside', in Harding, A. (ed.), *Experiment and design*, Exeter: Short Run Press, 20–9

Barclay, G.J. 2005, 'The "henge" and "hengiform" in Scotland' in Cummings, V. & Pannett, A. (eds), *Set in Stone: new approaches to Neolithic monuments in Scotland*, Oxford: Oxbow, 81–94

Brophy, K. 1998, 'Cursus monuments and bank barrows of Tayside and Fife', in Barclay, G.J. & Maxwell, G.S., *The Cleaven Dyke and Littleour*, Edinburgh: Soc Antiq Scot Monogr Ser 13, 92–108

Brophy, K. 2000, 'Excavation of a cropmark site at Milton of Rattray, Blairgowrie, with a discussion of the pit-defined cursus monuments of Tayside', *TAFAJ* 6, 8–17

Cameron, K. 2002, 'The excavation of Neolithic pits and Iron Age souterrains at Dubton Farm, Brechin, Angus', *TAFAJ* 8, 19–76

Kendrick, J. 1995, 'Excavation of a Neolithic enclosure and an Iron Age settlement at Douglasmuir, Angus', *PSAS* 125, 29–68

For stone circles and cup-and-ring-marked stones, good start points are:

Barclay, G.J. & Ruggles, C.L.N. 1999, 'On the frontier? Recumbent stone circles in Kincardineshire and Angus', *TAFAJ* 5, 12–22

Burl, H.A.W. 1988, *Four Posters*, Oxford: British Archaeol Rep. 195

Burl, H.A.W. 2000, *The Stone Circles of Britain, Ireland and Brittany*, New Haven & London: Yale University Press

Sherriff, J.R. 1995, 'Prehistoric rock-carving in Angus', *TAFAJ* 1, 11–22

Sherriff, J.R. 1999, 'Five Neolithic carved stones from Angus', *TAFAJ* 5, 7–11

For long barrows:

Collier, L., Hobbs, B., Neighbour, T. & Strachan, R. 2003, *Resistivity Imaging Survey of Capo Long Barrow, Aberdeenshire*, Scottish Archaeological Internet Report 6 (www.sair.org.uk)

Piggott, S. 1972, 'Excavation of the Dalladies long barrow, Fettercairn, Kincardineshire', *PSAS* 104, 23–47

For Neolithic material culture:

Saville, A. 1999, 'An exceptional polished flint axe-head from Bolshan Hill near Montrose, Angus', *TAFAJ* 5, 1-6

Wickham-Jones, C. & Mackenzie, J. 1996, 'An unusual lithic assemblage from Lunanhead, Angus', *PSAS* 126, 1-16

For Bronze Age burials and their products:

Dalland, M. & Carter, S. 1998, 'The evaluation of a prehistoric mound damaged by rabbit burrowing at Maryton Law, Angus', *TAFAJ* 4, 20-30

Hutcheson, A. 1898, 'Notice on the discovery of a burial-place of the Bronze Age on the Hill of West Mains of Auchterhouse', *PSAS* 32, 205-20

Russell-White, C.J., Lowe, C.E. & McCullagh, R. 1992, 'Excavations at three Early Bronze Age burial monuments in Scotland', *Proceedings of the Prehistoric Society* 58, 285-323

Sheridan, A. 2004, 'Scottish Food Vessel chronology revisited', in Gibson, A. & Sheridan, A. (eds), *From Sickles to Circles*, Stroud: Tempus, 243-67

Sheridan, A. (forthcoming) 'Dating the Scottish Bronze Age: "There is clearly much the material can still tell us"', in Burgess, C., Topping, P. & Lynch, F. (eds), *Essays on the Bronze Age in honour of Colin Burgess*, Oxford: Oxbow, 162-85

Taylor, D.B., Rideout, J.S., Russell-White, C.J. & Cowie, T.G. 1998, 'Prehistoric burials from Angus: some finds old and new', *TAFAJ* 4, 31-66

4 THE TRANSITION TO LATER PREHISTORY IN ANGUS

For Bronze Age metalwork see:

Burgess, C. & Colquhoun, I. 1988, *The Swords of Britain*, Munich: Beck (Prähistorische Bronzefunde IV/5)

Schmidt, P.K. & Burgess, C.B. 1981, *The Axes of Britain*, Munich: Beck (Prähistorische Bronzefunde IX/7)

Sheridan, A. 1999, 'Drinking, driving, death and display: Scottish Bronze Age artefact studies since Coles', in Harding, A. (ed.), *Experiment and Design*, Exeter: Short Run Press, 49-59

Overviews of the Scottish Iron Age include:

Armit, I. 2005, *Celtic Scotland*, London: Batsford. rev. edn

Harding, D.W. 2005, *The Iron Age in Northern Britain. Celts and Romans, Natives and Invaders*, London: Routledge

Hingley, R. 1992, 'Society in Scotland from 700 BC to AD 200', *PSAS* 122, 7-53

5 UP HILL AND DOWN DALE — THE FORTS OF ANGUS

For a recent overview of hillforts in Britain and beyond:

Ralston, I. 2006, *Celtic Fortifications*, Stroud: Tempus

For previous examinations of Scottish hillforts, including some Angus sites:

Christison, D. 1900, 'The forts, "camps", and other field-works of Perth, Forfar and Kincardine', *PSAS* 34, 43-120

Feachem, R.W. 1966, 'The hill-forts of northern Britain' in Rivet, A.L.F. (ed.), *The Iron Age in Northern Britain*, Edinburgh: Edinburgh University Press, 59-87

Feachem, R.W. 1971, 'Unfinished hill-forts' in Hill, D. & Jesson, M. (eds), *The Iron Age and its Hill-forts*, Southampton (Univ. Southampton Monograph 1), 19-39

Ralston, I. 2004, *The Hill-forts of Pictland since 'The Problem of the Picts'*, Rosemarkie: Groam House Museum

Further information on the principal forts discussed here:

Alexander, D. 2002, 'The oblong fort at Finavon, Angus: an example of the over-reliance on the appliance of science?' in Ballin Smith, B. & Banks, I. (eds), *In the Shadow of the Brochs. The Iron Age in Scotland*, Stroud: Tempus, 44-54

Alexander, D. & Ralston, I.B.M. 1999, 'Survey work on Turin Hill, Angus', *TAFAJ* 5, 36-49

Driscoll, S. 1995, 'Excavations on Dundee Law, 1993', *PSAS* 125, 1091-1108

Dunwell, A. & Strachan, R. 2007, *Excavations at Brown Caterthun and White Caterthun Hillforts, Angus, 1995-1997*, Perth: TAFAC Monogr 5

Ralston, I.B.M. 1986, 'The Arbroath Antiquaries Club's excavations at Castle Rock promontory fort, Auchmithie, Angus District', *PSAS* 116, 101-15

Strachan, R.J., Hamilton, J.E. & Dunwell, A.J. 2003, 'Excavation of cropmark enclosures at Mains of Edzell, Edzell and Hawkhill, Lunan', *TAFAJ* 9, 34-64

Taylor, D.B. 1982, 'Excavation of a promontory fort, broch and souterrain at Hurly Hawkin, Angus', *PSAS* 112, 215-53

Wilson, E.M. 1980, 'Excavations at West Mains of Ethie, Angus', *PSAS* 110, 114-21

6 ROUND THE HOUSES. IRON AGE SETTLEMENT AND FARMING

An overview of Iron Age settlement archaeology in Scotland:

Ralston, I. 1996, 'Recent work on the Iron Age settlement record in Scotland', in Champion T.C. & Collis J.R. (eds), *The Iron Age in Britain and Ireland: Recent Trends*, Sheffield: J.R Collis, 133-53

For key discussions of timber roundhouses:

Harding D.W. 1982, (ed.) *Later Prehistoric Settlement in South-East Scotland*, 133-53 Edinburgh (Univ Edin Dept Archaeol Occas Pap 8)

Hill, P.H. 1984, 'A sense of proportion: a contribution to the study of double-ring roundhouses', *Scottish Archaeological Review* 3.2, 80-6

Previous commentators on later prehistoric settlement patterns in Angus include:

Macinnes, L. 1982, 'Pattern and purpose: the settlement evidence', in Harding, D.W. (ed), 57-73

Pollock, D. 1985, 'The Lunan Valley Project: medieval rural settlement in Angus', *PSAS* 115, 357-99

For recent settlement excavations in Angus and nearby:

Cameron, K., Rees, A., Dunwell, A. & Anderson, S. 2007, 'Prehistoric pits, Bronze Age roundhouses, an Iron Age promontory enclosure, Early Historic cist burials and medieval enclosures along the route of the A92, Dundee to Arbroath', *TAFAJ* 13, 39-73

Cook, M. & Dunbar, L. (forthcoming) *Rituals, Roundhouses and Romans. Excavations at Kintore, Aberdeenshire 2000-2006: Vol 1 Forest Road*, Edinburgh: Scottish Trust for Archaeological Research Monograph

Driscoll, S.T. 1997, 'A Pictish settlement in north-east Fife: the Scottish Field School of Archaeology excavations at Easter Kinnear', *TAFAJ* 3, 74-118

Kendrick, J. 1995, 'Excavation of a Neolithic enclosure and an Iron Age settlement at Douglasmuir, Angus', *PSAS* 125, 29-67

McGill, C. 2003, 'The excavation of a palisaded enclosure and associated structures at Ironshill East, near Inverkeilor, Angus', *TAFAJ* 9, 14-33

Pollock, D. 1997, 'The excavation of Iron Age buildings at Ironshill, Inverkeilor, Angus', *PSAS* 127, 339-58

Rees, A. (forthcoming) 'The excavation of an Iron Age unenclosed settlement and an Early Historic multiple burial and metalworking area, at Hawkhill, Lunan Bay, Angus', *TAFAJ*

Rees, T. 1998, 'Excavation of Culhawk Hill ring-ditch house, Kirriemuir, Angus', *TAFAJ* 4, 106-28

Watkins, T. 1980, 'Excavation of an Iron Age open settlement at Dalladies, Kincardineshire', *PSAS* 110, 122-64

For overviews of eastern Scottish crannogs see:

Dixon, N. 2004, *The Crannogs of Scotland, an Underwater Study*, Stroud: Tempus

Morrison, I. 1985, *Landscape with Lake Dwellings*, Edinburgh: Edinburgh University Press

Overviews of the context of the southern brochs (see Chapter 5 for Hurly Hawkin):

Armit, I. 2003, *Towers in the North: The Brochs of Scotland*, Stroud: Tempus

Macinnes, L. 1984, 'Brochs and the Roman occupation of lowland Scotland', *PSAS* 114, 235-49

For the use of plants in Iron Age and other contexts:

Dickson, C. & Dickson, J.H. 2000, *Plants and People in Ancient Scotland*, Stroud: Tempus

Miller, J. 2002, 'Oakbank crannog: building a house of plants', in Ballin Smith, B. and Banks, I. (eds), *In the Shadow of the Brochs: The Iron Age in Scotland*, Stroud: Tempus, 35-43

Many accounts explore the character, date and functions of souterrains. These provide an introduction:

Armit, I. 1999, 'The abandonment of souterrains: evolution, catastrophe or dislocation?', *PSAS* 129, 577-96

Barclay, G.J. 1980, 'Newmill and the souterrains of southern Pictland', in Watkins, T. 'Excavation of a settlement and souterrain at Newmill, near Bankfoot, Perthshire', *PSAS* 110, 200-8

Miket, R. 2002, 'The souterrains of Skye' in Ballin Smith, B. & Banks, I. (eds), *In the Shadow of the Brochs. The Iron Age in Scotland*, Stroud: Tempus, 77-110

Wainwright, F.T. 1963, *The Souterrains of Southern Pictland*, London: Routledge & Kegan Paul

More recent souterrain excavations of note include:

Alexander, D. 2005, 'Redcastle, Lunan Bay, Angus: the excavation of an Iron Age timber-lined souterrain and a Pictish barrow cemetery', *PSAS* 135, 41-118

Anderson, S. & Rees, A.R. 2006, 'The excavation of a large double-chambered souterrain at Ardownie Farm Cottages, Monifieth, Angus', *TAFAJ* 12, 14-60

Cameron, K. 2002, 'The excavation of Neolithic pits and Iron Age souterrains at Dubton Farm, Brechin', *TAFAJ* 8, 19-76

Cameron, K. 2003, 'A new investigation at West Grange of Conon souterrain', *TAFAJ* 9, 65-73

7 WHERE ARE ALL THE HOUSES? EARLY HISTORIC SETTLEMENT

General accounts of the archaeology and history of the Early Historic period in northern Britain include:

Alcock, L. 2003, *Kings and Warriors, Craftsmen and Priests in Northern Britain AD 550-850*, Edinburgh: Society of Antiquaries of Scotland

Foster, S.M. 2004, *Picts, Gaels and Scots*, London: Batsford, rev. edn

Previous volumes of Pictish studies include:

Friell, J.G.P. & Watson, W.G. (eds) 1984, *Pictish Studies: Settlement, Burial and Art in Dark Age Northern Britain*, Oxford: Brit Archaeol Rep, Brit Ser 125

Henry, D. (ed.) 1997, *The Worm, the Germ and the Thorn: Pictish and Related Studies Presented to Isabel Henderson*, Balneaves, Angus: Pinkfoot Press

Small, A. (ed.) 1987, *The Picts: a New Look at Old Problems*, Dundee: University of Dundee

Wainwright, F.T. (ed.) 1955, *The Problem of the Picts*, Edinburgh: Nelson (Reprinted 1980, Perth: Melven Press)

An examination of houses and settlement patterns can be found in:

Cottam, M.B. & Small, A. 1974, 'The distribution of settlement in southern Pictland', *Medieval Archaeology* 18, 43-65

For post-souterrain settlement, the following provide additional information (see also souterrains, Chapter 6 above):

Coleman, R. & Hunter, F. 2002, 'The excavation of a souterrain at Shanzie Farm, Alyth, Perthshire', *TAFAJ* 8, 77-101

Small, A., Cottam, M.B. & Dunbar, J.G. 1975, 'Souterrain and later structures at Northwaterbridge, Kincardineshire', *PSAS* 105 (1972-4), 293-6

Watkins, T. 1984, 'Where were the Picts?' in Friell, J.G. P. & Watson, W.G. (eds), 63-86

For rectangular buildings:

Maxwell, G.S. 1987, 'Settlement in southern Pictland – a new overview', in Small, A. (ed) 31-44

McGill, C. 2004, 'Excavations of cropmarks at Newbarns, near Inverkeilor, Angus, *TAFAJ* 10, 94-118

Ralston, I.B.M. 1997, 'Pictish homes' in Henry, D. (ed.), 18-34

8 BURIAL TRADITIONS IN THE FIRST MILLENNIA

Overviews are available in Alcock (2003) and Foster (2004) (see above). The following also address the burial record:

Alcock, E. 1992, 'Burials and cemeteries in Scotland', in Edwards, N. & Lane, A. (eds), *The Early Church in Wales and the West*, Oxford: Oxbow Monogr 16, 125-9

Close-Brooks, J. 1984, 'Pictish and other burials', in Friell, J. & Watson, G. (eds), 328-45

Key studies of the contexts and distribution of long cist cemeteries include:

Henshall, A.S. 1956, 'The long cist cemetery at Parkburn sand pit, Lasswade, Midlothian', *PSAS* 89 (1955-6), 252-83

Proudfoot, E. & Aliaga-Kelly, C. 1997, 'Aspects of settlement and territorial arrangements in south-east Scotland in the late prehistoric and early historic periods', *Medieval Archaeology* 41, 33-50

Important antiquarian long cist discoveries in Angus include:

Hutcheson, A. 1903, 'Notice of the discovery of a full-length stone cist, containing human remains and a penannular brooch, at Craigie, near Dundee', *PSAS* 37 (1902-3), 233-40

Jervise, A. 1863, 'Account of the excavation of the round or "Bee-hive" shaped house, and other underground chambers, at West Grange of Conan, Forfarshire', *PSAS* 4 (1860-2), 492-9

Recently excavated Angus long cist cemeteries are not yet published in full, but for an interim account see:

Hall, D. 2007, 'The lost lairds of Ballumbie', *Current Archaeology* 207, 46-8

For other important excavations of long cist cemeteries in Eastern Scotland see:

Proudfoot, E. 1996, 'Excavations at the long-cist cemetery on the Hallow Hill, St Andrews, Fife 1975-7', *PSAS* 126, 387-454

Rees, A.R. 2002, 'A first millennium AD cemetery, rectangular Bronze Age structure and late prehistoric settlement at Thornybank, Midlothian', *PSAS* 132, 313-55

Key sources relating to barrow cemeteries are:

Alexander, D. 2005, 'Redcastle, Lunan Bay, Angus: the excavation of an Iron Age timber-lined souterrain and a Pictish barrow cemetery', *PSAS* 135, 41-118

Murray, D. & Ralston, I. 1997, 'The excavation of a square-ditched barrow and other cropmarks at Boysack Mills, Inverkeilor, Angus', *PSAS* 127, 359-86

Stevenson, J.B. 1984, 'Garbeg and Whitebridge: two square-barrow cemeteries in Inverness-shire', in Friell, J.G.P. & Watson, W.G. (eds), 145-50

Wedderburn, L.M.M. & Grime, D.M. 1984, 'The cairn cemetery at Garbeg, Drumnadrochit', in Friell, J.G.P. & Watson, W.G. (eds), 151-67

For the Hawkhill burial see Chapter 6 references

9 CELTS, ROMANS, PICTS AND SCOTS IN ANGUS

Issues of Celticity have generated a substantial amount of literature over recent years. Among the best and most measured start points remains:
Sims-Williams, P. 1998, 'Genetics, linguistics and prehistory: thinking big and thinking straight', *Antiquity* 72, 505-27

There are many accounts of the history and archaeology of the Roman military occupation in Scotland. Good introductions can be found in:
Breeze, D.J. 2006, *Roman Scotland*, London: Batsford. New edn
Breeze, D.J. 1982, *The Northern Frontiers of Roman Britain*, London: Batsford
Keppie, L.J.F. 2004, *Scotland's Roman Remains*, East Linton: John Donald. 3 edn

For an alternative account of the Flavian occupation see:
Woolliscroft, D.J. & Hoffmann, B. 2006, *Rome's First Frontier: The Flavian Occupation of Northern Scotland*, Stroud: Tempus

Examples of approaches to the assessment of Roman–native interaction can be found in:
Hanson, W.S. 2002, 'Zones of interaction: Roman and native in Scotland', *Antiquity* 76, 834-40
Hunter, F. 2001, 'Roman and native in Scotland: new approaches', *Journal of Roman Archaeology* 14, 289-309

For studies of the Roman influence on the emergence of the Picts, useful starting points are provided by:
Hunter, F. 2005, 'Rome and the creation of the Picts', in Visy, Z (ed.), *Limes XIX: Proceedings of the XIXth International Congress of Roman Frontier Studies, Pécs*, (Hungary): University of Pécs, 235-44
Mann, J. 1974, 'The northern frontier after AD 369', *Glasgow Archaeological Journal* 3, 34-42

For overviews of key sites and events related to Early Historic Angus see:
Aitchison, N. 2006, *Forteviot: a Pictish and Scottish Royal Centre*, Stroud: Tempus
Driscoll, S.T. 2002, *Alba: the Gaelic Kingdom AD 800–1124*, Edinburgh: Birlinn/Historic Scotland: The Making of Scotland series
Fraser, J.E. 2000, *The Pictish Conquest: The Battle of Dunnichen 685 and the Birth of Scotland*, Stroud: Tempus
Wainwright, F.T. 1948, 'Nechtanesmere', *Antiquity* 22, 82-97
Woolf, A. 2006, 'Dún Nechtan, Fortriu and the geography of the Picts', *Scottish Historical Review* 85, 182-201

For Pictish stones and other sculpture see:
Driscoll, S.T. 2000, 'Christian monumental sculpture and ethnic expression in early Scotland', in Frazer, W. & Tyrrell, A. (eds), *Social Identity in Early Medieval Britain*, 233-52, Leicester: Leicester University Press
Duncan, A.A.M. 1996, 'Early Christianity', in McNeill, P.G.B. & McQueen, H.L. (eds), *Atlas of Scottish History to 1707*, Edinburgh: Scottish Medievalists, 330-2
Fernie, E. 1986, 'Early church architecture in Scotland', *PSAS* 116, 393-411
Gondek, M. 2006, 'Investing in sculpture: power in early-historic Scotland', *Medieval Archaeology* 50, 105-42
Henderson, G. & Henderson, I. 2004, *The art of the Picts: sculpture and metalwork in Early Medieval Scotland*, London: Thames and Hudson
Jervise, A. 1857, 'Notices descriptive of the localities of certain sculptured stone monuments in Forfarshire … Part II', *PSAS* 2, 242-51
Laing, L. 2001, 'The date and context of the Glamis, Angus, carved Pictish stones', *PSAS* 131, 223-39
Laing, L. 2006, *The Archaeology of Celtic Britain and Ireland c.AD 400-1200*, Cambridge: Cambridge University Press

Mack, A. 1997, *Field Guide to the Pictish Symbol Stones*, Balgavies, Angus: Pinkfoot Press

Mack, A. 2002, *The Association of Pictish Symbol Stones with Ecclesiastical, Burial and 'Memorial' Areas*, Balgavies, Angus: Pinkfoot Press

RCAHMS 2003, *Early Medieval Sculpture in Angus Museums*, Edinburgh: RCAHMS Broadsheet 11

RCAHMS 2007, *Early Medieval Carved Stones at Brechin Cathedral*, Edinburgh: RCAHMS

Places to visit

I. SITES

Most sites in Angus are in private hands and in many cases – most obviously in the case of cropmarks – there will be nothing, or at least nothing coherent, to see at ground level. Archaeologists, being perverse creatures, nonetheless sometimes like to visit such sites to get a realistic feel of their position in the landscape – still not deliverable, at least to old lags, via Geographic Information Systems, fly-throughs or other of the tricks of computer animation. They are trying to appreciate what the Ancient Monuments legislation refers to as the setting of the site. Rather coyly, both the legislation and ensuing government guidance fail to define what precisely is meant by the 'setting' of a site. In other cases, there are good, coherent, physical remains to be pondered over; in some cases sites are laid out for public visits. Many sites, however, lie between these extremes.

Publicly accessible sites are highlighted below; as with other archaeological sites their positions in the landscape may make disabled access less than straightforward. In other cases, visitors should ask permission of landowners or tenants before visiting, wherever this is feasible. Visitors should conform to the Country Code, taking additional care at appropriate seasons; however well-behaved the family Labrador is, he's unlikely to be appreciated amongst sheep at lambing time.

The nearest reconstructions of archaeological sites of the kinds considered here are at Archaeolink Prehistory Park near Oyne in Aberdeenshire (www.archaeolink.co.uk) and at the Scottish Crannog Centre near Kenmore on Loch Tay in Perthshire (www.crannog.co.uk).

It is also worth remarking that visitors to archaeological sites, or others out walking, may come across archaeological remains in the landscape that have simply not been recorded at any time. A good way to check whether you might have spotted something entirely new is to consult the National Monuments Record, accessible at no cost over the web from the Royal Commission on Ancient and Historical Monument of Scotland's website. The system is called CANMORE, and it is now additionally underpinned by a map-based system called PASTMAP, both of which are well-explained on the RCAHMS website (www.rcahms.gov.uk). Curatorial responsibility for archaeological sites in Angus is held in practical terms under a service agreement by the Aberdeenshire Sites and Monuments Record (www.aberdeenshire.gov.uk/archaeology/index) and they can be contacted by e-mail at archaeology@aberdeenshire.gov.uk. They would appreciate being advised of any new discoveries within the county of Angus as it is now constituted. Their record of Angus sites is accessible over the web at www.aberdeenshire.gov.uk/archaeology/ang/smr_search.

For sites in State care and for sites scheduled under Ancient Monuments legislation, the enquirer's first port of call should be Historic Scotland. Historic Scotland is based at Longmore House, Salisbury Place, Edinburgh EH9 1SH. Historic Scotland's website is www.historic-scotland.gov.uk.

Those interested in the archaeology of Angus may wish to become involved with a local archaeological or heritage society. For up-to-date information on these, contact the Council for Scottish Archaeology,

Causewayside House, 160 Causewayside, Edinburgh EH9 1PR; www.scottisharchaeology.org.uk. A national period society, the Pictish Arts Society, is presently based in Angus at Pictavia, see www.pictart.org.

ABERLEMNO. Class I and Class II Pictish sculptured stones. NO 522 555, NO 522 558 and NO 522 559. Historic Scotland. Free. Restricted parking. Of the three that stand on the verge beside the B 9134, one, an unshaped boulder, carries incised symbols of Class I type, whereas the most substantial example is an elaborate Class II cross-slab. This has a relief carving of a cross on one major face, a hunting scene, Pictish symbols and other details on the other face, as well as subsidiary carving on its edges. The remarkable sandstone cross-slab in the nearby kirkyard has an elaborate cross in deep relief on one face, and Pictish symbols and a battle scene on the other. This latter is considered to commemorate a battle between long-haired, tunic-wearing Picts and helmeted Angles, suggested to be Nechtansmere believed by many to have been fought near Dunnichen. A more recent theory would, however, place that particular battle much further north, in the central Highlands. Not visitable October to early April, when protective covers are in place.

ARDESTIE. Souterrain or earth-house. NO 502 344. Historic Scotland. Free. Roadside parking only. This curving underground stone-lined passage has lost its capstones, making access easy. Its stonework includes a reused cup-and-ring-marked boulder. Above-ground dry-stone structures associated with the souterrain lie in its immediate vicinity.

AUCHTERHOUSE. West Mains of Auchterhouse cairn. NO 315 376. Private land. On the summit of West Mains Hill at nearly 300m and widely visible from its surroundings, this huge Bronze Age cairn is some 70m in diameter and 2.5m high. Late Victorian excavation demonstrated that the cairn had been built in several stages to cover the central double cist, which had two compartments. One held cremated bone only, the other cremated bone and an elaborate bronze dagger and even its handle and parts of the sheath made of ox horn (now in Royal Museum of Scotland). This interment has been dated by radiocarbon, as is discussed in the main text.

BRECHIN CATHEDRAL. Brechin seems to have become increasingly important as a Christian centre late in the tenth century AD, and a number of surviving features there show something of its likely importance by the following century. Most conspicuous is the 25m tall round tower (NO 596 601; its conical roof is more recent) beside the cathedral, one of only two to survive in Scotland. It is likely to have served as bell-tower and place of safety. In the cathedral itself are two very different sculptures of proabable eleventh-century date: one, the 'Mary Stone' is a fragment of a reused Pictish cross slab, the other is a damaged hogback gravestone. Both the form and some of the designs on the latter betoken Scandinavian influences. The Cathedral is open daily. The tower, cared for by Historic Scotland, can be viewed from the outside only.

CAPO. Long barrow, Inglismaldie Forest. Although technically in south Aberdeenshire, this site is included as an example of the original size and scale of earth-, turf- and wood-built Neolithic monuments, most of which have long since been ploughed flat in the lowlands of Angus. Positioned at NO 633 664, it is clear of trees within the woodland east of the unclassified road running north-east from Northwaterbridge.

CARLUNGIE. Souterrain or earth-house. NO 511 359. Historic Scotland. Free. Roadside parking only. This curving underground stone-lined passage is unroofed making access easy. Its walling includes a cup-and-ring-marked boulder, reused from an earlier monument. Whether the roof was originally slabbed over or covered in timbers in uncertain. F.T. Wainwright's excavations here nearly 60 years ago revealed above-ground structural evidence too, in the form of paved areas.

THE CATERTHUNS. Two substantial later prehistoric hillforts, set on prominent detached hills close to the Highland edge. Historic Scotland. Free. For both, a small car park is provided at the roadside on the saddle between the two summits. The Brown Caterthun (NO 555 668) involves a longer walk, but rewards the visitor with an elaborate series of ramparts and the greatest number of entrances of any Scottish site of this class. Accessing the White Caterthun (NO 547 660) involves a shorter, if steeper, walk. The outer ramparts here have many similarities to those on the Brown Caterthun, but the major, innermost wall, seemingly gateless, and measuring some 140m by 60m, is the best-preserved feature of this kind in Scotland. Inside the stone-walled fort, very feebly marked, are two circular enclosures perhaps of Early Historic date and a rock-cut cistern, probably contemporary with the (undated) principal wall, some 12m thick. Amongst the fortification lines on the south side can be seen the stances of timber houses and further examples, marked by a near-circular ditch can be spotted on the moorland between the fort and the road. On the west side, near the second circuit, is a substantial cup-marked boulder which has undoubtedly been displaced from an earlier monument.

EASSIE. A Class II Pictish sculptured stone. NO 352 474. Historic Scotland. Free. Easy roadside parking off the A94. The relief carvings on this slab depict a cross, angels, hooded figures (probably priests), animals, a warrior and Pictish symbols; those on the back are worn. The stone is within a protective case inside the old, roofless, church at Eassie.

FINAVON. Hillfort. NO 556 506. Private land. Limited roadside parking. The site lies north of the minor road from Finavon to Aberlemno and, whilst fenced, is accessible via a stile at its east end. This oblong fort, approximately 150m by 50m, sits on top of a conglomerate hillock that is partially edged by rocky outcrops. In places the stonework is heavily fused, indicating the vitrification of the upper portion of an elaborate timber-laced wall, originally some 6m thick. The shape of the site does not conform as closely to the local topography as is normal for hillforts. There is a substantial outwork at its eastern end. Excavation in the mid 1930s and again in 1966, produced a range of Iron Age finds (most are now in the Museum of Scotland in Edinburgh, although a few are in Dundee), a little structural evidence (mostly hearths) and radiocarbon dates suggesting occupation early in the Iron Age. The major internal feature is a rock-cut cistern at its eastern end. Another dating technique would attribute the burning of the defences to Pictish times, but this is controversial.

GLAMIS MANSE. Cross-slab. NO 385 468. Free, in the garden of the manse. Access is via the Kirkwynd of Glamis village, which houses the Angus Folk Museum; park adjacent to the church. This huge slab is the finer of two at Glamis (the other is on Hunters Hill at NO 393 465) which display the key characteristics of both Class I and Class II sculpture. On one side are the incised outlines of three Pictish symbols; the other is dominated by a huge relief cross, filled with interlace designs, and surrounded by a range of figures and symbols.

MAIDEN CASTLE, ARBROATH. Free. The most splendidly defended of the Angus promontory forts sits at the south end of Carlingheugh Bay, east of East Seaton Farm at NO 670 422. Its massive bank and accompanying external ditch are located seaward of the coastal footpath running north from Arbroath.

RESTENNETH. Priory. NO 482 515. Historic Scotland. Free. The date of the earliest stonework here, forming the lowest 3m of the 14m high tower, is disputed. It has been claimed as a surviving fragment of the stone-built church of early eighth-century AD date built by masons despatched north from the Anglian monastery of Wearmouth-Jarrow in Northumbria, but most recent commentators suggest that it is of more recent date. By the later twelfth century this was an Augustinian priory and was where Robert the Bruce's son John was buried at his father's wish. Much of the remaining architecture is thirteenth-century, with the elaborate broach spire being added in the fifteenth century.

ST ORLAND'S STONE. A Class II Pictish sculptured stone. NO 400 500. Historic Scotland. Free. This cross-slab stands on the margin of a field, overlooking lower ground. It is near the steading at Cossans Farm, 4.5m west of Forfar off A926 by rough tracks. One face depicts an ornate cross in relief, whereas the other shows Pictish symbols, a hunting scene and – interestingly so far from the sea – a ship.

TEALING. Souterrain or earth-house. NO 412 381. Historic Scotland. Free. Park in the steading near Tealing dovecot, also in the care of HS, from which the souterrain is a short walk. This curving underground stone-lined passage, found by chance in the 1870s, has lost its capstones since its discovery, making access easy, whilst giving an excellent impression of the scale of these features. The passage is around 2.3m wide and over 24m long. The walls, generally of smaller stones set above large boulders are slightly corbelled in at the surviving wall-head, thereby giving an indication of the original height of the structure. Noteworthy is a reused early prehistoric cup-and-ring-marked stone, forming the lowest part of the north wall near the entrance.

2. MUSEUMS

Angus Council runs a comprehensive museum service, with relevant museums at Arbroath, Forfar, Kirriemuir and Montrose and a visitor centre, Pictavia, near Brechin. Apart from Pictavia, admission to all Angus museums is free of charge. Important collections of material from Angus are also held in Dundee and in the Museum of Scotland (the latter including the Balmashanner hoard). Historic Scotland runs a museum containing early historic sculpture from the important site at St Vigeans. Perth Museum displays additional material directly relevant to the archaeology of Tayside.

ARBROATH: Signal Tower Museum, Ladyloan, Arbroath, DD11 1PU. Tel: 01241 875598; email: signal.tower@angus.gov.uk

BRECHIN: Pictavia, Haughmuir, by Brechin. Entrance charge, concessions, group rates. Tel: 01307 473785; website: www.pictavia.org.uk

BRECHIN: Brechin Museum, 10 St Ninians Square, Brechin DD8 7AA. Tel: 01307 464123

FORFAR: Meffan Museum & Gallery, 20 West High Street, Forfar, DD8 1BB. Tel: 01307 464123 / 467017; email: the.meffan@angus.gov.uk

KIRRIEMUIR: Gateway to the Glens Museum, The Old Town House, High Street, Kirriemuir DD8 4BB. Tel: 01575 575479; email: kirriegateway@angus.gov.uk

MONTROSE: Museum, Panmure Place, Montrose, DD10 8HE. Tel: 01674 673232; email: montrose. museum@angus.gov.uk

ST VIGEANS (Historic Scotland): In the village of St Vigeans. Tel: 01241 878756 for information

DUNDEE: McManus Galleries and Museum, Albert Square, Dundee, DD1 1DA. Tel: 01382 432350; website: www.mcmanus.co.uk

EDINBURGH: National Museum of Scotland, Chambers Street, Edinburgh, EH1 1JF. Tel: 0131 247 4422 ; email: info@nms.ac.uk; website: www.nms.ac.uk

PERTH: Perth Museum and Art Gallery, 78 George Street, Perth, PH1 5LB. Tel: 01738 632488; email: museum@pkc.gov.uk

Index

Italicised entries denote figures or colour plates.
Where no county name is given, sites are within Angus.